Sharing Freedom

The French have long self-identified as champions of universal emancipation, yet the republicanism they adopted has often been faulted for being exclusionary – of women, foreigners, and religious and ethnic minorities. Can republicanism be an attractive alternative to liberalism, communism, and communitarianism, or is it fundamentally flawed? *Sharing Freedom* traces the development of republicanism from an older elitist theory of freedom into an inclusive theory of emancipation during the French Revolution. It uncovers the theoretical innovations of Rousseau and of revolutionaries such as Sieyès, Robespierre, Condorcet, and Grouchy. We learn how they struggled to adapt republicanism to the new circumstances of a large and diverse France, full of poor and dependent individuals with little education or experience of freedom. Analyzing the argumentative logic that paradoxically led republicans to justify the exclusion of many, this book renews the republican tradition and connects it with the enduring issues of colonialism, immigration, slavery, poverty, and gender inequality.

Geneviève Rousselière is a Franco-American political theorist. She is Assistant Professor of Political Science at Duke University and the coeditor of *Republicanism and the Future of Democracy* (Cambridge University Press, 2019).

Sharing Freedom

Republicanism and Exclusion in Revolutionary France

GENEVIÈVE ROUSSELIÈRE
Duke University

Shaftesbury Road, Cambridge CB2 8EA, United Kingdom

One Liberty Plaza, 20th Floor, New York, NY 10006, USA

477 Williamstown Road, Port Melbourne, VIC 3207, Australia

314–321, 3rd Floor, Plot 3, Splendor Forum, Jasola District Centre, New Delhi – 110025, India

103 Penang Road, #05–06/07, Visioncrest Commercial, Singapore 238467

Cambridge University Press is part of Cambridge University Press & Assessment, a department of the University of Cambridge.

We share the University's mission to contribute to society through the pursuit of education, learning and research at the highest international levels of excellence.

www.cambridge.org
Information on this title: www.cambridge.org/9781009477314

DOI: 10.1017/9781009477291

First published 2024

A catalogue record for this publication is available from the British Library

Library of Congress Cataloging-in-Publication Data
NAMES: Rousselière, Geneviève, 1977– author.
TITLE: Sharing freedom : republicanism and exclusion in revolutionary France / Geneviève Rousselière, Duke University, North Carolina.
DESCRIPTION: New York, NY : Cambridge University Press, 2024. | Includes bibliographical references and index.
IDENTIFIERS: LCCN 2023046276 (print) | LCCN 2023046277 (ebook) | ISBN 9781009477314 (hardback) | ISBN 9781009477291 (ebook)
SUBJECTS: LCSH: Republicanism – France – History. | Political science – France – Philosophy. | Republics. | France – Politics and government – History. | France – History – Revolution, 1789–1799.
CLASSIFICATION: LCC JA84.F8 R677 2024 (print) | LCC JA84.F8 (ebook) | DDC 320.44409–dc23/eng/20231226
LC record available at https://lccn.loc.gov/2023046276
LC ebook record available at https://lccn.loc.gov/2023046277

ISBN 978-1-009-47731-4 Hardback
ISBN 978-1-009-47727-7 Paperback

Contents

Acknowledgments

This book does not have much in common with the dissertation I wrote at Princeton. Yet it certainly would not exist without the work I did then under the supervision of an exceptional committee. My greatest debt is to Philip Pettit, who advised my dissertation with care and generosity, inspired me to work on republicanism, and encouraged me to find my own intellectual path. I also benefited from the rigorous advice and generous guidance of Alan Patten, Nadia Urbinati, Alan Ryan, and Annie Stilz. I feel very lucky and grateful for what they have each taught me in their different styles.

I have also been fortunate to have had great colleagues in my postdoctoral position at the University of Chicago, my first tenure-track job at the University of Wisconsin-Madison and now at Duke University. I thank in particular Jennifer Pitts, Sankar Muthu, John McCormick, and Gary Herrigel as well as the Harper Schmidt fellows, who made my postdoctoral years intense and intellectually rewarding. At Madison, I am grateful to Dan Kapust, who has since become a mentor and friend, and Rick Avramenko for always stepping in when needed. I have found a welcoming and enriching political theory community at Duke University. Michael Gillespie, Jack Knight, Alex Kirshner, and Ruth Grant have been very generous with their intellectual advice, time, and good humor. They also have given me extensive and precious feedback on this manuscript. I have felt very much supported since I arrived at Duke. I am thankful to colleagues at the University of Chapel Hill, North Carolina, in particular Jeff Spinner-Halev, Susan Bickford and Alex Oprea who have contributed in making these last years intellectually rich. I am also grateful to the graduate students who have provided editorial assistance to this book, in particular Charlie Nathan, Brian Spisiak, Wanning Seah, Jihyun Jeong, and Katie Martin-Browne.

I owe much to the political theorists who became my friends in graduate school and beyond. They have shared their intellectual insights on my projects and have made my life happier with their friendship, humor and wit: Loubna El Amine, Yiftah Elazar, Sandra Field, Ben McKean, Julie Rose, and Charles Girard. A special thanks to Torrey Shanks who has always been there as friend and has helped me navigate academia through thick and thin. These last years would also have been hard without the support of my dear friends, Emmanuelle Audebrand, Félicia Fournier and Elif Uras.

I am indebted to the many people who read drafts or essays related to this book manuscript. To mention some who mattered particularly, I want to thank Arash Abizadeh, Annelien de Dijn, Hugo Drochon, Bryan Garsten, Alex Gourevitch, Ryan Hanley, Sharon Krause, Frank Lovett, Chris Meckstroth, Laura Montanaro, Ryan Pevnick, Juliette Roussin, John T. Scott, Melissa Schwartzberg, Will Selinger, Céline Spector, and David Williams. Many more inspired me, and I am sorry I cannot list all of them. Thanks to audiences that have given me invaluable feedback in workshops at Stanford, McGill, Yale, Brown, New York University, Georgetown, Princeton, Yale, the University of Chicago, and the Hebrew University of Jerusalem.

I am grateful to my family – my parents, Raymond and Bernadette, my siblings and their family, Damien, Samira, Manoue and Dimitri – and my in-laws – Shenny, Shahid, Aamir and Mariam. They have supported me throughout the years and never questioned my choices. Zakir Paul has been with me every step of the way. He read countless versions of this manuscript and encouraged me throughout. Our son, Adam, has been an immense source of joy in the years I wrote this book. I know that both of them cannot wait to see this book finally in print.

Note on Editions, Translations, and Abbreviations

References to the parliamentary archives of the French Revolution (*Archives Parlementaires*) are taken from the edition of Émile Laurent and Jérôme Mavidal. They will be noted with the letters *AP* followed by the volume and page number as well as the date of the parliamentary session when applicable. Since all of the 102 volumes of the *Archives* (1789–1794) have not yet been digitalized, I have supplemented them with the *Moniteur* when necessary.

For books and articles, I have privileged original published editions over the truncated versions available in collected volumes or English translations. Most of the original publications I refer to can be found in the digital archives of the Bibliothèque Nationale de France, *Gallica*, and the website devoted to the digitalization of the parliamentary archives of the Revolution, *Persée*.

Unless I explicitly refer to a published English translation in the footnotes, translations are my own.

ABBREVIATIONS

Montesquieu's Texts

CC *Considerations on the Causes of the Greatness of the Romans and Their Decline*. Edited and translated by David Lowenthal. Indianapolis: Hackett Publishing Company, 1999.

SL *The Spirit of the Laws*. Edited by Anne M. Cohler, Basia C. Miller and Harold S. Stone. Cambridge: Cambridge University Press, 1989.

Rousseau's Texts

DPE *Discourse on Political Economy*. In *The Social Contract and Other Later Political Writings*, translated by Victor Gourevitch, 3–38. Cambridge: Cambridge University Press, 2010.

E *Emile or On Education*. Edited by Allan Bloom. New York: Basic Books, 1979.

FD *Discourse on the Sciences and Arts (First Discourse)*. In *The Discourses and Other Early Political Writings*, translated by Victor Gourevitch, 1–28. Cambridge: Cambridge University Press, 2010.

GM *Geneva Manuscript*. In *The Social Contract and Other Later Political Writings*, translated by Victor Gourevitch, 153–161. Cambridge: Cambridge University Press, 2010.

GP *Considerations on the Government of Poland*. In *The Social Contract and Other Later Political Writings*, translated by Victor Gourevitch, 177–260. Cambridge: Cambridge University Press, 2010.

LM *Letters from the Mountains*. In *Œuvres Complètes Tome III*. Paris: NRF Gallimard (Pléiade), 1964.

OC *Œuvres Complètes Tome III*. Paris: NRF Gallimard (Pléiade), 1964.

SC *Of the Social Contract*. In *The Social Contract and Other Later Political Writings*, translated by Victor Gourevitch, 39–152. Cambridge: Cambridge University Press, 2010.

SD *Discourse on the Origin and Foundations of Inequality Among Men (Second Discourse)*. In *The Discourses and Other Early Political Writings*, translated by Victor Gourevitch, 111–222. Cambridge: Cambridge University Press, 2010.

SW *State of War*. In *The Social Contract and Other Later Political Writings*, translated by Victor Gourevitch, 162–176. Cambridge: Cambridge University Press, 2010.

Introduction

On the Universalization of Republican Freedom

This book is about an enduring moral and political wrong: exclusion. If contemporary republican democracies have efficient political institutions capable of securing private and public freedom for their citizenry, why are some of their members persistently deprived of what should be a common good – the status of being an equal and undominated citizen?

Looking at the historical case of France, I ask this question by examining republicanism, the political theory that promised to end domination, or, as I phrase it, the theory that envisions freedom as a common good to be equally shared among all. I argue that, in the French example, republicanism failed to acknowledge its own origins and, therefore, its own shortcomings. As a result, despite its explicitly universal framing as a theory of emancipation, republicanism justified forms of exclusion from full citizenship.

This book may be interpreted as an indictment of republicanism. To the extent that this is the case, it is only because, like many revolutionaries in the late eighteenth century, I contend that republicanism is the best theory of freedom that we currently have and the most powerful political discourse of mobilization against domination. Its normative attractiveness, which I present in this book, is the very reason we should attempt to save it from its failings. We need to dissect the historical forces that shaped it and face its shortcomings to understand how it could become what revolutionaries hoped it would be.

THE CRISIS OF REPUBLICANISM TODAY

"We are the Indigenous People of the Republic!" In their 2005 call, a French radical decolonial group, the *Parti des Indigènes de la République*, wanted a few truths to be heard:

Discriminated for work, housing, healthcare, education and recreation, people of former or present colonies and post-colonial immigration are the first victims of social exclusion and increased precarity. Independently of their real origins, populations from the "hoods" (*quartiers*) are "indigenized" (*indigénisées*), pushed aside to the margins of society. "Projects" (*banlieues*) are said to be "lawless zones" (*zones de non-droit*) that the Republic is called to "conquer back" (*reconquérir*).

For the *Indigènes*, to redress injustice is not only to address the urgent situation of exclusion in which minorities are denied basic rights and common goods but also to question the values and political ideas that have justified this situation: "It is time for France to question its Enlightenment (*Lumières*) and for the egalitarian universalism affirmed during the French Revolution to stamp down this nationalism erected on the "jingoism of the universal" (*chauvinisme de l'universel*) supposed to "civilize" old and young savages (*"civiliser" sauvages et sauvageons*)."[1]

The Call of the Indigènes prompted an intense political debate in France, as controversial personalities signed it[2] and accusations of extremism arose.[3] The word "indigène" was a direct reference to the colonial past of the country and its lasting use to designate a status of exception for the colonized, who were excluded from citizenship.[4] For its proponents, the Call was a much-needed anti-racist manifesto. For its detractors, the Call signaled the emergence of anti-republican identity politics, or more exactly a "reactionary, anti-republican, clerical, *antilaïque*, communitarian, and ethnicist movement on the left."[5] It marked a high point in an ongoing political crisis – a call to the whole nation to face its history, reckon with its failures and critically assess its dominant

[1] My translation. See the whole text on http://indigenes-republique.fr/le-p-i-r/appel-des-indigenes-de-la-republique. The two main authors of the Call are Houria Bouteldja and Youssef Boussoumah. The text can also be found in Robine, "Les 'indigènes de la république': nation et question postcoloniale," 118–48.

[2] For instance, Tariq Ramadan, a controversial Swiss Muslim scholar.

[3] On this debate, see Madec et al., "A propos des indigènes de la république," 112–26. For the accusation, see Fourest, *La tentation obscurantiste*. The debate intensified by the end of the 2010s. A manifesto against the decolonial movement was posted in the newspaper *Le Point* on November 28, 2018 and signed by number of prominent French intellectuals. The debate was further inflamed by Bouteldja's publication of a virulent antizionist pamphlet, *Les Blancs, les Juifs et nous: Vers une politique de l'amour révolutionnaire* (2016).

[4] Code de l'Indigénat (set in 1874 and repeatedly modified). See Le Cour Grandmaison, *De l'indigénat. Anatomie d'un monstre juridique: le droit colonial en Algérie et dans l'Empire français* and Shepard, *The Invention of Decolonization*.

[5] Jean-François Kahn, in the republican and "laïciste" journal *Marianne*, in January 2005.

political discourse, republicanism. The crisis seized academic and public debate, and overflowed, violently, into the streets.[6]

The Call of the *Indigènes* expressed the growing uneasiness of part of the French population vis-à-vis republicanism, despite the latter being deeply entrenched politically and overwhelmingly supported by the population. By January 2015, when the Parisian headquarters of the satirical newspaper Charlie Hebdo were attacked by terrorists, republicanism had been established in France for almost 140 years. After the Third Republic (1870–1940), France had remained under a republican regime with constitutional changes (the Fourth Republic [1946–1958] and the Fifth Republic [1958–now]), with the "only" interruption being the collaborationist regime of Vichy during World War II.[7] The French allegiance to republicanism was still so strong in 2015 that on the Sunday following the terrorist attack, a "Republican demonstration" (*une marche républicaine*) was organized across the country and turned into one of the largest demonstrations in French history.[8] Its main slogan that soon appeared worldwide on social media, *Je suis Charlie,* was meant to express both the attachment to republican political values, in particular freedom of expression, and the commitment to republican national solidarity, which stated that harming some citizens was tantamount to harming the whole body politic.[9] At the core of the debate surrounding the demonstration was, of course, the question of Islamist terrorism, but also the trial of republicanism as the official doctrine of French institutions.

[6] The "état d'urgence" (state of emergency) was declared to deal with the "urban riots" of November 2005.

[7] For a controversial account of the role of republicanism in explaining Vichy, see Noiriel, *Les origines républicaines de Vichy.*

[8] In Paris, the demonstration was centered on the Place de la République. On this point see Laurentin, "Pourquoi la république?" Though exact numbers are unknown, up to four million people may have gathered in more than 250 towns. For a controversial critique of the *marche républicaine* as a hysterical phenomenon showing the division of France rather than its unity, see Todd, *Qui est Charlie? Controverse d'une crise religieuse.* Jacques Rancière also argued that the motivations of the demonstrators could not be summarized under one heading and that the demonstration included individuals with radically opposed political views (interview in the *Nouvel Obs* in January 2015).

[9] The nature of the values endorsed by the *Je suis Charlie* slogan have been debated both in France and internationally. An important aspect of the controversy is that several of Charlie Hebdo's caricatures can be characterized as Islamophobic and that many saw in this newspaper a vehicle of hatred. Even though they endorsed freedom of the press, many refused the identity statement of the *Je suis Charlie* slogan because they rejected what they saw as the intolerant ideology expressed in the cartoons published in this journal. As a typical example, see Brenner, "Je ne suis pas Charlie Hebdo," in the *Huffington Post.*

A core concern of public debate was the normative attractiveness and social effectiveness of republicanism. Indeed, the two gunmen, Saïd and Chérif Kouachi, were children of the republic: they had attended public schools, traditionally institutions promoting *intégration,* that is, secular republican assimilation.[10] How could institutions meant to promote republican citizenship produce individuals who violently rejected republican values to the point of committing acts of domestic terrorism? This dramatic event intensified an already nagging doubt: that there was something wrong either with the republican ideal itself or with its historical and institutional implementations. Instead of taking the attacks as an instance of a global problem of Islamist terrorism, as many other countries did, the French questioned the nature and strength of their republicanism.[11] In doing so, they turned inwards, locating the root of the problem in the substantive tenets of their national political ideology rather than in a religious or cultural clash, or deep-seated economic disparities.

The public discussion that ensued was one of the latest episodes in what can be called the legitimacy crisis of French republicanism. From 1989 till the 2000s, the hijab question triggered an impassioned debate on the principle of *laïcité* – a specific French version of secularism and a defining element of republican discourse since the Third Republic.[12] In 2005, the whole world witnessed with astonishment the spectacle of Paris suburbs burning in response to the deaths of Bouna Traoré and Zyed Benna, two Black and North-African teenagers who were chased by the police. The burning of the suburbs revealed the degree to which a part of the population felt that they were unfairly treated, subjected to police brutality, and effectively excluded from national belonging. In 2018, after a French woman of West Indian origin posted an online petition about the rising cost of fuel, the movement of the Yellow Vests (*Gilets Jaunes*) transformed into a year-long protest that has been interpreted as both a revival of an old republican spirit and its populist rejection, raising the question of whether republicanism was an institutional doctrine or its contestation.[13] During this period, the existence of an entrenched

[10] I return to the notion of "integration" in the book's conclusion.

[11] Attacks perpetrated by homegrown terrorists have massively and disproportionally affected Asia, Africa, South America, and the Middle East rather than Europe. See the Global Terrorism Database (open-source database).

[12] See Baubérot, *Histoire de la laïcité* and Laborde, *Critical Republicanism: The Hijab Controversy and Political Philosophy.*

[13] See for instance Sudhir Hazareesingh's comments in Bouniol, "Les gilets jaunes représentent la part de rêve de la révolution française." See also Noiriel, *Les gilets jaunes à la lumière de l'histoire.*

social division – *la fracture sociale* – became a central subject of public discourse and national concern.[14] French journalists and intellectuals framed these issues in terms of the "lost territories of the Republic"[15] and debated who exactly were the "*exclus*" (the excluded, or left-behind) that the republic had failed.[16] For the *Indigènes* and their supporters, this very discourse proved the existence of exclusion: the republicans believed in the chimera of their universalism and egalitarianism, and reiterated the colonial discourse of civilization, nationalism, and imperialism without reflecting on their own actions.

The Indigenous People's claim that French republicanism fell short of its universal aspirations can be easily confirmed by a range of significant historical events. In August 1789, all men were declared free and equal in rights by the French Constituent Assembly. It became immediately clear, however, that this "universal" declaration did not include the black men and women from the French colony of Saint-Domingue, who remained slaves.[17] It also excluded a wide range of metropolitan residents from equal political rights, especially women, free people of color and domestic servants.[18] After slavery was reestablished by Napoleon, the Second Republic once more abolished slavery and decreed a universal declaration of equal political rights. Yet Algeria's colonized inhabitants were given a "special status," which amounted to a status of exclusion – the "Muslim Indigenes" and "Jewish Indigenes" of Algeria were French nationals but not citizens.[19] Exceptions to the universal are still present today. The Fifth Republic guarantees the equality of all yet perpetuates or tolerates exclusionary practices.[20]

Each time, specific contextual reasons could be provided to explain why exceptions from the universal rule were needed, and why exclusions

14 Chabal, *A Divided Republic. Nation, State and Citizenship in Contemporary France*, 88.

15 See Brenner, *Les territoires perdus de la république*; Kepel, *Quatre-vingt treize*; Kepel, *Banlieue de la république: société, politique et religion à Clichy-sous-Bois et Montfermeil.*

16 Jennings, "Citizenship, Republicanism and Multiculturalism in Contemporary France."

17 The first abolition of slavery in Saint-Domingue occurred only in August 1793 to avoid the military defeat that followed the slave uprising of August 1791. See Dubois and Garrigus, *Slave Revolution in the Caribbean, 1789–1804*. The abolition of slavery in all colonies occurred only in February 1794, and even then, it was not applied properly.

18 The law of September 29, 1789 introduced the distinction between active citizenship and passive citizenship, which did not include political rights. Women, children, foreigners, the poor, the propertyless, and domestic servants were passive citizens. This question is the topic of Chapter 4 of this book.

19 See Saada, "The Republic and the Indigenes," 225.

20 Mazouz, *La république et ses autres. Politiques de l'altérité dans la France des années 2000*.

were warranted. Let us consider the example of the immense constitutional work accomplished by the Constituent Assembly in the summer and fall of 1789. The same revolutionaries who dared to declare the abolition of privileges thought that they needed to set aside the complex question of the special status of colonies in order to overthrow the social structure of privileges in metropolitan France. Their decision may appear self-interested: taxes needed to be collected in an almost bankrupt state, and the colonies were a huge financial resource.[21] It may also have been strategic – the colonies had a special legal status under the *Ancien Régime*, which made legislating them a complex and divisive issue that was bound to stall the revolutionary process.[22] But contextual reasons can only provide ad hoc explanations. They do not explain why some issues were plagued by self-interest and strategic considerations, while others were not. We need to understand the reasons that the agents were giving to themselves and to each other to understand how and why the universalization of freedom did not occur as planned in the mind of revolutionaries themselves.

Since the nineteenth century, critical discourses across the social sciences and humanities – Marxism, feminism, and postcolonial studies, for instance – have analyzed relations of power at a systemic rather than contextual level, providing wide-ranging explanations for the phenomenon of exclusion presented in this book. These theoretical resources have gone a long way in accounting for the logic of otherwise incoherent events and led to a deeper investigation, in recent decades, of the colonial archives of the French Republic. I have used these resources and followed their inspiration, though mostly with quite different methods. In particular, I give priority to the analysis of reason-giving in discourses, whether scholarly treatises or parliamentary archives.

For their part, political theorists have critically considered the extensive endorsement of colonialism by republicans.[23] The failure of republican France to consider residents from former colonies or from the Antilles as full citizens further demonstrates its exclusionary nature.[24]

[21] On the state's huge debt and its role in the Revolution, see Sonenscher, *Before the Deluge*. On the colonies as a source of wealth, see Dubois, *A Colony of Citizens*, Ch. 2.

[22] For other considerations why the revolutionaries stalled the process of abolition, see Cooper, *Slavery and the French and Haitian Revolutionists*.

[23] Pitts, *A Turn to Empire. The Rise of Imperial Liberalism in Britain and France*.

[24] Hajjat, *Les frontières de l'identité nationale. L'injonction à l'assimilation en France métropolitaine et coloniale*; Conklin, *A Mission to Civilize: The Republican Idea of Empire in France and West Africa, 1895–1930*; Saada, *Empire's Children: Race, Filiation, and*

This exclusionary logic shows how ideas ostensibly rejected by republicans – such as the concept of "race" today in France – have shaped republicanism unbeknownst to its proponents.[25] In these frameworks, however, the trajectory of France does not singularly differ from other European countries and officially "liberal" countries. Exclusion, one could object matter-of-factly, is not a unique feature of republicanism. What remains particular to the French republican case, however, is the contradiction between general claims of inclusion and circumstantial justifications of exclusion. It is this theoretical inconsistency that is of interest to me here.

How are we to explain this Janus-faced dimension of republicanism – at once emancipatory and exclusionary? The question may seem trivial initially. After all, it is hardly surprising that the history of France, like so many other European countries, would show its complicity with oppression. It would be miraculous if republicans, in contrast with everybody else, happened not to have been racist, misogynistic, or elitist on the sole basis of their lofty ideals, as if they alone could escape the structural inequality of the eras that shaped their lives and determined their privileges.

A common way of dealing with this conundrum has been to chalk it up to human imperfection, that is, to present republicanism as a promise of freedom that imperfect men encumbered with prejudices failed to attain. In the narrative of failed promise, republicanism – epitomized by the French motto liberty, equality, fraternity – remains normatively attractive because it is unsoiled by the imperfections of reality: it is the theory according to which individuals are free and equal under the rule of law, regardless of, or abstracted from, their differences. The slow emancipation of slaves, women, the poor, the colonized, and other minorities, is ascribed to the fact that the republic has not yet lived up to its promises. Yet the republic is perfectible and perpetually moving in the right direction. The "failed promise narrative," which supposes the perennial opposition between theory and practice, relies on and reinforces the redemptive hope of progress.

The frame of the "failed promise" dominates most attempts by republicans to take stock of and reckon with the troubled past and the difficult present of republicanism in France. This might make sense if there were an actual difference between discourse and practice. But,

Citizenship in the French Colonies; Larcher, *L'autre citoyen*. See also Mame-Fatou Niang's movie, "Mariannes noires."

[25] Vergès, *Monsters and Revolutionaries. Colonial Family Romance and Métissage*; Mazouz, *La république et ses autres. Politiques de l'altérité dans la France des années 2000*.

as I will show in this book, discourse, not only that of professional politicians but also of intellectuals and philosophers, has consistently justified the practices of preventing minorities from accessing universal suffrage in the name of safeguarding freedom for all, of promoting colonialism in the name of emancipating the colonized, and of slowing down the abolition of slavery in the name of protecting slaves. This is the historical reality this book takes as a point of departure.

It remains to be explained why republican discourse has been able to justify the repeated exclusion of large parts of the population while claiming its universalism and what, within republican theory, enables such arguments. In what follows, I do not endorse the narrative of failed promises. Instead, I focus on the argumentative structures that made it possible to endorse both the emancipation of all and justify the exclusion of many on the grounds of freedom itself. Less a matter of unrealized potential, the problem remains, I argue, the struggle to interpret the meaning of republican freedom and spell out its conditions of possibility. Claiming universalism while justifying exception and claiming freedom yet justifying domination – these are the internal tensions that I track within the very idea of republicanism at the moment of its formation.

WHAT IS REPUBLICANISM?

I have so far presented the problem of this book as if we all know what republicanism in France, and republicanism *tout court*, are. This is far from being the case. Defining this term is surprisingly difficult if one starts, as I do, from both a French and transatlantic point of view. These two points of view – from within "the Hexagon" (France), and from without – have so little in common that one may wonder whether they share anything. We need, however, to connect them to determine the theoretical content of French republicanism, as well as its place in the broader tradition.

Let us start with the consensus. Republicanism designates a European political tradition that provided a powerful language of political emancipation and contestation against tyrannical power from antiquity till the Atlantic Revolutions. A first methodological difficulty arises from the geographical and temporal extents of this tradition, which includes Ancient Rome, the Italian Renaissance, early modern England, and the American founding period. Such utterly different contextual situations necessarily generate important, if not overwhelming, conceptual discrepancies in the formulation of republican theory.[26] A second difficulty arises out of naming "republicanism" a contemporary political theory inspired by this tradition, yet systematizing it into a coherent and normatively attractive set of principles.[27] Beyond the idea of a political tradition, republican theory has been mobilized in the past decades as a normative political discourse offering an alternative to liberalism, socialism, and communitarianism.[28] Considering the diversity of the tradition, historians have tended to embrace an all-inclusive approach (any theory claiming to be republican can be explored as such), while theorists and philosophers have tended to adopt a more selective strategy (only works endorsing specific theoretical tenets can be counted as republican).

Internationally, both approaches have been at play in what has been called the neo-republican revival, which has been influential in many academic disciplines in the last fifty years around the world, but in particular in the Anglo-American sphere.[29] Initially, a range of revisionist historians challenged the liberal orthodoxy and uncovered a diverse yet consistent republican discourse from antiquity through Machiavelli and the English "commonwealthmen," and to the American founders.[30] In this all-inclusive approach, historians of political thought tend to identify a

[26] For a synthesis, see Hammersley, *Republicanism. An Introduction.*

[27] The main representatives are Philip Pettit (*Republicanism* and *On the People's Terms*) and Frank Lovett (*A General Theory of Domination and Justice* and *The Well-Ordered Republic*).

[28] There are alternative names, such as "civic republicans" or "contemporary republicans," used for instance by Lovett. I prefer the term neo-republican to simply mark the existence of a revival of republicanism. There are important conceptual differences within neo-republicanism, but this should not concern us here.

[29] Pocock, *The Machiavellian Moment: Florentine Political Thought and the Atlantic Republican Tradition*; Skinner, "The Paradoxes of Political Liberty"; Pettit, *Republicanism* and *On the People's Terms*; Dagger, *Civic Virtues*; Laborde and Maynor, *Republicanism and Political Theory*; Laborde, *Critical Republicanism: The Hijab Controversy and Political Philosophy*; Lovett, *A General Theory of Domination and Justice* and *The Well-Ordered Republic*; Bellamy, *Political Constitutionalism: A Republican Defence of the Constitutionality of Democracy;* Gourevitch, *From Slavery to the Cooperative Commonwealth: Labor and Republican Liberty in the Nineteenth Century*; Taylor, *Exit Left;* Viroli, *For Love of Country;* Elazar and Rousselière, *Republicanism and the Future of Democracy.*

[30] Van Gelderen and Skinner, *Republicanism: A Shared European Heritage*; Wood, *The Creation of the American Republic, 1776–1787*; Robbins, *The Eighteenth Century Commonwealthman*; Baron, *The Crisis of the Early Italian Renaissance: Civic Humanism and Republican Liberty in an Age of Classicism and Tyranny*; Bailyn, *The Ideological Origins of the American Revolution*; Pocock, *The Machiavellian Moment: Florentine Political Thought and the Atlantic Republican Tradition*; and Skinner, *The Foundations of Modern Political Thought.*

range of traits shared by republican theories, though not all can be found in each variation. This method of classification has sometimes been called a "family resemblance" approach.[31] Among such partially shared traits figure antimonarchism, the rule of law ("the empire of laws"), self-government, the idea of the free citizen, the common good or public thing (the "res publica"), the rejection of domination, the ideal of the virtuous citizen, the fear of corruption, and the mixed constitution.[32]

In turn, philosophers and political theorists have used this historical research to rethink issues of justice, public policy, and institutional design.[33] As a consequence, they tend to privilege the identification of a clear and robust set of normative principles. For them, the all-inclusive approach is unlikely to be successful methodologically, as it paints republicanism as a family-resemblance. Neo-republican theorists are thus making choices in the historical tradition, choices that are intended to facilitate the elaboration of more systematic thinking than history provides. They therefore opt for a principle-based approach, which counts as republican only a narrow set of works that are best suited to what they consider the most promising ideas for contemporary republican theory.[34]

The normative approach has been championed by Philip Pettit, whose landmark 1997 *Republicanism* transformed the field. Pettit proposes to build republican theory around the notion of freedom as non-domination: the idea that freedom is the robust protection against the arbitrary or uncontrolled will of another. While the idea of freedom as protection against arbitrary power was commonly used as a marker for republican theory in earlier scholarship, it had always been accompanied by a range of other concepts (the rule of law, the common good, the virtuous citizen, self-government, the fear of corruption, etc.) and was not singled out as the core of the theory.[35] This shift is important because after Pettit's *Republicanism*, the notion of "freedom as non-domination" became commonly used as the new standard to determine the extent to

[31] Lovett, *The Well-Ordered Republic*, 2.

[32] Hammersley, *Republicanism. An Introduction*. Another work with a similar approach is Honohan, *Civic Republicanism.*

[33] Lovett and Pettit, "Neo-Republicanism: A Normative and Institutional Research Program."

[34] Some have chosen an intermediary solution. Lovett, for instance, proposes a reflective equilibrium between canonical and contemporary republican writings to define a coherent tradition (Lovett, *The Well-Ordered Republic*, 1–3).

[35] Pettit, *Republicanism*, 51.

which specific historical works or doctrines could be adequately called republican, reversing, so to speak, previous methods that went from history to norms, rather than using norms to classify historical works.

It should be noted that for Pettit, as well as for other neo-republicans such as Lovett, republicanism entails fundamental principles beyond freedom as non-domination. For Pettit, these principles are the mixed constitution and the contestatory citizenry;[36] for Lovett, they are the empire of laws and the popular control principle.[37] These variations account for small differences with non-negligible theoretical and policy implications, but certainly no schism. An important evolution of Pettit's theory is its clearer commitment to democracy as an implication of republicanism in *On The People's Terms* (2012): "If we start from the republican concept of freedom as non-domination, then we can derive the need for democracy, under a suitable characterization, from the requirements of freedom."[38] While the first formulations of neo-republican theories left room for interpretation, the recent trend has been toward a full-throated endorsement of republican democracy.[39]

A puzzling feature of this vast and diverse body of mainly Anglo-American scholarship is the remarkable absence of French political thought in both its historical and contemporary forms.[40] When it is not absent, it is rejected.[41] Take for instance works by Pocock and Skinner, which stop before the entry of French revolutionaries on the stage of history.[42] Or take the normative work of Pettit, who places Rousseau outside of the Italian-Atlantic tradition because of his endorsement of popular sovereignty and thick citizenship.[43] For Pettit, the exclusion of

[36] Pettit, *On the People's Terms*, 5.

[37] Lovett, *The Well-Ordered Republic*, 3–8.

[38] Pettit, *On the People's Terms*, 22.

[39] Elazar and Rousselière, "Introduction: Republicanizing Democracy, Democratizing the Republic," In *Republicanism and the Future of Democracy*, 1–10.

[40] Recent scholarship has started to integrate French republicanism within the international history of republicanism. This book places itself within this movement, though its thesis differs in detail from these works. See Laborde, *Critical Republicanism: The Hijab Controversy and Political Philosophy*; Audier, *Les théories de la république*; Spitz, *Le moment républicain*; Hamel, "L'esprit républicain anglais adapté à la France du XVIIIe siècle: un républicanisme classique?"; Miqueu, "Le Républicanisme. Présentation d'un champ de recherches en philosophie politique." An important exception in the earlier wave of neo-republican research is Venturi, *Utopia and Reform in the Enlightenment*.

[41] Lovett associates French republicanism with the "excesses of the French Revolution" (*The Well-Ordered Republic*, 5).

[42] Pocock, *Virtue, Commerce, and History: Essays on Political Thought and History, Chiefly in the Eighteenth Century*; Skinner, *Liberty Before Liberalism*.

[43] Pettit, *On the People's Terms*, 11–18. Lovett concurs in this exclusion.

Rousseau and his followers from the Italo-Atlantic canon of republicanism is a matter of normative classification. From this perspective, while Rousseau and some continental philosophers like Kant are republicans in a sense, as they continued the republican quest to alleviate domination, they nonetheless betrayed the idea of a vigilant citizenry always keeping public power accountable, and the idea of a mixed constitution in which public power is divided and balanced.[44]

Setting aside the particularity of Pettit's reading of Rousseau (I offer an alternative reading in Chapter 2), it is important to step back to assess the strangeness of this position from the other side of the Atlantic. Indeed, for French historians and theorists (that is both historians of France and French scholars), not only are Rousseau and his followers republican, but in fact republicanism is part of French national identity, if not a distinctively French invention. How can one make sense of such a striking interpretive difference in the international scholarly community? It is all the more baffling that while republicanism has also undergone a revival in France, it has done so by and large without communication with the international trend.[45] What is at stake in this interpretive dissensus?

Let us then look to the French side for a response. Republicanism there is commonly identified with the triad *liberté, égalité, fraternité,* the historical motto of the French Republic,[46] with the addition of *laïcité,* a notion that became important at the end of the nineteenth century. It is now an integral part of the national narrative, one that started in 1789 with the birth of the modern French nation and has been attached to its identity.[47] While there are numerous books on French republics, such as the studies of Maurice Agulhon and Pierre Nora, most of them are written as political, social, or cultural history.[48] There is surprisingly little written by the French themselves about republicanism as a political theory, unless it is considered as a form of ideology. This is the case, for instance, in Nicolet's landmark study, which "considers the history of the Republic as

44 Pettit, "Two Republican Traditions."

45 Prochasson, "Introuvable Modèle Républicain." An important exception is Jean-Fabien Spitz (see Spitz, *La république? Quelles valeurs?*)

46 The motto is officially adopted in the constitution of the Second Republic (1848). It had already been proposed by Robespierre in 1790 (in his *Discours sur l'organisation des gardes nationales*).

47 Weil and Truong, *Le sens de la république*; Peillon, *Liberté, égalité, fraternité. Sur le républicanisme français.*

48 Agulhon, *Marianne au combat: l'imagerie et la symbolique républicaine de 1789 à 1880*; Agulhon, *La république au village*; Nora, *Les lieux de mémoire. Tome I, la république.*

the history of an ideology, that is of an opinion, of a *representation*."[49] It may be that the idea of republicanism has acquired the status of a sacred credo, which is taboo to question, or a state ideology whose critics risk being accused of treason.[50]

Furthermore, philosophers are wary of focusing on a corpus with mostly minor authors, whose treatises appear ideologically oriented and lacking in theoretical substance or systematicity.[51] The situation has recently changed as a few French scholars have aimed to rehabilitate the tradition by analyzing the works of Third Republic thinkers.[52] Yet such important historical work still struggles to draw a systematic picture of the republican tradition in France, which remains diverse and context-specific.

This book provides a bridge between the national narrative of the French and the neo-republican negative assessment of French republicanism. This bridge can be created, I contend, by looking at the historical and conceptual intersection between the shaping of the French tradition and the classical and modern (Greek, Roman, Italian, English, and American) traditions embraced by neo-republicanism. The wager of this book is that to understand the specificity of French republicanism (or *républicanisme à la française*), we should look at its transformation in the first years of the Revolution. Studying this period of innovation reveals the particular shape of French republicanism, marked by both its radical form as a theory of emancipation and its enduring problems as a structure of exclusion. Understanding this moment can also explain *how* this specific tradition differs from its ancestors, whose precepts it adapted, translated, and transformed.

Interpreting the beginning as carrying meaning is in itself a typically republican approach. In this case, what does the beginning tell us? How and when does French republicanism begin? A central claim of this book is that the "beginning" of French republicanism is not a birth, but rather a transformation of an older language, the reconfiguration of an inherited

[49] Nicolet, *L'idée républicaine en France: Essai d'histoire critique (1789–1924)*.

[50] For the idea that republicanism is a state ideology, see Hazareesingh, *Political Traditions in Modern France*, 65–97 and *Intellectual Founders of the Republic*.

[51] Among authors who may appear minor from an international perspective, I should mention Charles Renouvier, Étienne Vacherot, Jules Simon, Jules Barni, Alfred Fouillée, Henri Marion, Léon Bourgeois and Célestin Bouglé.

[52] Spitz, *Le moment républicain*; Audier, *La pensée solidariste. Aux sources du modèle social républicain*; Audier, *Léon Bourgeois*; Blais, *La solidarité: histoire d'une idée*.

way of thinking. I argue that during the Revolution, early republicans found themselves under the necessity of adapting a language that did not immediately fit the task it was called to accomplish. They chose the powerful yet elitist republican language of the freedom of the few to achieve the new task of emancipating everyone. This task required new devices – the creation of a thick notion of citizenship and the embrace of popular sovereignty – to overcome the considerable obstacles it encountered.

For most French historians, republicanism is an original ideological creation born with the Revolution, which gives France its idiosyncratic political form. If we want to investigate the beginnings of French republicanism, it goes without saying that we should look at the revolutionary event that shaped it.[53] For many historians, and certainly in the shared national narrative, the French Revolution marks the absolute beginning of modern France, which subsequently takes the form of a succession of republics. The fusion between republicanism and the Revolution is such that all republicans have felt the need to provide an interpretation of the Revolution, and, in turn, the interpretation that one gives of the Revolution has been key to determining one's political stance. French thinkers and politicians have provided time and again their reading of the Revolution to place themselves politically. This was as true in the nineteenth century, when republicans, such as Louis Blanc wrote histories of the Revolution, as it is today for intellectuals like Marcel Gauchet.[54] It is even true of politicians – see, for instance, the political leader Jean-Luc Mélenchon, who sees Robespierre as the hero of his preferred radical left-wing populism, and the right-of-center president Emmanuel Macron, who embraces a strong executive function and has not hesitated to praise Napoleon, despite the latter's association with imperialism and slavery. However one interprets the Revolution, from the left-wing endorsement of Robespierre by historians like Mathiez to the rejection of Jacobinism by Aulard, French republicans have been in the habit of claiming "exceptionality," arguing that nowhere else on the face of the Earth had there ever been such a monumental emancipatory event.[55]

[53] In linking French republicanism and the Revolution, I join most of the scholarship. In this regard, see Furet, *Penser la Révolution française* and *La Révolution en débat*; Nicolet, *L'idée républicaine en France: Essai d'histoire critique (1789–1924)*; Jennings, "Citizenship, Republicanism and Multiculturalism in Contemporary France."

[54] Gauchet, *Robespierre: l'homme qui nous divise le plus.* See among many other examples, Lamartine, Maurras, Jaurès, and so on.

[55] For claims on the exceptionality of French republicanism, see Vovelle, *Révolution et république. L'exception française*; Nicolet, *L'idée républicaine en France: Essai*

The "exceptionality claim" can be traced back to the insistence of revolutionaries that they were building anew. Despite their emphatic references to antiquity, and in particular to the Roman Republic, they claimed that no model could be adequate for their enterprise. Their avowal to have broken with the past, I contend, repressed the inherited burdens ensconced in their notion of republicanism. It was this claim to radical *invention* that in large part prevented the French over and over from coming to terms with the hidden premises of the political language they adopted, with the fact that the past had bequeathed more than they imagined. Republicanism, which quickly became the central political language of revolutionaries and soon of all French politics, was far from being a spontaneous creation of the French Revolution. It was, on the contrary, a multifaceted inheritance that weighed heavily on the way republicanism came to be conceptualized in the new context of late eighteenth-century France.

UNIVERSALISM AND EMANCIPATION

From the critics of republicanism – like the *Indigènes* of the Republic – to its more devoted proponents, French republicanism is always seen as universalist in its core intent. The claim that French republicans' main exploit was the universalization of freedom is not a recent one. In 1794, the First French Republic, only in its second year of existence, was supposed to become the beacon of the free world. Or at least, this is what Robespierre hoped when he announced the necessity of implementing the reign of virtue and terror,

> so that France, once illustrious among enslaved countries, eclipsing the glory of all the free peoples that have existed, may become the *model for all nations*, the terror of oppressors, the consolation of the oppressed, the ornament of the universe; and that in sealing our work with our blood, we may at least glimpse the shining dawn of *universal felicity*.[56]

Liberated from its abject past of subjection to monarchy, republican France was to lead the world into a future of universal freedom and happiness. Universalism here takes the form of exemplariness: France is

d'histoire critique (1789–1924); de Saint-Victor and Branthôme, *Histoire de la république en France*.

56 Discourse of February 5, 1794 (18 Pluviôse Year II) ("Sur les principes de morale politique qui doivent guider la Convention nationale dans l'administration intérieure de la République,"*Œuvres*, vol. X, 350–66); Robespierre, *Robespierre. Virtue and Terror*, 110. My emphasis.

universal because it shows what all free people in the world could hope to realize for themselves.

Robespierre not only praised France for setting the example of a virtuous republic, but he also underlined the reason for its exceptionality among republics, which made it the universal leader of freedom: "The French are the first people in the world to have established true democracy, by calling *all men* to equality and the plenitude of citizens' rights; and that, in my opinion, is the reason why all the tyrants allied against the Republic will be vanquished."[57]

The glory of France was thus to set out popular sovereignty and extend freedom equally to the whole of its citizenry, that is to say to make a democracy out of a republic. While early modern thought had carefully separated republics and democracies, French republicans like Robespierre saw democracy as the very realization of the republic as a universal regime of free and equal citizens. Because the principles are universal, that is, valid for all in the world, they should start with being applied at home to all, that is, *generalized* to all French citizens.

The timing of Robespierre's declaration will give readers pause. In early 1794, having suspended the republican constitution a few months before, the revolutionary government was battling external enemies on all its borders, and was trying to end the civil war in Vendée, a large rural and royalist region in Western France, with incendiary battalions aiming to destroy everything in their wake (the infamous "*colonnes infernales,*" literally, the battalions from Hell.)[58] Yet, even a couple of years before this bloodbath, the claim that France was special for being the first republican democracy and the leading light toward freedom still seemed odd.

Republicanism as a theory of freedom was not born with the French Revolution – it had a long history both of existing regimes and of extensive theorization before Robespierre converted to republicanism in the relatively later stages of the Revolution.[59] Robespierre was well aware of the republican tradition, to which he frequently referred. Given the long history of republics in Europe, France's regime was hardly a novelty. Yet what was singular in the French case, Robespierre claimed, was neither the idea of republican freedom, which it indeed took from an illustrious republican past, nor its liberation from monarchy, since antimonarchism

[57] Idem. My emphasis.

[58] See Furet's article on "Vendée," in *Dictionnaire critique de la Révolution française.*

[59] Scurr, *Fatal Purity. Robespierre and the French Revolution*; McPhee, *Robespierre. A Revolutionary Life*; Rousselière, "Can Popular Sovereignty Be Represented? Jacobinism from Radical Democracy to Populism."

had been an important part of the tradition. Rather, it was its appeal to inclusive emancipation, that is, the universal application of freedom. The French were transforming a theory of the freedom of the few into a theory of emancipation of all. Republicanism was moving from a theory of exclusion to a theory of inclusion.

Even a cursory look at the history of republics confirms Robespierre's suggestion that republicanism was historically based on a less-than-universalist theory of freedom. Sparta was famous for its small number of citizens, and its large number of helots whose labor made it possible for citizens to devote themselves to the cultivation of virtue and military skills. Athens restricted citizenship exclusively to men of free birth with two Athenian parents, and left metics with no path to citizenship despite their active engagement in civic and economic life.[60] Even eighteenth-century republics, such as the cities of Venice and Geneva, had elitist governmental structures and highly exclusionary rules, which left some of its native-born population without any hope of acquiring citizenship.[61]

Yet, one may object that republicanism had surely not only served the preservation of freedom for those lucky enough to have been born male citizens in a republic. It was also fundamentally a theory of emancipation, and that is what made it attractive for reformers and lovers of liberty throughout history. Take the example of Rome, which had a conception of citizenship that was not exclusively tied to kinship. Roman law granted citizenship to some of conquered cities.[62] Being a republican meant believing in overthrowing tyrants and freeing peoples from subjection. Take the example of the English republicans of the mid-seventeenth century, such as Milton and Nedham, who used republican ideas against tyrannical monarchy.[63]

At stake was not whether republicanism as a theory could be mobilized against domination, which it undoubtedly had, but rather whether it could be applied universally. In these two examples, Rome and seventeenth-century England, freedom was not a concept that intrinsically commanded a norm of universal application. Roman republicans did not object to the fact that many were deemed unworthy

[60] Kasimis, *The Perpetual Immigrant and the Limits of Athenian Democracy*, 5–6.

[61] Grubb, "Elite Citizens"; Kirk, "Genevan Republicanism"; Rosenblatt, *Rousseau and Geneva*, 18.

[62] See for instance the 188 Law to expand citizenship to Fundi, Formiae, and Arpinum (Lintott, *The Constitution of the Roman Republic*, 27.)

[63] Milton, *The Tenure of Kings and Magistrate;* Nedham, *The Case of the Commonwealth of England, Stated* and *The Excellencie of a Free State.*

of citizenship, nor did they reject the existence of slavery in itself. In turn, English republicans used republicanism as a theory of emancipation from monarchy – but they did not object to private domination.[64] Sidney, for instance, did not see a contradiction between his fight for public freedom and his endorsement of the private domination of servants.[65] Harrington's first order in *Oceana* sorts out freemen and servants: those who cannot "live of themselves" cannot be citizens.[66] In all these cases, republican freedom was sought after – but only for the happy few who were deemed worthy of it, and in a strictly political domain. It lacked universality both in terms of those considered fit to be free (the extent of freedom), and the kinds of practices that ought to be protected (the domain of freedom).

The proclamation of the American Republic might seem to eclipse the exceptionality of French republicanism and render Robespierre's claim preposterous. From the late 1960s on, the neo-republican revival in U.S. history has shown the formidable importance of republican ideas at the end of the eighteenth century in America.[67] An important part of the scholarship suggests that the republican transformations of France and the United States come from the same revolutionary moment.[68] More radically than any other states before, the two sister republics both embraced popular sovereignty and sought to combine republic and democracy. It has been argued that the success of the American Revolution inspired the French one.[69] Already for James Madison, popular sovereignty came from an American impulse: "In Europe, charters of liberty have been granted by power. America has set the example and France has followed it, of charters of power granted by liberty."[70] Of the two, America was clearly the elder republic clearing the path to freedom.

64 Gourevitch, "Labor Republicanism and the Transformation of Work," 15.

65 Sidney, *Discourses Concerning Government*, 41.

66 Harrington, *The Commonwealth of Oceana and A System of Politics*, 75.

67 Bailyn, *The Ideological Origins of the American Revolution*; Wood, *The Creation of the American Republic, 1776–1787*; Hont and Ignatieff, *Wealth and Virtue: The Shaping of Political Economy in the Scottish Enlightenment*; Shalhope, "Republicanism and Early American Historiography."

68 Palmer, *The Age of the Democratic Revolution: A Political History of Europe and America. 1760–1800*; Godechot, *France and the Atlantic Revolution of the Eighteenth Century, 1770–1799*.

69 Kloppenberg, *Toward Democracy: The Struggle for Self-Rule in European and American Thought*, 2.

70 Madison, For the *National Gazette*, January 18, 1792.

Contrary to many other French revolutionaries – in particular the ones later called "Girondins" such as Clavière, Brissot, and Condorcet – Robespierre knew very little about the American Revolution and did not participate in the trans-Atlantic intellectual discussions around its state constitutions.[71] His ignorance may explain, to some extent, his misunderstanding of the importance of the American revolution and of American constitutionalism, and his inflation of the role of the French Revolution with regard to the transformation of republican theory and the principles of modern government.

Yet in his ignorance, he anticipated a long-standing political debate on the difference between the two revolutions.[72] Conceding that the Americans had given "an imperfect example" (Discourse of April 15, 1793), Robespierre claimed that French republicanism had a more pronounced claim to universalism – to which the *Declaration of the Rights of Man and the Citizen* bore witness – and to social and material equality – as the abolition of privilege in August 1789 and Robespierre's own *Draft Declaration of the Rights of Man (1793)* showed. While Robespierre doubtlessly got a lot wrong, and despite his blind spot about the American Republic, he was right in singling out the specificity of French republicanism as a theory of the emancipation of all with a universalist vocation and an egalitarian dimension beyond the strictly political domain.

The American case was further marked by the existence of slavery on their national soil. Viewed from France, the Constitution of the United States betrayed a fundamental contradiction between the universality of its claim to freedom and its interpretation accepting vast exclusions.[73] Even for Condorcet, the one who most deeply admired the American endeavor and its constitutional inventiveness, this contradiction stained the American example.[74] One should temper, however, the self-glorification: French revolutionaries took a long time to end slavery in their colonies, and only did so when forced to by powerful insurrections from slaves. Just like the Americans, the French were not exempt from self-contradiction.

71 On the French discussion of American constitutions, see Appleby, "America as a Model for the Radical French Reformers of 1789"; Palmer, *The Age of the Democratic Revolution: A Political History of Europe and America. 1760–1800*. I discuss this in Chapter 1.

72 See, for instance, Arendt, who claims that in the French Revolution, in contrast with the American one, "freedom had to surrender to necessity, to the urgency of the life process itself" (*On Revolution*, 60).

73 The literature on the question is of course immense. See Wood, *Power and Liberty: Constitutionalism in the American Revolution*, 100–25.

74 Condorcet, "Influence de la révolution de l'Amérique sur les opinions et la législation de l'Europe," 13.

In the two following centuries, an increasing number of French thinkers and politicians, however critical most of them were of Jacobinism and the Terror, reasserted Robespierre's fundamental belief that the republican ideal served the cause of universal emancipation. During this period, the republic appeared to yield many successes: free and public education turned peasants into citizens,[75] universal suffrage was achieved,[76] and outside of the Hexagon, France pursued a "civilizing mission" of expanding freedom in the world that gave it considerable cultural, political, and economic powers.[77] The bicentenary of the revolution in 1989 offered an occasion to renew France's commitment to republican democracy. François Furet and Mona Ozouf's *Critical Dictionary of the French Revolution*, a monumental commemorative volume published for the occasion, celebrated the French Revolution in a lapidary statement: it was, simply, "the birth of democracy."[78] The bicentenary festivities were lavish and unabashedly self-congratulatory. Yet one distinguished guest, the British Prime Minister Margaret Thatcher, found the French arrogance out of place and expressed a Burkean reluctance at the idea of the Revolution. "The rights of men did not start with the Revolution," she said, as they were developed in the course of British history with the Magna Carta of 1215 and the Glorious Revolution. The importance of the storming of the Bastille should not be exaggerated, she claimed, as "there were only seven prisoners in there." And most importantly, for Thatcher, the Revolution devolved into the Terror on the ground of ideas that the Communists would later endorse.[79] The French may be self-satisfied but, for Thatcher, the meaning of the Revolution was still open to skeptical interpretation. Needless to say, she was booed during the celebrations.

FREEDOM AND ITS PARADOXES

I have so far defined French republicanism as a form of political theory that sought to rework the republican tradition to universalize freedom and combine republicanism with democracy. I have not yet specified the

[75] Weber, *Peasants into Frenchmen. The Modernization of Rural France, 1870–1914*; Agulhon, *La république au village*.

[76] Rosanvallon, *Le sacre du citoyen: histoire du suffrage universel en France*.

[77] Conklin, *A Mission to Civilize: The Republican Idea of Empire in France and West Africa, 1895–1930*.

[78] Furet and Ozouf, *A Critical Dictionary of the French Revolution*.

[79] Thatcher's interview was published in the national newspaper *Le Monde* on July 13, 1989. I was not able to locate the original English, and I had to translate her words from French back into English. These are therefore not Thatcher's exact words.

meaning of freedom at play in this enterprise, though I mentioned that the neo-republican revival overwhelmingly privileges the definition of freedom as non-domination as the central feature of the theory. When looking at the French Revolution, however, the question of what is meant by freedom is surprisingly difficult to ascertain. Given the extent of the scholarship on both republicanism and the French Revolution, one would expect some scholarly consensus on the definition of republican freedom in the late eighteenth century. Nothing of the sort can be found.[80]

Let us start with the contemporary assessment. On the one hand, as we saw earlier, the neo-republican revival has provided one clear and powerful answer: republican freedom is best defined as non-domination. The idea of "non-domination" was elaborated as an alternative to the liberal view most clearly expressed by Isaiah Berlin in his *Two Concepts of Liberty* (1958).[81] For Berlin, there are two main conceptions of freedom, one negative (non-interference) and the other positive (self-mastery). This conceptual framework was the point of departure for neo-republicans to articulate what the republican idea of freedom was by contrast: neither a negative concept of non-interference nor a concept of positive freedom, but rather, robust protection against the uncontrolled will of others. Freedom as non-domination, as Pettit came to call it, entails that someone is unfree if she is under the control of a master, even if the latter happens to be a "good master" who does not interfere with her. It also means that one is free under the rule of (just) laws since laws are not an arbitrary or uncontrolled type of interference in a republic. Laws are thus necessary for freedom to be possible.[82] Republican freedom entails being under "the empire of laws."

It is important to note here that the claim that republican freedom is primarily freedom as non-domination is a move against a trend in the early republican revival, mostly led by Baron and then Pocock: the civic humanist idea that freedom was political participation.[83] For Pettit, such an idea of freedom is mostly a romanticized idea of participation in the

[80] This is what De Dijn notes, though she provides an answer against the grain of neo-republican scholarship: "the freedom fought for by the Atlantic revolutionaries was of a particular kind: it was the antique freedom to govern themselves" (Dijn, *Freedom: An Unruly History*, 188). I partially agree with her, as will become clear.

[81] Berlin, "Two Concepts of Liberty."

[82] Pettit, *Republicanism*, 17–79.

[83] Baron, *The Crisis of the Early Italian Renaissance: Civic Humanism and Republican Liberty in an Age of Classicism and Tyranny*; Pocock, *The Machiavellian Moment: Florentine Political Thought and the Atlantic Republican Tradition.*

community; it obfuscates what freedom really is. That is to say: it perpetuates a normatively inadequate, or mistaken idea, of freedom.

The neo-republican understanding of freedom should be contrasted with the definition of republican freedom in the immediate aftermath of the French Revolution. Berlin's theory of the two freedoms refers to and reformulates an idea central to Benjamin Constant's lecture at the Athénée Royal in 1818.[84] In his discourse, Constant contrasts the freedom of the moderns (the freedom to enjoy individual rights) and the freedom of the ancients (the freedom to participate collectively in government). The freedom of the moderns has been interpreted as *liberal freedom*, a form of non-interference consisting in enjoying rights and liberties in the silence of the laws and under a limited government. But what is exactly the freedom of the ancients?

Understanding Constant's discourse requires putting it in its strategic, polemical context. A republican during his youth, that is, during the Thermidorian Convention, Constant moved away from republicanism toward a more liberal position.[85] While Constant presents the contrast between the two liberties under descriptive garb, his goal is clearly prescriptive: he aims to show what freedom should and should not be. Obviously, it should *not* be what led to the Terror: a form of collective and unlimited political power that trampled individual freedoms. For Constant, this is how we should understand the heart of Jacobin politics, a form of republican power that disregarded the importance of limiting the sphere of government action and popular sovereignty. The "freedom" embodied in the Jacobin vision of politics was unacceptable to Constant, who had been a direct witness to the Terror. More than an analytical distinction, the opposition of the two liberties was a political intervention, directly targeting the revolutionary enterprise of thinking about freedom as coming from membership in the popular sovereign, which for Constant gave rise to bloody chaos.

Yet Constant himself did not ascribe the whole of republican thought to this ancient way of thinking. Rather, as has been argued by recent scholarship, Constant noted the excess of both types of freedom, and the need for an association of the two if one hoped to maintain a free government and not fall prey to counterrevolutionary forces.[86] He was

84 Constant, *Political Writings*, 308–28.

85 On Constant's republicanism, see Rousselière, "On Political Responsibility in Post-Revolutionary Times: Kant and Constant's Debate on Lying."

86 Fontana, *Benjamin Constant and the Post-Revolutionary Mind*, 48–67; Kalyvas and Katznelson, *Liberal Beginnings: Making a Republic for the Moderns*.

careful to say that modern freedom would not be sufficient to preserve an uncorrupted government. Participation in government was necessary for moderns to be free. Constant can thus be interpreted as a liberal republican.

Constant furnished an influential way of understanding what republican freedom meant before the Atlantic revolutions: a form of self-government and participation in politics. Importantly, this understanding converges with the assessment of many eighteenth-century thinkers, notably Montesquieu. As I show in Chapter 1, Montesquieu's reception of republicanism provides a largely polemical analysis of republicanism by claiming it was unfit for modernity at least for a large country like France, which could never be a federation. Importantly, for Montesquieu, republican freedom – understood as the freedom of the ancients – is outdated as it supposes a sacrifice of the self that modern individuals are unwilling to make.

Both the Montesquieu-Constant and the neo-republican approaches define republican freedom *normatively* either as what it ought *not* to be (a positive conception of political participation in self-government) or what it *ought* to be (a protected status against domination). While they claim to be historically accurate, both approaches are in fact focused on providing an attractive and coherent vision of freedom rather than embracing the complexity and possible incoherence of the notion of freedom as it was conceptualized by "classical" republicans, that is republicans before the Atlantic revolutions.

Where does this leave our understanding of the nature of republican freedom in eighteenth-century France and during the Revolution? On the eve of the Revolution, the republican understanding of freedom is nowhere near as clearly defined as neo-republicans would argue. Rather, I claim, what prevails is an ambivalent definition that oscillates between the idea of non-domination (freedom as non-domination) and the notion of self-government (freedom as self-government). The two notions are not taken to be analytically distinct by eighteenth-century thinkers, even though neo-republicans are correct in maintaining that they ought to be distinguished. For eighteenth-century thinkers, as well as revolutionaries that took up and reworked the republican discourse, the fight against domination and the endorsement of self-government necessarily came together. I analyze this idea in Chapter 1.

An important aspect of this ambivalence is that the idea of self-government supposes a range of conditions. It should be noted that eighteenth-century republicans and revolutionaries did not understand self-government as self-mastery, that is, an ideal notion of perfect self-control. Nor did they necessarily think of self-government as democracy, a notion of which many were initially wary.[87] Rather, they saw self-government as a capacity that not everyone exhibited – an idea that cut across different strands of the republican tradition: some citizens are free because they "live of themselves," as Harrington wrote, whereas others behave like dependents, that is, unfree individuals.

For eighteenth-century thinkers and revolutionaries, freedom as self-government

(1) required material and economic independence ("private independence")
(2) required moral and cognitive skills ("agency competence")
(3) did not preclude the necessity of dominating others privately and possibly required it in many circumstances ("asymmetrical domination").

To be a republican citizen, one must first be rid of private dependence, that is to say economic and social dependence. The citizen needs to have some property to rely on and he cannot be a domestic servant. In eighteenth century France, many men did not meet these conditions. Women were bound not to have this type of material and economic independence, as they were dependent on men for their subsistence and social status.

Next, the republican citizen needs to have the moral and cognitive skills that make self-government possible, though he does not have to be in mastery of all his passions (which would be an unrealistically high goal). He needs to have sufficient virtue and knowledge to govern himself, which sets the idea of "agency competence" as a threshold rather than an ideal. He needs to be educated (possess epistemic competence) and virtuous (show moral competence).

Finally, the republican citizen may have to dominate others in order not to be dominated. One can see how this makes sense intuitively. As a matter of practical reality in the eighteenth century, an independent man capable of self-government relies on others (such as his wife and servants) to provide himself with the resources necessary for his freedom. He needs to rely on dependents so that he himself can be free from dependence.

87 Most revolutionaries started to explicitly endorse the notion of "democracy" in the course of the Revolution, not before.

Given the difficulty of acquiring such private independence and agency competence, denying the possibility of dominating others to achieve this status seems simply to deny the possibility of freedom itself.

Once we recognize these three conditions, which I analyze in Chapters 4 and 5, we can better understand the nature of the difficulty encountered by revolutionaries. They could not simply proclaim the universalization of freedom as non-domination. They had to think through how to get rid of social and political dependence, and how to restructure relations of dependence that made large parts of the population ineligible for freedom as self-government.

The work of universalizing a conception that was intrinsically structured in an exclusive and elitist way led French revolutionaries into two paradoxes: the paradox of republican emancipation and the paradox of national universalism. These paradoxes, I contend, are enduring problems that plague French republicanism. They come from a contradiction between a universal premise (Premise 1) and an exclusive one (Premise 2).

The "paradox of republican emancipation" (which I present in Chapter 4) can be articulated in the following way:

(1) Freedom ought to be universalized.
(2) Freedom requires private independence and agency competence.

The two premises are in tension with another. They create a paradox:

Paradox of Republican Emancipation: only those who are not dependent, that is, those who are already free, are eligible to be emancipated.

The second paradox, the paradox of national universalism, takes a somewhat different form.

(1) *Republican citizenship* is universal: it is an inclusive status that demands allegiance to republican political principles and not a particular culture.
(2) *National belonging* is an exclusive status that requires sharing a common culture.

The citizen of a particular country, here France, has thus to abide by both general and particular rules, on the basis of belonging to both an inclusive community and an exclusive community, each of which is definitionally different yet claims to include the same people. This may seem to be a tension rather than a logical paradox. However, as I show in Chapter 5, the confusion between the two notions creates a practical paradox for the members of the political community who are torn between two different injunctions.

CHAPTER SUMMARIES

In Chapter 1, I discuss the state of the debate about republicanism before the French Revolution. While coming out of different strands of European thought, republicanism in this period mostly appeared as a political theory of a virtuous elite devoted to the pursuit of freedom. The republican tradition at that time was generally seen as inapplicable to modern circumstances. In what I call the "scale thesis," Montesquieu questioned whether republicanism could fit a large and modern country.

Montesquieu saw challenges to the possibility of applying the republican ideal to the circumstances of modernity. He argued that there would be three great obstacles to establishing a large, successful republic, which I call the unity, epistemic, and motivation objections. Montesquieu, however, did not consider all the resources that were available in the tradition to overcome these obstacles. I show how the republican tradition, in its wide temporal and geographical diversity, contained important elements beyond those Montesquieu underlined. These different traditions (Italian, English, American) informed the French republicans on key issues (conquest, freedom, commerce, institutions). In Chapter 1, I retrace the context in which the myth of outdated republicanism was born, but also how its elitism and martial dimension durably impacted its transformation during the Revolution.

Thinking of Rousseau as an "author of the Revolution" is a well-trodden idea. Without making such a causal claim, I note that he is nonetheless constantly invoked and often followed by revolutionaries, be they Girondins, Jacobins, or pretty much any other kind, with the exception of the *Monarchiens*, who were not fond of him. Rousseau radically transformed the fate of republicanism in France by democratizing it and adapting it to a large country. Under Rousseau's pen, republicanism moved from an elitist language to the language of all the people, and from defining freedom as the status of not being dominated to the rejection of domination altogether. Chapter 2 presents this formidable conceptual transformation.

Rousseau responded to Montesquieu by arguing that a republic would be a solution for a large and modern country because it is rational for individuals to want equality as a condition for their freedom. In his theory, virtue is transformed into a rational feeling of allegiance to a polity of free and equal citizens, and the unity and epistemic challenges are met with a new theory of citizenship. By laying out a theory of interdependence on an egalitarian basis, Rousseau explained how solidarity can emerge in a republican democracy. These advantages notwithstanding, Rousseau's theory also carried an ambivalence that has plagued French republicanism ever since. On the one hand, it presented a rational and universalist project of equal freedom for all, but on the other hand, it required an emphasis on particularism and nationalism as a condition of its maintenance, as Rousseau himself lucidly acknowledged.

Chapter 3 presents the emergence of a new form of republicanism in the revolutionary period. I argue that this theory was called upon to address a problem that was historically foreign to it: enabling the emancipation of a large and diverse people that had just lost the unifying power of their King. After examining the arguments of the first republican treatises (in particular those of Condorcet, Robert, and Billaud-Varenne), the chapter lays out the solutions republicans imagined to the problem that arose with the defection of the King. This included the attempt to create a united popular sovereign to replace him, and, in response to Montesquieu's challenges, the creation of a virtuous and educated citizenry that was ready to defend the republic. Revolutionaries imagined a republic based on an abstract notion of citizenship and a representative system without representation of particular interests. I conclude this chapter by revisiting the debate between Sieyès, Condorcet, and Robespierre about how to represent the people in a republic.

Chapter 4 confronts the paradox of republican emancipation. This paradox is due to the ambivalence of republican freedom, which revolutionaries interpreted in two different ways. On the one hand, republican freedom is the status of those who are already masters of themselves (as well as "masters" of slaves, wives, and other dependents). Freedom is independence and it is this independence that makes them capable of governing with competence and virtue. On the other hand, freedom is the newly claimed right of everyone, or anyone, not to be dominated – regardless of their virtue or their socio economic situation, that is, regardless of their capacity to self-govern. But how can one reconcile the universal claim of freedom as non-domination with the republican premise that the free person ought to be already socially, economically, and intellectually independent to be able to self-govern? If the many are incapable of self-governing and must be subordinated to the few, how can they ever become independent from the government of the few – how can they ever emancipate themselves? This chapter presents four instances of this paradox: the debate on passive/active citizenship; Condorcet's position on the emancipation of slaves; Guyomar's argument for the emancipation of women; and Grouchy's proposal for changing the way we think about human dependence.

Chapter 5 examines the possible reasons for French republicanism's historical tendency to exclude foreigners and minorities. After retracing the formation of the discourse of "nation" alongside that of "people," I argue that the development of nationalism alongside the discourse of universalism created what I call a "national universalist logic." Different forms of republican universalism (cosmopolitanism, exemplariness, and generalization) turned into their opposite exclusionary movements (respectively xenophobia, conquest, and homogenization). The chapter presents educational policies and civil religion as two instances that manifest the national universalist logic of revolutionary republicanism. I then argue that this internal tension leads to the paradox of national universalism.

The conclusion offers an overview of French republicanism as a theory of sharing freedom. I argue that its originality lies in its being a theory of emancipation, of republican democracy, and solidarity.

SHARING FREEDOM

This book project began with the goal of defining the conceptual architecture of French republicanism and determining whether it was a coherent and normatively attractive theory. Such an enterprise proved too vast. It would require looking at over two centuries of intellectual, political, economic, and social history in addition to providing a normative demonstration of this theory. The more modest argument of this book takes a narrower aim: to determine some of the key historical and conceptual patterns that have made republicanism, in its French form, the paradoxical theory that it is. I have limited my work to the formative years of the Revolution, where I believe most of the answers lie.

One might ask why this study stops before the end of the First Republic, which technically comes only when Napoleon Bonaparte proclaimed himself Emperor of the French in May 1804. The First Republic officially entails the Thermidorian Convention (July 1794–October 1795), the Directory (October 1795–November 1799, that is "the 18th Brumaire"), and the Consulate (November 1799–May 1804). This period is rich in transformations for republicans. The Thermidorian Republic, often considered the beginning of the "bourgeois" republican period,[88] opens a

[88] See Dunn, "The identity of the bourgeois liberal republic." For an analysis of post-Terror republicanism, see Jainchill, *Reimagining Politics after the Terror*.

new dimension of republicanism, one that I plan to explore in future work. During the Thermidorian Convention, republicanism can be seen as embodying the quest for institutional stability, that is, being on the side of order rather than change. This recurring tendency of republicanism remains to be fully analyzed.[89] The choice to focus on the period preceding the Revolution until 1794 is dictated by my theoretical goal. I focus on the intensely revolutionary period before 1794 where republicanism is characterized by ambivalence: both an attempt to bring about radical change and emancipation to all and an attempt to stabilize institutions through potentially exclusionary measures. This is the formative tension I am interested in exploring. Once this tension is dissolved, another dimension of republicanism – an institutional form of republicanism aiming for social order – becomes prevalent. This important transformation, however, is not the object of this study.

The matrix of French republicanism, as I contend in Chapter 2, can be found in the work of Rousseau, whose social contract theory shows how freedom can exist in a modern country of interdependent and self-interested individuals, as long as their association is based on a principle of equality promoting individual freedom and citizens' solidarity. Rousseau should be credited for laying out a new social ontology of interdependence. Since political beings are by necessity in a relation of dependence with one another, they should aim to build up this interdependence in a way that avoids dominating relations, that is, in a properly republican way.

Rousseau's legacy to French republicans is immense. They became focused on the conditions of possibility for freedom to be realized in a modern country of interdependent, self-interested individuals. The project of "expanding" freedom as non-domination turned out to be much more: it entailed a restructuring of social and economic relations of dependence into relations of mutually beneficial interdependence. Such a restructuring required seizing popular sovereignty, creating a thick sense of citizenship through education, and imagining ways of improving social and economic equality. I explore these ideas in Chapter 3.

I develop this model in what follows as "the republican model of sharing freedom." The idea of "sharing" freedom captures the two dimensions of this political project: that freedom has to belong to all, and not to the few, and that it needs to entail an act of solidarity that actively binds those who are sharing it. No one emancipates anyone; yet

[89] For an argument about the contemporary tendency of French republicanism to be on the side of order, see Spitz, *La république? Quelles valeurs? Essai sur un nouvel intégrisme*.

each is freed by all. French republicanism provides, in my view, a valuable contribution to the revival of republican theory, that is, a reflection on the economic and social conditions of freedom and the ways in which the social bond can be created through egalitarian institutions and policies in a large and diverse country.

French republicanism, though, has its risks and shortcomings. *Sharing Freedom* thus provides a critical approach rather than a laudatory one. Modifying our understanding of the history of republicanism does not require creating yet another myth, but rather taking into consideration the real history of popular emancipation. By doing this, we prize open a new conceptual possibility for republicanism as a theory not only of freedom but of emancipation.

1

Plural Beginnings

A long-standing narrative among French historians takes republicanism to be the political theory that defines their national history: The modern French nation and the idea of republicanism arose together in the storming of the Bastille.[1] An idea without a past, republicanism for them was created by sheer French genius – or rather, if a republican past existed, it was so different in kind from the modern form of republicanism that took shape in France that it was pure homonymy. In this national narrative, republicanism is an idiosyncratic invention of the French, whose revolution opened a path for the emancipation of oppressed peoples, or so the story goes. With the advent of the French Republic came the birth of the free French people, as the revolutionary calendar acknowledged, resetting the beginning of time to September 1792, the start of the First French Republic.

The birth of French republicanism, taken to coincide with the birth of the French nation as a free people, is essentially a national myth, which became popular at times of national consolidation, most notably in the Third Republic which needed to strengthen domestic unity after the defeat in the Franco-Prussian war (1870–1871). In this politically charged context, the historian Ernest Renan, later dubbed "the Third Republic's God,"[2] argued in his influential *What Is a Nation?* (1882) that the idea of the nation ought not to be based on race, ethnicity,

[1] Nicolet, *L'idée républicaine en France: Essai d'histoire critique (1789–1924)*; Vovelle, *Révolution et république. L'exception française.* This opinion is reflected in popular weekly newspapers such as *Marianne.*

[2] Compagnon, "Le dieu de la IIIe République."

language, religion, or geography, but on the *will* of the people, that is, on the "clearly expressed desire to live a common life," which amounted for him to "a daily plebiscite." The idea of patriotic republicanism was thus made compatible with the modern idea of the nation.[3] Renan, however, importantly added that

> [T]he act of forgetting, I would even say historical error, is an essential factor in the creation of a nation, which is why progress in historical studies often constitutes a danger for nationality. Indeed, historical inquiry brings back to light the deeds of violence that took place at the origin of all political formations, even of those whose consequences have been the most beneficial.[4]

Renan may be right that "unity is always achieved brutally" in the history of nations – it is beyond the scope of this book to assess this sweeping claim. Yet in the light of the contemporary sentiments of exclusion and the debates over the colonial past of the French Republic, his injunction that we ought to forget the past and embrace historical error for the sake of national unity appears wrongheaded.

In the Introduction, I put forth the hypothesis that French republicanism suffered from internal tensions that could be found at its beginnings. This chapter thus interrogates the prerevolutionary foundations of French republicanism at the risk of exposing the "deeds of violence," which, according to Renan, may better remain hidden and ignored. Yet I contend that there is greater violence in forgetting itself, as it informs our political way of thinking unbeknownst to us. If the French foundation narrative is historically false, as I will argue, it is due to a self-inflicted blindness that carries with it detrimental ideas bound to perpetuate the violence of foundation.

One could argue, as the great historian of the French Revolution, François Furet, did, that the myth was not one invented after the facts, but was the creation of the Revolution itself. For Furet, the Revolution "wanted it that way" in order to affirm "the regeneration of humanity through individual liberty," and thus "*erased from the national memory everything that came before.*"[5] In Chapter 3, I will argue that this assessment, which certainly contains an important element of truth, is however inadequate to characterize the relation of revolutionaries to republicanism

[3] See Viroli, *For Love of Country: An Essay on Patriotism and Nationality*, 159–60. For Viroli, Renan was central to the historical constitution of republican patriotism in the nineteenth century.

[4] Renan, *What Is a Nation? And Other Political Writings*, 251.

[5] Furet, "The Ancien Régime and the Revolution," 111. My emphasis.

itself. Republicanism was a tradition that revolutionaries intentionally aimed to retrieve as well as transform. They needed the past to create the future, and they consciously anchored their revolutionary endeavor in the lineage of previous attempts at fighting against domination.

Indeed, revolutionaries were deeply aware of republicanism, and for good reasons. Not only was republicanism alive in many different countries and periods from antiquity onward, it was also the object of intense debate in the reformist milieux of eighteenth-century France.[6] While it is hardly necessary to demonstrate the importance of Enlightenment in the intellectual formation of revolutionaries, the idea that the Enlightenment had a primary *causal* role in the Revolution has been debated at length and it is not my object here to take position on it.[7] The terms of the question are methodologically fraught. Rather than asking whether ideas can cause political events, I am specifically concerned with the elaboration of a specific political theory and its mobilization during the Revolution and its aftermath. I focus, so to speak, on the reasons for action given by revolutionary thinkers and agents, refraining from making claims about causation itself. Instead of arguing that certain ideas caused some events, I retrace the arguments the revolutionaries elaborated to make sense of and justify the formidable changes they both witnessed and realized.

This chapter reconstructs the landscape of republican ideas in eighteenth-century France and makes two overarching arguments.[8] First, I argue that, prompted by Montesquieu, the idea circulated that republicanism, a tradition constituted and reconstituted from antiquity onwards, was unfit for the modern circumstances of a large, unequal,

[6] Among the texts asking about the possibility of republics in large and commercial countries: Montesquieu, *The Spirit of the Laws* and *Considerations on the Causes of the Greatness of the Romans and Their Decline*; Rousseau, *The Social Contract*; Jacques Necker, *On Executive Power in Great States*; Paine, *Lettre au peuple français sur la journée du 18 Fructidor*. In England and in America, the question was also being asked: Hume, *The Idea of a Perfect Commonwealth*; Publius, *The Federalist Papers*; Adams, *A Defense of the Constitution of the United States of America*. For an excellent overview of the question, see Levy, "Beyond Publius: Montesquieu, Liberal Republicanism and the Small-Republic Thesis."

[7] On this debate, see Lefebvre, *The Coming of the French Revolution*; Cobban, *The Social Interpretation of the French Revolution*; Furet, *Penser la Révolution française*; Israel, *Democratic Enlightenment: Philosophy, Revolution, and Human Rights, 1750–1790*.

[8] Needless to say, I make no claim to exhaustivity. I only retrace elements that provide a helpful background for the revolutionary period.

diverse, modernizing, and democratizing country. This is the "scale thesis." Montesquieu raised a tripartite challenge to any modern republicanism, which I dub the "unity," "epistemic," and "motivation" objections. He offers a critical portrait of what after the revolution came to be known as "classical republicanism," one that relies on a virtuous and educated elite in a small tight community.

Second, I argue that contrary to Montesquieu's description, republicanism was a heterogeneous tradition that stretched in different theoretical directions on crucial concerns (I focus here on imperialism, freedom and commerce). This diversity – which finds its sources in Greek and Roman antiquity, the Italian Renaissance, seventeenth-century England, the different eighteenth-century European republics as well as the newly erected American Republic – created layers of complexity that directly impacted the revolutionary reflection on republicanism, as revolutionaries mobilized different aspects of the tradition to answer *ad hoc* concerns. History did not tell revolutionaries that there was only one way of arguing from a republican point of view: Rather it suggested that the complexity of political situations would warrant different conclusions on republican grounds.

While this chapter provides the historical basis to debunk the French myth of national republican invention, it also provides the theoretical background for the immense difficulty of revolutionaries' task: appropriating and modifying a theory which was not immediately suited for the role they wanted it to play. In this rich tradition, they found a range of options that not only stimulated them but also fostered the confusion associated with indeterminate guidance in the face of new circumstances.

WHAT IS A REPUBLIC?

During the eighteenth-century debate on whether republicanism could be an appropriate model for political reform, the most widespread thesis was what we can call the "scale thesis," that is, the claim that republics could only be city-states, or, even better, small rural communities.[9] In a century of growing commerce and in a continent of increasingly large states, this thesis made republicanism look anachronistic and useless. Viewed from the twenty-first century, the scale thesis appears patently false. With hindsight, we know that large republics came not only to exist but also to thrive,

[9] Nelson, *The Greek Tradition in Republican Thought*, 76; Levy, "Beyond Publius: Montesquieu, Liberal Republicanism and the Small-Republic Thesis." These two perspectives are quite different from mine.

and, in the case of the United States, have an uninterrupted constitutional existence. Yet even in the eighteenth century, this thesis was already odd, or at least should have appeared so. There had been large republics in the past, most spectacularly the long-lasting Roman Republic, but also, in more recent memory, short-lived ones like the English Commonwealth. And there were distinctly modern republics in the eighteenth century, such as the United Provinces of the Netherlands. The existence of such Republics was well known to any educated European and abundantly commented upon in the literature and press of the time.[10]

The "scale thesis" was also surprising because republican ideas, widespread in Europe at the time, were bound to be attractive to the many reformers who wanted to find an alternative to the immense arbitrary power of the French monarch. We find such tendencies long before the Revolution in the work of someone like Fénelon, who, in his 1699 *Telemachus* (a didactic book written for Louis XIV's grandson, which eventually became a bestseller), presented the advantages of commercial republics through thinly veiled allegories.[11] Internationally, republican ideas also flamboyantly came to the forefront with the successful formation of the American republic, which French naval support had made possible.

We shall start our inquiry with Montesquieu, the author who did the most to set the terms in which republicanism was to be understood later, and provided the most influential formulation of the scale thesis.[12] Following the publishing success of the *Spirit of the Laws* (*SL* hereafter), Montesquieu undeniably had an immense influence on French political thought.[13] His moderation, his endorsement of intermediary bodies and the separation of powers, and his thesis of the "fit" of regimes to their circumstances, as well as his interpretation of the English constitution, durably shaped the development of liberalism in France.[14] There is much

10 As Jaucourt notes in the article "République" of D'Alembert's *Encyclopédie*, "Holland, Germany and the Swiss Leagues are considered eternal republics in Europe."

11 Fénelon, *Télémaque*. For an excellent analysis of Fénelon's political ideas, see Hanley, *The Political Philosophy of Fénelon*.

12 Nelson, *The Greek Tradition in Republican Thought*, 76; Levy, "Beyond Publius: Montesquieu, Liberal Republicanism and the Small-Republic Thesis"; Shklar, "Montesquieu and the New Republicanism."

13 Courtney, "*L'Esprit des Lois* dans la perspective de l'histoire du livre (1748–1800)."

14 Bandoch, *The Politics of Place: Montesquieu, Particularism and the Pursuit of Liberty*; Craiutu, *A Virtue for Courageous Minds*; Dijn, *French Political Thought from Montesquieu to Tocqueville: Liberty in a Levelled Society*; Levy, *Rationalism, Pluralism, and Freedom*. For the idea that Montesquieu's account of the English constitution was fundamentally flawed, see Selinger, *Parliamentarism. From Burke to Weber.*

disagreement however on whether Montesquieu was a republican, largely because his method does not easily allow us to capture his normative position. Many scholars interested in his influence on American political thought tend to believe he was a republican.[15] Many others have argued that he was not.[16] This controversy turns in part on textual interpretation and, to a larger extent perhaps, on the role Montesquieu's work played in the intellectual formation of America's "founding fathers."[17] The complexity of his view hangs on to the fact that while he rejected classical republicanism, he also proposed ideas for a moderate regime adequate for modern times. Scholars, however, have disagreed on whether such a regime should be counted as a form of modern republicanism.

I do not mean to describe Montesquieu as a fervent anti-republican, or even an anti-republican *tout court.* My point is rather that, regardless of his ultimate position, he mounted an impressive rationale to demonstrate that republicanism, in its classical form, was impracticable and obsolete. What interests me here is the articulation of his challenge to would-be republicans, which laid out the obstacles reformers were facing. His challenge presented three arguments against the relevance of republicanism in a large country in modern Europe: the need for a strong sovereign ("unity argument"); the incapacity of a large and diverse people to know the common good ("epistemic argument"); and the absence of virtue in large and commercial states ("motivation argument"). Apart from recrafting institutions, Montesquieu argued that a modern republic would also need to create a united, knowledgeable, and virtuous citizenry, which was simply not possible in modern circumstances.

Following the expository method of the *Spirit of the Laws*, Montesquieu defines the republican government as one of three possible forms of governments (republic, monarchy, and tyranny): "There are three kinds of government (...). A republican government is that in which the people

[15] Pangle, *Montesquieu's Philosophy of Liberalism: A Commentary on the Spirits of the Laws*; Rahe, *Republics Ancient and Modern: Classical Republicanism and the American Revolution*; Lutz, "The Relative Influence of European Writers on Late Eighteenth-Century American Political Thought"; Sellers, *American Republicanism: Roman Ideology in the United States Constitution.*

[16] Monnier, *Républicanisme, patriotisme et Révolution française*; Spector, "Montesquieu: Critique of Republicanism?"; Wright, "Montesquieuan Moments: The Spirit of the Laws and Republicanism"; Douglass, "Montesquieu and Modern Republicanism"; Dijn, "Was Montesquieu a Liberal Republican?"

[17] Cohler, *Montesquieu's Comparative Politics and the Spirit of American Constitutionalism*; Rahe, *Republics Ancient and Modern: Classical Republicanism and the American Revolution.*

as a body, or only a part of the people, have sovereign power" (*SL* II.1). We should note that Montesquieu takes this statement to be a description rather than a definition, as his method relies on the observation of existing regimes.

The classification of regimes is organized along two criteria. The first is the origin of sovereign power in all, the few or one man: "In a republic when the people as a body have sovereign power, it is a *democracy*. When the sovereign power is in the hand of a part of the people, it is called an *aristocracy*" (*SL* II.2). The second criterion is whether government functions with or without established laws: "Monarchical government is that in which one alone governs, but by fixed and established laws; whereas in despotic government, one alone, without law and without rule, draws everything along by his will and his caprices" (*SL* I.1).

Despite its apparent familiarity, Montesquieu's presentation is disconcerting for anyone familiar with the genealogy of republicanism, as it subtly displaces familiar classifications inherited from Aristotle and Polybius. I'll mention here five distinctive and highly controversial features of republics in Montesquieu's "description." According to him, republics are: (1) simple constitutions defined by the origin of sovereign power, (2) democracies or aristocracies, (3) self-sacrificial, (4) unfree, and (5) rigid and authoritarian. These characteristics all converge to make republics unattractive and unstable forms of government.

Let us consider the first characteristic: republics are simple forms of sovereignty instead of mixed regimes. In several passages, Montesquieu notes that democracies are characterized by their lack of moderation precisely because they are simple regimes. This is a very serious shortcoming. Furthermore, this description contradicts the traditional analysis of republicanism in antiquity. In Book 6 of his *Histories*, the Greco-Roman historian Polybius, who later became known as one of the first theorists of republicanism, praised the Roman constitution for its balance between the aristocratic and democratic forces, "so that none of the principles should grow unduly and be perverted into its allied evil, but that the force of each being neutralized by that of the others, neither of them should prevail and outbalance another but that the constitution should remain for a long time in a state of equilibrium."[18] Based on his theory of *anakyklosis*, the cycle of regimes, Polybius argued that the most balanced regime combined the elements of all the simple ones: "For it is plain that we must regard as the best constitution that which partakes of all

[18] Polybius, *The Histories*, VI,10,7.

three elements" (Bk III.6). Such a balance fostered the two most important aspects of republics for Polybius: long-term stability and the capacity to expand. In like manner, Cicero insisted on the mixed constitution that moderated democratic elements with a strong senate.[19] In *On the Commonwealth*, he evoked the harmony that comes from blending these forces. Roman freedom and order could be maintained only through the harmony of the different classes and social components.

In addition to running against the tradition that attaches the mixed constitution to republican regimes, Montesquieu also seemed to vacillate on this question in the rest of his work. His description of republics in the *Spirit of the Laws* contrasts with many passages in the *Considerations on the Causes of the Greatness of the Romans and Their Decline*, where he analyzes the Roman Republic as being composed of popular and aristocratic institutions as its motto *SPQR* – *Senatus Populusque Romanus* – attested. Repeatedly describing the Roman Republic as a mixed constitution, Montesquieu ran the risk of self-contradiction when he described republicanism as based on a simple form of sovereignty. By insisting on this point, Montesquieu emphasized the institutional fragility of republics in contrast with not only mixed constitutions like England's but also the historical resilience of the Roman Republic.

Second, Montesquieu categorized republics into democracies or aristocracies. The partial conflation with democracies is notable because of the careful distinction between the two made by so many different republican authors in antiquity and early modernity. The same conflation also made republics seem more unstable. Democracies have been historically associated with chaos and the incapacity to make wise decisions.[20] For Polybius, Cicero, and Machiavelli, republics are precisely *not* democracies: They are based on a mixed constitution, which combines elements of popular, aristocratic, and monarchical governments.[21] In rejecting the most authoritative sources on republicanism, Montesquieu's presentation appeared deliberately polemical.

Furthermore, Montesquieu insisted on the elitist dimension of republics, notably aristocratic ones. The people, he wrote, "is not capable of

[19] Craiutu, *A Virtue for Courageous Minds*, 23.

[20] See Cicero's dismissive description of democracies as lacking any kind of social order in *On the Commonwealth*, I.67–68. In addition, Thucydides' description of Athens' disastrous Sicilian expedition was read for centuries as symptomatic of the democratic lack of wisdom.

[21] Cicero, *On the Commonwealth*, 2.57.

discussing public business," which "is one of the great drawbacks of democracy" (*SL* XI.6). Montesquieu's position seemed to be antidemocratic in this sense, though he clearly endorsed the importance of a certain level of self-government within a balanced system of institutions. Self-government and democracy are, however, not the same concept. While republicans endorsed the former, they rejected the latter until the eighteenth century.[22] There is a wide range of political possibilities of self-government that do not entail the entire population participating in law-making, let alone doing so *equally*.

Montesquieu's position implied that humans were not equally capable of self-governing because they were unequal in epistemic capacities: "Just as most citizens, who are competent enough to elect, are not competent enough to be elected, so the people, who are sufficiently capable to call others to account for their management, are not suited to manage by themselves" (*SL* II.2). He followed Cicero's view that the people were adept at choosing good leaders, even though they could not self-govern adequately.[23]

This view is also characteristic of an inegalitarian world, where the lower class of citizens can still find contentment in being assigned a lower role. Harmony comes from the fact that each is assigned a role that fits their status in the city and that the most qualified are given a more important role in government. There was thus an important gap between the egalitarian and democratic vision that Montesquieu assigned to republics, and the traditional one – like Cicero's – that was fundamentally inegalitarian.[24]

In the end, Montesquieu conceded that republicanism relied on a deeply entrenched elitism despite its claim to be based on equality. For him, this elitism was so deeply engrained in the people that even when given power, they self-effaced and gave it to patricians because they recognized their higher "merit":

> It is known that in Rome, though the people had given themselves the right to elevate plebeians to posts, they could not bring themselves to elect them; and in

[22] See Urbinati, "Competing for Liberty: The Republican Critique of Democracy" for the argument that republicanism and democracy have not always been strong allies.

[23] This is a characteristic of the Roman Republic according to him (he develops this view in the *Considerations of the Causes of the Greatness of the Romans and Their Decline*). In this regard, he follows Polybius, who makes a similar argument in *Histories*, 6.

[24] Wood, *Cicero's Social and Political Though*, 90–104; Gourevitch, *From Slavery to the Cooperative Commonwealth: Labor and Republican Liberty in the Nineteenth Century*, 27–30.

Athens, although, according to the law of Aristides, magistrates could be drawn from any class, Xenophon says that it never happened that the common people turned to those classes that could threaten their well-being or glory. (*SL* II.2)

At the same time as he described republics as either democracies or aristocracies, Montesquieu carefully noted that successful republics had to be aristocratic, that is, elitist in their form of government. This unequal conception of the capacity to self-govern weighed heavily on later republican conceptions, as I will argue in Chapters 3–5.

Third, and possibly most strikingly, Montesquieu claimed that republics were "not free states by their nature" (*SL* 11.4), echoing the famous assessment of republicans' archenemy, Hobbes.[25] Montesquieu, however, meant something different than Hobbes. He did not claim that individuals did not enjoy the status of free citizens in republics. On the contrary, he noted with admiration that Rome guaranteed a fair trial to all its citizens, an uncommon procedure in any other nation in the history of mankind. Yet he argued that republics were not free by their nature because "political liberty is found only in moderate governments" (*SL* 11.4). Montesquieu doubted that freedom could be found in any government primarily based on virtue. "[Political liberty] is present only when power is not abused, but it has eternally been observed that any man who has power is led to abuse it; he continues until he finds limits. Who would think it! Even virtue has need of limits" (*SL* 11.4).

Montesquieu therefore argued that republics, as simple forms of government, were intrinsically incapable of durably securing political freedom. Montesquieu noted that in Italian Republics, there was less freedom than in "our" monarchies because these republics had no separation of powers. The absence of separation of powers meant that the legislature, should it become tyrannical, did not find anything to stop its power. It could therefore "crush any citizen" (*SL* XI.6).

This view was commented at length by Jaucourt in his *Encyclopédie* article on "République."[26] Jaucourt's reasoning is important for our purpose. In a republic, he argued, magistrates are both legislating and executing the laws: "[The body of magistrates] can destroy the state through its general wills, and as it still has the power of judging, it can destroy each citizen by its particular wills."[27] Using the vocabulary of the

[25] Hobbes, *The Leviathan*, Ch. 21.

[26] *Encyclopédie ou Dictionnaire raisonné des sciences, des arts et des métiers* (1765), édition Mazarine, tome XIV, 150. The scientific digital edition (*Edition Numérique Collaborative et Critique de l'Encyclopédie*) is available at enccre.academie-sciences.fr.

[27] Jaucourt copied Montesquieu's *SL* XI.6.

"general will," which became ubiquitous during the Revolution, though it was not prevalent in Montesquieu's work, Jaucourt suggested that a republic would fail to prevent tyranny because it had no institutional dams against its governing magistrates.

Fourth, Montesquieu argued that the spring of republics, that is, "the human passion that sets it in motion," was virtue, "a moral virtue in the sense that it points towards the general good" (*SL*, 3.5 fn9). Montesquieu closely followed the tradition here. Virtue had always been considered a key element in republics, igniting the patriotism of citizens and preventing corruption.[28] In Montesquieu's lexicon, virtue can be simply understood as "the love of the republic," that is, "a sentiment and not a result of knowledge" (*SL* 5.2). In a democratic republic, this meant love of equality and frugality (*SL* 5.3). In an aristocratic republic, it meant embracing a spirit of moderation (*SL* 5.8).

Virtue, Montesquieu argued, is a very powerful tool of political regulation. When the people is virtuous, there is no need to have a draconian system of penalties (*SL* 6.11). In the Roman Republic, for instance, very little repression was needed: "often the legislator needed only to show them the good to have them follow it." Even after removing most of penalties from laws, "the republic was no more poorly ruled and no injury to its police resulted" (*SL* 6.11). Virtue is more efficient for social order than the negative fear of punishment.[29]

Yet Montesquieu's definition of virtue is noteworthy and sets him apart from the traditional interpretations. Republican virtue, he argued, is self-renunciation and sacrifice. "Political virtue is a renunciation of oneself, which is always a very painful thing" (*SL* 4.5).[30] It is thus an undesirable feature of politics, incompatible with the demands of modern individualism.[31] In a republic, virtue means the love of equality – and the love of equality, according to Montesquieu, means the sacrifice of

[28] See Pocock, *The Machiavellian Moment: Florentine Political Thought and the Atlantic Republican Tradition*. See MacGilvray, *The Invention of Market Freedom*, for the claim that "republican thought centers around the problem of securing the practice of virtue through the control of arbitrary power" (22).

[29] Montesquieu's understanding of virtue heavily borrows from the tradition of civic humanism. See Spector, "Montesquieu: Critique of Republicanism?," 41.

[30] See also *SL* V.19.

[31] Many commentators have noted that Montesquieu is critical of "virtue." See Krause, *Liberalism with Honor*, 35–38; Pangle, *Montesquieu's Philosophy of Liberalism: A Commentary on the Spirits of the Laws*, 82–83; Sullivan, *Montesquieu and the Despotic Ideas of Europe: An Interpretation of the "Spirit of the Laws,"* 141–59; Douglass, "Montesquieu and Modern Republicanism."

one's own interest. This description is in sharp contrast with the understanding of political virtue in antiquity, which was accompanied by a high sense of accomplishment. Equality and virtue thus have a cost in modern times that they did not have in antiquity: one renounces one's self-interest for the sake of the common good. By contrast, in antiquity, the citizen was *rewarded* for his virtuous act by the public esteem it generated.

We should note the considerable transformation that the concept underwent in Montesquieu's interpretation. His description of virtue highlighted its incompatibility with modernity. Republican citizens devote themselves to the good of the polity, not to pursue their private interests. Virtue is thus incompatible with the development of commerce, which depends upon people pursuing their self-interest.[32] As a consequence, a republican polity will not be pluralist, as moderns demand, but perfectionist as it posits the superiority of one good (the common good) over others (private interests).

Finally, for Montesquieu, a republic tends to be authoritarian. The necessity of having a virtuous citizenry has many undesirable implications. Since virtue does not come naturally to humans, inculcating virtue demands a strict and authoritarian public system of education. Republican education supposed training "the body of the people like a single family" (*SL* IV.6). This required mobilizing considerable forces to educate the people. But how could such a demanding education be implemented in a large state? "Attention of this kind cannot be expected in the confusion and multitude of affairs in which a large nation is entangled" (*SL* IV.6).

Because a republic depends on the love of equality and frugality, it also requires the existence of agrarian and inheritance laws that secure this love within the citizenry. Laws, however, do not suffice and mores need to support the social order. Censorship has an important role to play. The censors "must re-establish all that has become corrupted in the republic, notice slackness, judge oversights and correct mistakes just as the laws punish crimes" (*SL* IV.4–8). Laws thus leave place to manners as the controller of virtue. The persistence of old customs serves the permanence of public values; when disrupted by the emergence of new social phenomena, old customs may fail to play this crucial function.[33] The corruption of virtue occurs unless there is a homogeneous and strong

[32] Hont, "The Early Enlightenment Debate on Commerce and Luxury."
[33] Spector, "Montesquieu: Critique of Republicanism?" 41.

public morality securing the republic. The reader of the *Spirit of the Laws* is thus left with the strong impression that republicanism, at least in the classical form, is maladapted to modernity, if not simply intolerable.

MONTESQUIEU'S CHALLENGE

Given this unorthodox presentation of republics, what are the challenges that would-be republicans would have to overcome according to Montesquieu? The response is largely attached to his understanding of modernity in all its dimensions – the evolution of European society and mores, as well as the international political order in Europe in his time. The "scale thesis," which I mentioned as the defining thesis about republicanism at the end of the eighteenth century, is essentially the argument that republics are unfit for modernity. In Montesquieu's words, the thesis can be simply formulated: "It is in the nature of a republic to have only a small territory; otherwise, it can scarcely continue to exist" (*SL* VIII.16).

The scale thesis relies on an assessment of the circumstances of modernity as adverse to the core of republican ideas and organizations. For Montesquieu, who often commented on the indelible differences between the ancients and the moderns, the nature of modernity was an important object of inquiry.[34] With modernity came principally the spirit of commerce, the rise of individual self-interest, and large states with complex administration. Being "modern" meant embracing the rise of commerce (rather than conquest) as the source of wealth, a transformation of individual behavior (self-interest rather than community orientation), and the political fact that large states by necessity supposed complex administration and a heterogeneous people. In Montesquieu's work, the notion of modernity characteristically straddled description and normativity.

The increase of trade in Montesquieu's time, for instance, was an economic fact, but commerce itself was normatively assessed as positive. *Doux commerce* substitutes peace for war: "commerce cures destructive prejudices, and it is an almost general rule that everywhere there are gentle mores, there is commerce and that everywhere there is commerce, there are gentle mores" (*SL* 20.1). The thesis of *doux commerce* should have appeared problematic to Montesquieu himself, as he was aware of the extensive slave trade in his time as well as the numerous "wars for empire" that accompanied the expanding international commerce.

[34] See for instance *SL,* IV.6; X.3; XXX.14.

Interestingly in Book VI, Montesquieu provides counterexamples of republics which have successfully engaged in commerce: "the republics of Tyre, Carthage, Marseilles, Florence, Venice, and Holland" (*SL* 20.4). Commerce in republics is not founded on the need for luxury but rather "real" economic needs. Some republics managed to be modern and adapted to commercial change.

As mentioned above, Montesquieu's claim that modern states were large was itself a mix of description and normativity. The alleged reason why states *should* not be small in general was military: small states cannot expect to remain free in a world of large states. Yet if a state needs to be large to resist conquest, its size brings serious impediments. In a large country, private interests are exacerbated; the common good is hard to discern; individuals cannot practice moderation; citizens become incapable of self-government; and patriotism declines.

In his *Considerations on the Causes of the Greatness of the Romans and Their Decline,* Montesquieu explicitly attributes to scale expansion the most important role in the fall of Rome.[35] The military expansion of Rome increased its size so much that it morphed into a qualitatively different form of political organization. In fact, no name would be adequate to describe such a behemoth. "Rome," Montesquieu noted, "was not properly a monarchy or a republic, but the head of the body formed by all the peoples of the world" (*CC* Ch. VI). In faraway territories, soldiers became loyal to their general rather than to the republic: soldiers "were no longer the soldiers of the republic, but of Sylla, of Marius, of Pompey, and of Caesar" (*CC* Ch. IX). In becoming an empire, the Roman republic lost its unity: "the unbounded extent of the Roman empire proved the ruin of the Republic" (*CC* Ch. IX).[36] Rome was thus a prime example confirming, rather than denying, the scale thesis: a large territory makes the republican form of government unsustainable.

Montesquieu's assessment of modernity primarily concerned the transformation of mores, which in turn made individual aspirations legitimated by public opinion. "The political men of Greece who lived under popular government recognized no other force to sustain it than virtue.

[35] My reading differs from Nelson (2004) who has an Harringtonian interpretation of *Considerations of the Greatness of the Romans and Their Decline,* and takes the decline of Rome to be due to unequal distribution of wealth.

[36] See also *SL* II.2 "In Rome, which started small and became great, Rome, made to endure all the vicissitudes of fortune, Rome, which sometimes had nearly all its citizens outside its walls and sometimes all Italy and a part of the world within them, the number was not determined; this was one of the great causes of its ruin."

Those of today speak to us only of manufacturing, commerce, finance, wealth and even luxury" (*SL* III.3).

Montesquieu's assessment of the circumstances of modernity (states will have to be large; and citizens feel entitled to a plurality of individual pursuits) creates one central concern: the uncertain bond between citizens and their common allegiance to their country. While Montesquieu does not articulate it as such, we can discern the problem of plurality of conceptions of the good and identities – a key issue not only for republics, but any modern state.

All states have to adapt to the circumstances of modernity. Yet republics, in particular, are unfit to endure them. Indeed, a republic requires virtue, and a large state cannot foster virtue.

> In a large republic, there are large fortunes, and consequently little moderation in spirits; the depositories are too large to put in the hands of a citizen; interests become particularized; at first a man feels he can be happy, great and glorious without his homeland; and soon that he can be great only on the ruins of the homeland. (*SL* VIII.16)

Montesquieu offered three different arguments against the possible existence of a republic in the modern context, that is, in a context of commerce, rise of self-interest, and large states. I call these three arguments taken together "Montesquieu's challenge," not to refer to Montesquieu's intention, but to designate the effective theoretical task that later reformists tempted by republicanism would have to face.

(1) *The unity argument.* In a large state, national unity is weaker. A large state needs a strong sovereign, which a republic cannot provide while remaining under democratic or aristocratic control.
(2) *The epistemic argument.* In a large state, citizens are unlikely to know what the common good is. Large states foster the development of a plurality of views and the legitimation of private interests. In this context, the common good required for a republic becomes hard, if not impossible, to know.
(3) *The motivation argument.* In a large state, citizens have a loose bond to their community and are unlikely to be motivated to sacrifice themselves for the common good. The rise of commerce exacerbates this tendency. A large republic would not have virtuous citizens to rely on.

Montesquieu's challenge meant one thing for sure: If republicanism wanted to survive in the circumstances of modernity, it would need to be considerably transformed.

Montesquieu arguably provides three solutions to his own challenge – but only two of them can be characterized as republican. The first one is based on an analysis of the constitution of England, which he famously described as a republic in the guise of a monarchy. Second, he envisions the possibility of a federation of republics. Finally, he offers his preferred solution, which he considered the most practical and highly efficient system of government: a constitutional monarchy.

Montesquieu's suggestion that England was a "nation where the republic hides under the form of monarchy" (*SL* V.19) dominated the imagination of postrevolutionary liberals in France. Montesquieu described England as a modern republic in the sense that individuals were freed by representative institutions and the separation of powers. It was a republic because it guaranteed the freedom of its citizens. And it was decidedly modern because it did not require active and virtuous participation. Montesquieu thus presented England as the freest of all nations (*SL* XI.6). On this basis, he has been presented as a covert republican.

The English monarchy, Montesquieu claims, is clearly distinct from other monarchies as it has freedom as its goal (*SL* XI.7). The importance of constitutionalism, intermediary bodies and the separation of powers for a free government became Montesquieu's most valued heritage. Many scholars – mostly those who have an eye on his influence on the founders of the American Republic – tend to emphasize his embrace of a liberal and commercial republic, one that would be based on, and expand, the institutions of England. This form of liberal republican alternative becomes the basis for American modern republicanism.[37]

Montesquieu is therefore often understood to be an *anglomane*, a proponent of a form of limited government *à l'anglaise*. A thinker of moderation by excellence, Montesquieu insisted on the importance of "limited power, the separation of powers and the rule of law."[38] Indeed he proposed to separate the three powers (XI.6), or rather to balance power by distributing those powers.[39] Separation of powers had been advocated by English republicans, such as Nedham in *The Excellencie of a Free State*. In contrast with the ancient republic that requires virtue, the modern

[37] Pangle, *Montesquieu's Philosophy of Liberalism: A Commentary on the Spirits of the Laws*.

[38] Craiutu, *A Virtue for Courageous Minds*, 33.

[39] Krause, "The Spirit of Separate Powers in Montesquieu," 231.

solution for a free state is one in which institutions are sufficiently well designed that they guarantee everyone's freedom by their mere existence.

The second model is the federal republic. Montesquieu proposed to solve the military problem of small republics, always the potential prey of larger states, by imagining "a kind of constitution that has all the internal advantages of republican government and the external force of the monarchy. I speak of the federal republic" (*SL* IX.1). Giving the examples of Holland, Germany, and the Swiss League as federal republics, Montesquieu described such a political organization as the perfect alloy of republicanism and monarchy: "this sort of republic, able to resist external force, can be maintained at its size without internal corruption: the form of this society curbs every drawback" (*SL* IX.1). The federal republic, combined with the English model, became a central inspiration for the Americans.[40] As I will argue in Chapter 3, the idea of federation, however, found no traction in France, where it became associated with the destruction of the unity of the nation.

While textual evidence shows Montesquieu's attraction to both English style government and the idea of federation, I see his preference to actually lie elsewhere. It has been a long-standing view in the French scholarship on Montesquieu that he endorsed a form of constitutional monarchy.[41] His disavowal of republics led to a praise of monarchy, the political system best suited to answer the challenge of a large nation of self-interested individuals.[42] The central advantage of monarchy is its absence of reliance on virtue, that is, on the constant necessity of individuals to sacrifice themselves. In monarchies, great outcomes are produced with very little force.

> In monarchies, politics accomplishes great things with as little virtue as it can, just as in the finest machines art employs as few motions, forces and wheels as possible. The state continues to exist independently of love of the homeland, desire for true glory, self-renunciation, sacrifice of one's dearest interests, and all those heroic virtues we find in the ancients and know only by hearsay. (*SL* III. 5)

Because they do not rely on the exhausting effort needed for virtue (*SL* III.5), monarchies are the most efficient system. Even better, they are

40 Larrère, "Montesquieu et l'idée de fédération."

41 Spector, *Montesquieu: Pouvoirs, richesses et sociétés*.

42 For an interpretation arguing that Montesquieu supports monarchy, see Dijn, "Was Montesquieu a Liberal Republican?" She writes: "Montesquieu's *Spirit of the Laws* defended not one but two political models as an alternative to the classical republics of antiquity: the modern republic of England and a French-style monarchy," 33.

capable of channeling apparently morally defective passions, like ambition, toward the greater good. "Whereas ambition is pernicious in a republic, it has good effects in a monarchy, it gives life to this government." (*SL* III.7)

Montesquieu describes something that sounds familiar, even though not usually associated with monarchy: in a modern state, particular interests self-coordinate on a large scale without individuals believing that they are acting for the common good. "Honor" plays an important motivational role but does not require individuals to be altruistic. Contrary to the vices described by Mandeville in the *Fable of the Bees,* honor, despite being "primarily self-serving,"[43] is not corrupting. Because honor "motivates principled disobedience to encroaching political power,"[44] it is a type of desire for distinction that can turn beneficial to society. "Honor makes all the parts of the body politic move; it connects them through its very action; and it so happens that everyone contributes to the common good all the while believing they follow their particular interests." (*SL* III.7) Monarchies are thus capable of generating a positive mechanism that strengthens the allegiance of all to the stability of the regime because it provides individuals with the satisfaction of peer recognition and does not exhaust them with the necessity of virtue, that is, the necessity of being motivated for the higher cause of the country. Constitutional monarchy also solves the unity problem: the figure of the King ensures the continual existence of the state and the allegiance of the citizens, as an embodiment of shared history and tradition. Constitutional monarchies thus appear the most versatile institutional solution and the best adapted to the circumstances of modernity.

In laying out a stringent critique of republicanism, Montesquieu mounted a considerable challenge. Any reformer wanting to take up the republican tradition and apply it in the circumstances of modernity would have to answer a set of related questions: (1) What will create the unity of the state? (2) What can replace virtue? (3) How will the people know the common good? Neither the example of the English Constitution nor the federalist option would be possible for the French – for Montesquieu, therefore, a constitutional monarchy would be the best path toward a free future as it offers clear response to these quandaries. Barring a constitutional monarchy, an attempt to create a large and modern republic would require something that cannot be had, according to Montesquieu: a virtuous, knowledgeable, and devoted citizenry ready to sacrifice themselves for the common good.

43 Krause, *Liberalism with Honor,* 33.
44 Ibid., 32.

IMPERIALISM

Montesquieu developed a cohesive and critical presentation of classical republics in a civic humanist light. Yet at the same time, he implied the existence of divergent views and offered his own modern republican alternatives. The diversity of republican theories was widely accepted in the eighteenth-century. This diversity, I contend, should give us a sense of the scope of conceptual possibilities that revolutionaries had at their disposal in their quest for adequate models. While I cannot give an exhaustive picture of republicanism in France in the eighteenth century, I propose here to look at topics debated in the scholarship that matter for the evolution of French republicanism: imperialism, freedom, and commerce.

Let us attend first to a crucial question about imperialism: whether republics can legitimately aim to extend their borders and colonize new territories to establish an empire. Following the wave of decolonization in the mid-twentieth century, European regimes, including republics, were abundantly criticized both for their colonial policies and their moral justification of colonialism. To understand the republican reasoning on colonialism, let us look more carefully at their arguments in the prerevolutionary period.

Recall that Montesquieu claimed that modernity and progress characterized the spirit of commerce rather than conquest (*SL* XX.1–2). He also attributed the fall of Rome to its hubristic conquests, suggesting that even though some ancient republics had been inclined toward expansion ("Rome was founded for grandeur," *CC* Ch. VIII), wars and conquest were ill-suited to modernity (*CC* Ch. VIII–IX). Montesquieu, however, did not endorse the only, or even the majority position on this question. In the prerevolutionary period, I contend, republicanism appeared as a tradition in which imperialism was largely compatible with republican liberty.[45] In the republican tradition, the moral justification to extend one's territory was based on two concepts, greatness (glory) and stability (longevity).

The legitimacy of republican imperialism can be traced to the ultimate model of republics, the martial Roman Republic. While Polybius is mostly remembered as the theorist of republican stability, his inquiry about Rome starts with the question of empire and conquest. Polybius

[45] The justification of imperialism seems to have been the dominant position historically. For the "anomalous" episode of the rich literature denouncing imperialism in the eighteenth-century, see Muthu, *Enlightenment against Empire*.

writes that he aims "to discover by what means and by what type of regime almost the entire inhabited world was conquered and in less than fifty-three years brought under the single rule of the Romans, an achievement which is without historical precedent."[46] In turn, in his *History of Rome,* Livy claims he wants to "contribute his share to perpetuate the achievements of a people, *the lords of the world.*"[47]

The early modern republican tradition continued the trend of analyzing the Romans' martial republicanism in order to understand how they achieved glory. Machiavelli, the author of *The Prince,* which Rousseau deemed "the book of Republicans" (*SC* III.6), devoted the second book of his *Discourses on Livy* to the "decisions of the Roman people pertaining to the increase of the empire." The model of the Roman Republic looms large in the imagination of ancient and early modern republican theories, asking the extent to which the greatness of its political institutions was connected to its military prowess.

Machiavelli was considered a republican early on in France, despite a sulfurous reputation that never entirely dissipated.[48] While significant work remains to be done on the transmission of Machiavelli's ideas in the revolutionary period in France, forays into this question have shown that he had a non-negligible influence on some revolutionaries, such as Desmoulins, Robespierre, and Condorcet.[49] The importance of his legacy to the French republican tradition is multifaceted, but I will focus only on the part of his work that touches on its commitment to an imperial or even martial republic.

The question of whether Machiavelli endorses an imperial form of republicanism is fiercely debated among scholars. One camp argues that Machiavelli is committed to praise military virtue and conquest, alongside his endorsement of republican freedom.[50] Others, like Maurizio Viroli, argue that "Machiavelli's republicanism is not a commitment to

46 Polybius, *The Histories.* I.I.5.

47 Livy, *The History of Rome,* Preface. My emphasis.

48 See for instance Bayle, *Dictionnaire historique et critique,* article "Machiavel."

49 Jaume, "Robespierre chez Machiavel? Le culte de l'Etre Suprême et le 'retour aux principes'"; Addante, "Machiavel et les jacobins." Machiavelli also had a strong influence on English republicans, who, in turn, were widely read in France. On Machiavelli in England, see Raab, *The English Face of Machiavelli: A Changing Interpretation 1500–1700.*

50 Hörnqvist, "Machiavelli's Three Desires. Florentine Republicans on Liberty, Empire, and Justice." See also Sullivan who writes that Machiavelli is "a partisan of a particular type of republic – that is an aggressive, acquisitive republic" (Sullivan, *Machiavelli, Hobbes and the Formation of a Liberal Republicanism in England,* 34).

the value of civic or military virtue, and even less devotion to the pursuit of military greatness and predation, but a commitment to the ideal of a well-ordered republic."[51]

There is considerable evidence that Machiavelli endorsed a martial vision of the republic as he deemed military affairs the prime object of government (*Prince* XIV). Surely, war should not be the only preoccupation of princes and republics, writes Machiavelli; yet it ought to have some priority. "The main foundations of all states (whether they are new, old, or mixed) are good laws and good armies. And since there cannot be good laws without good armies, and where there are good armies there are good laws, I shall refrain from discussing the topic of laws, and discuss armies" (*P* XII).

The first reason for the priority of good armies in the art of government is the fundamental and uncontrollable uncertainty that Machiavelli sees in all human enterprises. If nothing can be mastered using rationality alone, it is crucial to have "fortune" on one's side. But for Machiavelli, there are proven ways to tame fortune, and to yoke it to on one's side: "It is better to be impetuous than circumspect because Fortune is a woman and you must, if you want to subjugate her, beat and strike her (...) Like a woman, she always befriends the young, since they are less circumspect and more brutal: they master her more boldly" (*P* XXV).

If Fortune favors the bold, then military expansion may be the best way to keep a country free. Rejecting expansion means exposing oneself to the fickleness of fortune; embracing it means increasing one's chance of mastering uncertainty and therefore vulnerability.[52] As Machiavelli describes fortune as a woman who likes being beaten into submission, military expansion is more than mere prudence: aggressiveness, violence, and demonstration of military superiority are justified by the mere existence of uncertainty.

Yet considering Machiavelli's sexual fantasy of a woman enjoying being assaulted,[53] it is hard not to see the glorification of violence as an end in itself because it provides pleasure to the perpetrators. This display of "manly" aggressivity does not only lead to the mastery of uncertainty. It is also the expression of superior power, otherwise known as greatness.[54] An aggressive conception of politics, in which dominating is a key strategy,

[51] Viroli, *Machiavelli*, 115.
[52] Pocock, *The Machiavellian Moment*, 198.
[53] For Machiavelli's sexual politics, see Pitkin, *Fortune is a Woman.*
[54] Skinner, *Machiavelli*, 34.

is initially justified for the sake of maintaining one's freedom. And at the same time as freedom is maintained, the glory of conquest is achieved, and with it the satisfaction of deep-seated impulses of domination.

One could object that this vision is exaggerated and based on existing yet limited textual evidence. Machiavelli's justification of conquest, the argument goes, is mostly based on necessity and not on some violent desire for domination.[55] Indeed, in the *Discourses* Book 2, Machiavelli defends the idea that expansion was important, essential indeed, for the mere survival of the Roman Republic. "It is impossible for a republic to succeed in staying quiet and enjoying its freedom and little borders. For if it will not molest others, it will be molested, and from being molested will arise the wish and the necessity to acquire" (*DL* II.19, p. 173).

Conquest is just preventive defensive war in a world with constant military conflicts, such as Europe in Machiavelli's time. Prevention is doubly important because it concerns both the international order and domestic politics. War, Machiavelli argues, may be the only outlet to prevent internal dissension. Without expansion, the argument goes, internal conflicts would signal the end of the Republic.[56] Several anecdotes warrant this conclusion. For instance, Machiavelli describes how the attack of the Veientes, who thought they could conquer Romans, who appeared disunited, ended up fostering their union: "For the cause of the disunion of republics is usually idleness and peace; *the cause of union is fear and war*" (*DL* II.25 my emphasis). War is thus a main instrument of domestic politics.

The importance of conquest comes down not only to the state of international politics but to the structure of domestic politics. Machiavelli's art of government is known for relying on a theory of political humors: "They do not consider that in every republic are two diverse humors, that of the people and that of the great, and that all the laws that are made in favor of freedom arise from their disunion, as can easily be seen to have occurred in Rome" (*DL* I.4). The perpetual conflict between the "ignobles" who do not want to be dominated and the "nobles" who want to dominate is a mere fact of politics (*DL* I.5), but one that can be exploited for beneficent ends ("keeping Rome free" *DL* I.4) as Rome managed to create institutional safeguards.

[55] Lovett, for instance, defends Machiavelli against accusations of being "militaristic and imperialistic" and argues that "Machiavelli may have been right to believe that a republic's best defense is a good offense" (article "Republicanism" in the online *Stanford Encyclopedia of Philosophy*).

[56] Hörnqvist, *Machiavelli and Empire*; Hulliung, *Citizen Machiavelli*.

Yet domestic conflicts cannot entirely be managed if the nobles' desire to dominate does not find a proper outlet. Machiavelli advises that war-oriented policies are necessary to channel the desire of ambitious men to rise above others. Without such outlets, these men will try to satisfy their ambition either by gaining undue power internally and threatening the freedom of citizens, or by plotting dangerous external wars (*DL* III.16, p. 255). Imperial politics is thus necessary to fuel the *grandi*'s desire to dominate and therefore make them accept to lower their oppression over the people.[57] Machiavelli thus clearly sees the goal of a republic as dual: "A city that lives free has two ends – one to acquire, the other to maintain itself free" (*DL* I.29).

It should be noted that Machiavelli does not advise a mode of acquisition that leads colonized subjects into a mode of subordination so intense that it will make them likely to resist unto death. Instead, he recommends a less directly violent mode of acquisition, the one used by the Romans, which consists in conquering and deceiving the conquered into believing they are allies. Neither glory nor the satisfaction of the *grandi* can be attained by utter destruction. Rather success necessitates a soft mode of acquisition relying on deceptive strategies:

> And republics and princes would believe that increasing the inhabitants of one's city, getting partners and not subjects, sending colonies to guard countries that have been acquired, making capital out of booty, subduing the enemy with raids and battles and not with sieges, keeping the public rich and the private poor, and maintaining military exercises with the highest seriousness is the true way to make a republic great and to acquire empire. (*DL* II.19)

Despite the aggressiveness endorsed elsewhere, Machiavelli considered that conquest ought to be done only in tactical ways to be successful. It ought to take into consideration the desire of conquered people to be free, which means that any unrestrained subordination would be humiliating to them and lead to a constant state of rebellion instead of cooperation. A successful kind of conquest, that is, one leading to stability, would need to include the colonized in the construction of a common good.

Imperialism, however, was not an unalloyed good for Machiavelli. Roman imperialism not only destroyed freedom wherever it was deployed, it also turned against Roman freedom itself.[58] The praise of

[57] McCormick, *Machiavellian Democracy*, 59.

[58] Zuckert, "Machiavelli's Democratic Republic," 271; McCormick, *Machiavellian Democracy*, 52.

martial republicanism and its adjacent goods, power and glory, does not mean that Machiavelli was unconcerned with the well-ordered republic. Laws and constitutionalism are crucial in this vision because Machiavelli does not believe a republic can entirely rely on virtue – on the contrary, he bases his republican theory on the inherent wickedness of man, whose impulses have to be controlled. Machiavelli thus insists on the republic as the government of *laws,* and not of men.

What matters for us here is that from the point of view of Machiavelli, the maintenance of freedom in a republic may require imperialism, that is the expansion of domination of others. In so far as Machiavelli was considered a republican in the later tradition, he transmitted a key idea to those who aimed to universalize freedom yet found themselves waging war both internally and externally, as the French revolutionaries did. Machiavelli insisted that in order not to be dominated, one may have to dominate. Dominating others is a justifiable necessity to achieve freedom, especially when a republic is attacked by foreign powers and when it has internal enemies ready to destroy the republic. Furthermore, keeping conquered territories may involve deception, such as making the conquered believe that their subjugation is for their own good. At the same time, dominating others may be necessary to achieve certain forms of glory. The heirs of the illustrious Machiavelli would thus need to ask whether his justifications for war and conquest were acceptable from their own republican point of view. As I argue in Chapter 5, it turns out that the French republicans of the revolutionary period were sensitive to several of these arguments.

FREEDOM AND DEPENDENCE

Let us now turn to another vexed question in the scholarship on prerevolutionary republicanisms: the definition of freedom. "In democracies," writes Montesquieu, "the people seem very nearly to do what they want" (*SL* XI.2). This common impression has an important theoretical consequence. "The power of the people has been confused with the liberty of the people" (*SL* XI.2). Yet for Montesquieu, following one's will without regard to rule or reason is license, not freedom. "Political liberty in no way consists in doing what one wants" (*SL* XI.3). Instead, he writes: "Political liberty in a citizen is that tranquility of spirit which comes from the opinion each one has of his security, and in order for him to have this liberty the government must be such that one citizen cannot fear another citizen" (*SL* XI.6).

This kind of liberty as security from oppression "is found only in moderate governments" (*SL* XI.4). Liberty is a form of individual freedom that consists in enjoying security and is not primarily associated with political control or collective decision-making. The form of government, however, is crucial in maintaining this security.

Through this distinction between democratic freedom (doing what one wants) and individual freedom (being secure against oppression), Montesquieu anticipates the later historiographical controversy about freedom at the center of both the early nineteenth-century rise of liberalism in France and the twentieth-century republican revival. In the immediate aftermath of the Revolution, early liberals, such as Benjamin Constant, Simonde de Sismondi, and Germaine de Staël rehabilitated this distinction for strategic purposes. In Constant's oft-cited formula in his *Discourse at the Athénée Royal*: "we can no longer enjoy the liberty of the ancients, which consisted in an active and constant participation in collective power. Our freedom must consist in the peaceful enjoyment of private independence (*la jouissance paisible de l'indépendance privée*)."[59]

In the Cold War era, Berlin proposed to think of this distinction as negative freedom ("freedom from," i.e., the absence of constraints) and positive freedom (itself defined either as the ability to pursue willed goals or autonomy). While slightly different, the distinction supports a liberal narrative about the dangers of positive freedom. A recent book by Annelien de Dijn revives this dichotomy, defining the dominant prerevolutionary idea of freedom as the "democratic conception of freedom" or "popular self-government" in contradistinction with the postrevolutionary idea of freedom as "being left alone."[60] De Dijn's distinction echoes Benjamin Constant's dual definition – with the important difference that for de Dijn, the modern conception of freedom is a detrimental loss of the original spirit of democratic freedom.

This distinction has been discredited by the neo-republican revival as historically and normatively wrong. Their central historical claim is now well-known. Neo-republican scholars distanced themselves from the liberal narrative that defined republican freedom as ancient freedom, positive

59 Constant, *Political Writings*, 316. Translation modified.
60 Dijn, *Freedom. An Unruly History*.

freedom, and participation in government.[61] As far as historical credentials are concerned, they have mostly relied on English republicans to argue that the appropriate way to understand freedom should be as the opposite of domination: to have a master is to be dominated; and to be free is not to have a master.[62] In doing so, they explicitly aimed at distancing themselves not only from the liberal idea of freedom as non-interference but also from some ideas central to civic humanism (the priority of civic virtue and the emphasis on political participation in particular).

My goal here is not to retrace the evolution of republican freedom as an idea before the era of the Atlantic revolutions to determine the extent to which the liberal narrative and its republican revision are based on a polemical reconstruction. Rather I want to make two more modest arguments that matter for our analysis of the revolutionary period and what I take to be its struggle with the conceptual ambivalence bequeathed by the tradition. These arguments are modestly revisionist – they nuance the current neo-republican position more than they object to it.

First, I contend that there was no unequivocal conception of republican freedom in use among all those who can reasonably be taken to be part of the republican tradition. Equivocally intertwined are ideas of self-government, non-domination, non-dependence, and participation in politics. Associated concepts of slavery and dependence are also used equivocally, sometimes in a strict legal sense and often in a broader non-legal sense, leaving ample space for theoretical divergence. Second, republican freedom was not essentially understood as universal in this period. Freedom primarily referred to a political status restricted to those meeting some conditions, and therefore was not considered attainable by all.

I develop my case by focusing first on Machiavelli and then on a group of thinkers who has recently been studied in light of their importance for French republicanism: the seventeenth-century English republicans. The latter include Marchamont Nedham (1620–1678), John Milton (1608–1674), James Harrington (1611–1677), and Algernon Sidney (1623–1683). Scholars tend to agree on the importance of this group of thinkers in the transmission of the republican tradition in France.[63] Their

[61] Pettit, *Republicanism*, 17–19.

[62] Lovett, *The Well-Ordered Republic*, 26.

[63] Baker, "Transformations of Classical Republicanism in Eighteenth-Century France"; Dijn, *French Political Thought from Montesquieu to Tocqueville: Liberty in a Levelled Society*, 12; Hammersley, "English Republicanism in Revolutionary France: The Case of the Cordelier Club." Compare with Goulemot, in *Le siècle de l'avènement révolutionnaire*, 45 who writes that England had no importance in the French republican

legacy, however, is hard to assess because this group of thinkers diverged on important points and did not have a unified reception.[64] One concern, however, was central to English Republicans and impacted French political thought: what exactly freedom was, and how it should be defined?

Before we turn to the English, we can first note that conceptual ambivalence on freedom can also be found in the work of Machiavelli, a key author in the constitution of English republicanism.[65] At first sight, Machiavelli's understanding of freedom may seem to fit the idea of freedom as non-domination. See for instance the oft-cited passage from the *Discourses on Livy*: "The common utility that is drawn from a free way of life is not recognized by anyone while it is possessed: this is being able to enjoy one's things freely, without any suspicion, not fearing for the honor of wives and that of children, not to be afraid for oneself" (*DL* I.16).

Freedom here is security from domination for oneself and for one's property and dependents. It should be noted, however, that the idea of being protected from domination is not presented as freedom itself, but as the "utility" drawn from being free. If the protection against domination, and therefore the tranquility of mind that accompanies it, are the *consequences* of a free life, then what is freedom itself?

Machiavelli defines freedom, more positively, as "being governed by one's own will," describing free cities as those who are governed by their own will, either as republics or principalities (*DL* I.2). This self-government is defined as the opposite of the subordination to an outside power. It does not specify, however, how a city needs to be self-governed to be free – it merely states, as a sufficient condition to be said "free," that it cannot be subjected to an alien city or state. It leaves open the meaning of "own will" and how this "will" ought to be expressed or organized. Being free here mostly supposes the condition of not being a colony or under the tutelary power of another state: it is a sovereign standing in the international order of states, and it does not specify what the internal arrangement of a state needs to be for it to qualify as a self-governed state.

In *DL* I.16, Machiavelli presents another feature of freedom. Freedom supposes a *capacity* for self-government and therefore some extent of self-reliance. If freedom requires a set of conditions, not all states or

psyche. Goulemot's claim is symptomatic of a twentieth-century tendency in French scholarship to deny the influence of English political thought in their own tradition.

64 Hammersley, *The English Republican Tradition and Eighteenth-Century France*.

65 Worden, "English Republicanism," 446.

individuals will be able to be free. One of these conditions is the preexistence of an anterior state of freedom. When individuals are unfree, they become used to servitude in such a way that becoming free is difficult, maybe impossible, for them:

> Infinite examples read in the remembrances of ancient histories demonstrate how much difficulty there is for a people living under a prince to preserve its freedom afterward if by some accident it acquires it, as Rome acquired it after the expulsion of the Tarquins. Such difficulty is reasonable; for that people is nothing other than a brute animal that, although of a ferocious and feral nature, has always been nourished in prison and in servitude. Then, if it is left free in a field to its fate, it becomes the prey of the first one who seeks to rechain it, not being used to feed itself and not knowing places where it may have to take refuge. (*DL* I.16)

Freedom may initially be a question of legal status, but psychological and moral dependence soon naturalize unfreedom. Freedom is thus not simply a legal concept (not being a slave under the law). It also designates a social, economic, moral, and psychological condition: being self-reliant and capable of independence. If humans are like animals, they can be fit for freedom like feral beasts, or unfit like pets and domestic cattle. Yet how can an unfree people be emancipated if being unfree makes one unfit for freedom? With this brief foray into Machiavelli's idea of freedom, we can already see two concerning issues: the indeterminacy of the sense of self-government and the complexity of the requirements of freedom, which cannot be reduced to a legal status.

Let us now turn to the way English republicans have defined freedom. The first concept used to frame freedom, neo-republicans write, is its opposite: slavery.[66] It may seem initially odd to think of a concept as understandable primarily by its opposite, as if it could not intuitively be grasped directly. This claim, however, is made by Skinner and supported by extensive textual evidence.[67] Republican thinkers, Skinner argues, were particularly keen on using the idea of slavery to designate positions of unfreedom as they were influenced by Roman law. Take for instance John Milton, whose ideas of freedom and slavery are taken directly from the *Codex* of Justinian. Slavery refers to the legal status of unfreedom: "slavery is an institution of the *jus gentium* by which someone is, contrary

[66] This idea guides contemporary republican description of republican freedom. See for instance: "This discussion of the liberty-servitude theme in the republican tradition should serve to support the claim that freedom is conceived there as non-domination, not as non-interference" (Pettit, *Republicanism*, 34).

[67] Skinner, "John Milton and the Politics of Slavery," 289–90.

to nature, subject to the dominion of someone else."[68] The free citizen is therefore he who is *sui juris*, because he is not a slave.

The trope of slavery, however, is indeterminate in two different ways. First, there were different kinds of non-slaves in antiquity. Most of the non-slaves were not entirely free. Let us mention, for instance, the helots, the foreigners and all non-slave women. When republicans say that being free is not being a slave, they have in mind only a small category of the non-slaves historically. Being a free citizen does not only imply not being a slave; it also implies not being a woman, not being a foreigner, not being an helot, and so on. That is to say, it supposes a range of positive requirements.

Second, republicans use the legal category of slavery, yet enlarge its meaning. For the seventeenth-century republicans, being the subject of a king means being a slave. This is an obvious extension of the idea of slavery beyond its legal meaning, especially given that seventeenth-century Englishmen were precisely *not* slaves, contrary to the slaves who were owned by the English themselves in the colonies. The use of the concept beyond its strict legal sense has been key to other republican emancipatory causes, for instance feminism. Wollstonecraft, for instance, describes the subordinated situation of middle-class women as slavery.[69] Nineteenth-century American republicans also used slavery to designate wage-working.[70] In these cases, slavery does not refer to the legal status of being owned in one's person by another person, but of being under their power to some important extent, which resembles slavery because in some aspects of their lives, they are under the domination of a master. It is precisely because they were not legally slaves that the republicans would use the concept as a powerful rhetorical tool to raise awareness of the unfreedom present in these situations of servitude.

The distinction between "being a slave" and "not being a slave" suffers from considerable levels of indeterminacy. In its narrow Roman definition, slavery is crucial for republicans because it implies three things about freedom: (1) that being free is a *legal* status which involves legal protection, (2) that it means not being under the dependence of another

[68] Watson (ed.), *The Digest of Justinian*, I.5.4 (vol. 1, 15).

[69] Wollstonecraft, *A Vindication of the Rights of Woman. A Vindication of the Rights of Men*, 67. See Coffee, "Mary Wollstonecraft, freedom, and the enduring power of social domination."

[70] Gourevitch, *From Slavery to the Cooperative Commonwealth: Labor and Republican Liberty in the Nineteenth Century*.

will, and (3) that it cannot be measured in terms of quantity of interference. These three ideas are illustrated in Algernon Sidney's definition of freedom in his *Discourses Concerning Government*, an influential text in the republican tradition: "Liberty solely consists in an independency upon the will of another, and by the name of slave we understand a man, who can neither dispose of his person nor goods, but enjoy all at the will of his master" (*DG* I.5).

Sidney insists that the amount of interference does not matter in determining whether someone is free. "He is a slave who serves the best and gentlest man in the world, as well as he who serves the worst" (*DG* III.21). Republicans define slavery as the domination of one person over another, that is to say the exercise of power over another person without them being capable of controlling it in any way, and regardless of whether the master uses their domination or not to interfere with the dominated. Using this idea as their core meaning, they enlarged the concept of slavery so that it could be used to describe situations involving domination beyond the legal status of slaves.

It remains to be shown, however, whether Sidney thinks of a slave only in these terms. Sidney sees slavery not only as a condition of unfreedom: it is also a natural condition, which arises when the slave is legally a slave *and* lacks the required qualities to be free. Consider for instance this passage about nations that are "slaves by nature":

> Other generous nations have been subdued beyond a possibility of recovery; and those that are naturally base, slide into the like misery without the impulse of an exterior power. They are slaves by nature and have neither the understanding nor courage that is required for the constitution and management of a government within themselves. They can no more subsist without a master, than a flock without a shepherd. They have no comprehension of liberty and can neither desire the good they do not know, nor enjoy it if it were bestowed upon them. (*DG* III. 4)

The opposite of slavery is thus not simply being protected from domination. It also means having a set of moral and epistemic qualities that imply a lack of servile character.[71]

[71] See also this passage, which similarly insists on the moral qualities necessary for self-government: "It has been hitherto believed in the world that the Assyrians, Medes, Arabs, Egyptians, Turks, and others like them, lived in slavery, because their princes were masters of their lives and goods. Whereas the Grecians, Italians, Gauls, Germans, Spaniards, and Carthaginians, as long as they had any strength, virtue or courage amongst them, were esteemed free nations, because they abhorred such a subjection. They were and would be governed only by laws of their own making" (*DG* I.5).

Sidney even goes further, describing as a slave "one who is transported by his own passions or follies" or his "lusts and vices" (*DG* III.25). A person who cannot control him or herself, he claims, is a "slave by nature" (*DG* I.2). Freedom is thus not only not being dominated; it means being *capable of self-government*, which is not something that all humans are going to possess without training, and maybe something that not all humans possess by nature.

The idea of freedom as self-government is central to Sidney's republican views. "We have no other way of distinguishing between free nations and such as are not so, than that the free are governed by their own laws and magistrates according to their own mind"(*DG* III.21). Self-government is not instrumental to freedom itself: it is part of its definition. It puts into question whether republican freedom is rightly understood as primarily a negative conception of freedom in the English republican tradition.[72]

The notion of "self-government" is not altogether clear either. For Sidney, being governed by one's own mind does not mean being governed by a *democratic* government. What is therefore the constitution of the political "self"? "If I should undertake to say, there never was a good government in the world, that did not consist of the three simple species of monarchy, aristocracy and democracy, I think I might make it good," he maintained (*DG* II. 16). Governing according to one's own mind means governing according to the principle of a mixed constitution.

The idea of self-government, however, is mostly associated with the idea of limiting the power of individual men and emphasizing the impersonal character of the law. Being self-governed therefore means being protected from the dominating tendency of parts of the polity by the establishment of impersonal laws. We also find the idea of the empire of the laws most famously in Harrington's work:

> Government (to define it *de jure* or according to ancient prudence) is an art whereby a civil society of men is instituted and preserved upon the foundation of common right or interest or (to follow Aristotle and Livy) it is the empire of laws and not of men.[73]

[72] The importance of the idea of freedom as self-government becomes particularly clear in the eighteenth century in the work of Richard Price, *Observations on the Nature of Civil Liberty, the Principles of Government, and the Justice and Policy of the War with America (1776)*. On this question, see Elazar, "The Downfall of All Slavish Hierarchies; Richard price on Emancipation, Improvement, and Republican Utopia."

[73] Harrington, *The Commonwealth of Oceana and A System of Politics*, 8. On this point, see Lovett, "Harrington's Empire of Law."

The English republican notion of freedom thus combines stable elements (the empire of laws) with ones that are less clearly defined (protection against domination, self-government, and self-control).

The other important aspect to note in these bodies of work is the limited domain of republican freedom. For Sidney, the sphere of application of republican freedom does not concern everyone, as it excludes all of those who are socially, economically, or psychologically dependent. According to Skinner, this is quite understandable since "neo-roman theorists (...) generally make it clear that they are thinking of the concept in a strictly political sense. They are innocent of the modern notion of civil society as a moral space between rulers and ruled and have little to say about the dimensions of freedom and oppression inherent in such institutions as the family or the labour market."[74] Because republican freedom deals mostly with "the relationship between the freedom of subjects and the powers of the state," it comes as no surprise that Sidney is not concerned by the domination between masters and servants.[75] This is why Sidney can write that part of the freedom that a free man enjoys is having as many servants as he wishes and "putting them away at [his] pleasure" (*DG* III.41).

This limitation of the sphere of application logically means the exclusion of parts of the population. The consequence is clearly drawn by Harrington, despite his reputation for being one of the most egalitarian republicans, and for being preoccupied with the importance of equal material possessions.[76] Even though agrarian laws are necessary to raise people to an equal political position, some would still be excluded from equal citizenship. In *The Commonwealth of Oceana* (1665), Harrington considered that those who were dependents could not be citizens:

> The materials of a commonwealth are the people; and the people of Oceana were distributed by casting them into certain divisions; regarding their quality, their ages, their wealth, and the places of their residence or habitation, which was done by the ensuing orders.
>
> *The first* distributing the people into freemen or citizens, and servants, while such; for if they attain unto liberty, that is to live of themselves, they are freemen or citizens.[77]

A free man could not be a servant – because it would mean that he had a master. Yet he could *have* servants and a wife. The same distinction

74 Skinner, *Liberty before Liberalism*, 16.

75 On this point, see Gourevitch, *From Slavery to the Cooperative Commonwealth: Labor and Republican Liberty in the Nineteenth Century*, 15.

76 Nelson, *The Greek Tradition in Republican Thought*, 87–126; Worden, "English Republicanism."

77 Harrington, *The Commonwealth of Oceana and a System of Politics*, 75.

is specified in earlier writings, *A System of Politics, Delineated in Short and Easy Aphorisms* (1660–1662): “If a man has some estate, he may have some servants or a family, and consequently some government, or something to govern; if he has no estate, he can have no government” (Ch. 2.4). Being free not only precludes *being* a servant, but it implies *having* servants or a family, that is, some dependents. The standard to be a free man thus appears to include ruling over others. Harrington notes that “the man that cannot live upon his own, must be a servant; but he that can live upon his own, may be a freeman” (Ch. 1.13). To be free, one must “live upon his own,” that is not relying on someone else for their subsistence. Freedom is thus not just protection against domination. It also demands a particular material condition: owning property that makes one self-reliant and ruling over either servants, tenants, or family members.

English republicans did not provide an immediately universalizable form of freedom as they anchored freedom in property and material independence. Rather they seemed to accept that private domination was an inescapable part of social and economic life: if an individual does not have the means to be independent, then he will be dependent on a master for his means of subsistence and preservation. This was not a *contradiction* of the general idea of freedom as non-domination, but rather a delimitation of private dependence as the outer boundary of freedom.

COMMERCE

Let us now consider another contentious issue in eighteenth century debates: whether republics could be commercial states. Montesquieu insisted that republics required the love of equality and frugality (*SL* V.3), whereas the moderns talked only about wealth and finance (*SL* III.3). The accusation here comes back to one I have analyzed at length: republics are outdated if they cannot adapt to the main events of modernity. The most important modern phenomenon, according to eighteenth-century thinkers themselves, was the rapid development of globalized commerce.[78] “The eighteenth century,” writes Istvan Hont, “produced a vision of the future as a global market of competing commercial states.”[79] As they saw it, there was no place in such a future for any regime that was not based on trade.

78 Reinert, *Translating Empire. Emulation and the Origins of Political Economy*; Hont, *Jealousy of Trade;* Cheney, *Revolutionary Commerce.*

79 Hont, *Jealousy of Trade*, 4.

With the rediscovery of the tradition dubbed "civic humanism," scholars have wondered about the compatibility between virtue and commerce in the republican tradition. The terms of the debate are, however, rather controversial. Pocock argued that in the civic humanist tradition, commerce was seen as corrupting the values necessary for the survival of republics.[80] With this argument, Pocock was opposing Hans Baron, who did not see the civic humanists as dissociating the terms of virtue and commerce as such – the most important opposition was rather between the active life, which included trade, and the contemplative life.[81]

Montesquieu did not argue that commerce and republics were incompatible. Republics could be martial, as Rome was, but could also be commercial like Holland. Commercial republics, however, needed to keep control of equality and frugality (*SL* V.6). Embracing commerce did not mean letting go of all regulations. It also meant that the economic organization on which republics would rely was open-ended in the eighteenth century, even in the eyes of a critic of republicanism like Montesquieu. In this section, I would like to make the case that the nature of commerce was indeed more open than it is often assumed in the republican scholarship. As with the questions of imperialism and freedom, the republican tradition did not provide a clear guidance to revolutionaries.

Here as in the other topics that interest us, liberal scholarship has loaded its retrospective narrative with normative stakes. In the aftermath of the Revolution, as I already mentioned, liberals such as Benjamin Constant built a case for the rejection of republican ideas as obsolete. Their argument was not simply about the nature of liberty but entailed another central aspect: the importance of commerce as a key area of personal achievement and happiness. The liberal narrative reimagined "classical republicanism" as a form of theory which did not just endorse freedom as collective decision-making, but also rejected commercial activity. This is how Benjamin Constant describes the author who is the most clearly associated with a purely French classical republicanism: the Abbé Mably. "The Abbé de Mably can be regarded as the representative of the system which, according to the maxims of ancient liberty, demands that citizens should be entirely subjected in order for the nation to be

80 Pocock, *Virtue, Commerce, and History: Essays on Political Thought and History, Chiefly in the Eighteenth Century*, 37–50.

81 Baron, *The Crisis of the Early Italian Renaissance: Civic Humanism and Republican Liberty in an Age of Classicism and Tyranny*; Jurdjevic, "Virtue, Commerce, and the Enduring Florentine Moment: Reintegrating Italy into the Atlantic Republican Debate."

sovereign, and that the individual should be enslaved for the people to be free."[82]

In addition to his "austerity" and "intolerance," Constant continued, Mably rejected commerce as shown in "his declamation against wealth and even against property."[83] What mattered ultimately was not Mably's anti-commercialism itself, though, but how it affected the revolutionaries, in particular the Jacobins. "We all know, Gentlemen, what has come of it," concluded Constant, sure that his audience of gentlemen would agree with him on the Terror.

Should we therefore see the prerevolutionary republican tradition, in particular in France, as anti-commercial? To understand why republicanism has been retrospectively associated with the rejection of commercialism and wealth, we need to go back to one of the most passionate intellectual debates of the eighteenth century, which concerned luxury.[84] I cannot retrace this vast debate and will only lay out the positions of some of the protagonists in order to illuminate how it impacted the republican tradition. The luxury debate did not show the republicans incapable of adapting to modernity; rather it bore witness to the republican struggle with keeping ethics, politics, and economics together. Yet, again, as in other issues, it did not propose one unitary solution to the question of how to integrate commerce within the republic and how to maintain material equality while preserving freedom.

The most important figure in this debate was Fénelon, the archbishop of Cambrai, personal tutor of Louis XIV's grandson and one of the most influential seventeenth-century authors. Fénelon cannot be called a republican – instead, he was a proponent of a constitutional and moderate monarchy and a sharp critic of the absolute monarchy of Louis XIV. Yet his criticism of absolutism, corruption, and luxury marked the republican tradition in France.[85] Rousseau was durably influenced by his ideas.[86] Fénelon argued, against Colbert, that the politics of luxury central to monarchical France's economic policy was disastrous for the country.

In the *Adventures of Telemachus* (1699), Fénelon offered veiled prescriptions to reform corrupt France. The love of luxury was like a disease

82 Constant, *Political Writings*, 318.

83 Ibid., 320.

84 On this debate, see Hont, "The Early Enlightenment Debate on Commerce and Luxury" and Jennings, *Revolution and the Republic*, 131–46.

85 Chérel, *Fénelon au XVIIIe siècle en France (1715–1820)*; Riley, "Rousseau, Fénelon, and the Quarrel between the Ancients and the Moderns."

86 Hanley, "Rousseau and Fénelon."

that encouraged the desire for domination and war, which unleashed violence against nations and hurt their prosperity. At the same time as it imagined a reformed monarchy for France, *Telemachus* proposed different visions of republics – the ancient and agrarian community of Bétique, and the commercial, Holland-like, republic of Tyre. Fénelon did not entirely reject commerce, contrary to what some scholars have implied. But he certainly condemned the vision of mankind as addicted to the endless pursuit of superfluous goods, which the economic plan of Colbert, Louis XIV's minister of finance, entailed.[87]

Fénelon became strongly associated with the anti-luxury camp in the eighteenth-century reception. The two most important proponents of luxury were Mandeville and Jean-Francois Melon, who were also widely read in eighteenth-century France. In his 1734 *Essay on Commerce,* Melon noted that luxury was already a well-trodden topic.[88] Completely uninterested in the moral dimension of the question, Melon mostly saw luxury as an economic incentive. Once they had acquired necessities, individuals in his view were motivated to work only out of a desire to acquire luxury and live in opulence. Coherently, Melon took luxury to be a relative notion, because the "superfluous" evolves as the quality of life rises. It was precisely this relativity that made luxury an enduring – unlimited – incentive.[89] Melon entirely rejected the republican narrative of the military glory of Sparta or Rome: "Austere Sparta was not better at conquest, better governed, nor produced greater men than voluptuous Athens."[90] Even more strikingly, Melon was unstartled by the relation between the production of the superfluous and the colonization necessary to produce it as he vehemently rejected "moral questions." Refusing to think "whether it is against justice to subjugate a barbarian nation,"[91] Melon did not see slavery as a problem either, since it was economically beneficial: "The use of slaves in our colonies teaches us that slavery is contrary neither to religion nor morality: we can therefore freely examine whether it would be useful to extend it everywhere."[92]

87 On Fénelon's economic views, see Hanley, *The Political Philosophy of Fénelon,* 49–82. Hanley convincingly argues that Fénelon should be understood as endorsing "a set of moderate commitments on three fronts: sufficiency in wealth, stability in growth, and mixed modes of production" (50).

88 Melon, *Essai politique sur le commerce [1734]*, 129. Chapter IX, "On Luxury."

89 For instance, "silk tights," which were considered common needs at the time of Melon, "were luxury at the time of Henry II" (*Essai Politique*, 131).

90 Ibid., 139.

91 Ibid., 51.

92 Ibid., 61.

In turn, Mandeville proposed a sharp and memorable description of commercial society with the image of a "grumbling hive."[93] The scandalous idea developed in this text was that by pursuing their self-interest and indulging in their vices, bees were contributing to the creation of a wealthy and powerful hive, even though they were not virtuous in any understanding of the term. Perceived as one of the great apologists of luxury, Mandeville had a durable influence on republicans, first of all on Rousseau, who shared most of his description of the moral torment of modern individuals in commercial society, although, in contrast to Mandeville, he condemned it instead of extolling it.[94]

In the debate on luxury, we find Mably, the "classical republican," opposing the arguments of Melon and Mandeville.[95] Yet I would like to deflate Benjamin Constant's argument that Mably was a typical "classical republican" and that he proposed the type of economic plan that the Jacobins followed. Instead I see him as an original thinker presenting a synthesis of republicanism and egalitarianism that did not find a strong following in the Revolution.

Surely, Mably was "classical" in his constant reliance on republican thinkers from antiquity.[96] We should note, however, that Mably's republicanism was also inspired by the English republican tradition. In *Des Droits et des devoirs,* Mably's character – a Commonwealthman Lord Stanhope – used discourses inspired from well-known English republican literature to make his points.[97] While Mably was undoubtedly inspired by antiquity, his republicanism was also indebted to English thought of the very kind that influenced Montesquieu. In this regard, there was no classical purity in his republicanism – his was

93 For a nuanced analysis of Mandeville's position on luxury, see Turner, "Mandeville against Luxury."

94 Jack, "One State of Nature: Mandeville and Rousseau"; Rasmussen, *The Problems and Promise of Commercial Society: Adam Smith's Response to Rousseau.*

95 For a description of Mably as a classical republican, see Wright, *A Classical Republican in Eighteenth-Century France. The Political Thought of Mably.*

96 It would be an understatement to say that Mably's political thought was inspired by ancient political thought. The names of many of his works bear witness to his interest in studying ancient regimes: *Parallèle des Romains et des Français par rapport au gouvernement* (1740), *Observation sur les Grecs* (1749), *Observations sur les Romains* (1751). Mably's preferred genre, the philosophical history, is also taken from a long tradition, whose model may be Machiavelli's *Discourses.* Because of the *Entretiens de Phocion,* he is considered a proponent of ancient virtues.

97 For the argument that Mably owed a lot to English republicanism, see Baker, *Inventing the French Revolution,* 86–106 and Hammersley, *The English Republican Tradition and Eighteenth-Century France,* 86–98.

very much the result of the mixed influences coming from different traditions.

What made Mably's thought distinctive is the egalitarian form of his republicanism. Nelson notes that he was a "Greek"-style republican, one whose hero was Lycurgus and his egalitarian, homogenous Sparta.[98] While Mably did not argue for complete material equality, he emphasized – just like Rousseau – that the difference between the poor and the rich should not be too great.[99] In this regard, Mably might be best described as an early critic of the emergent classical political economy. In *Doutes proposés aux philosophes économistes*, he criticized Lemercier de la Rivière for the priority he gave to the production of goods and for his insistence that the property over one's person cannot be detached from the property over land. Because of his reluctance to embrace the traditional republican association between freedom and private property, Mably argued in favor of collective ownership. For instance, he described with admiration the Jesuit communities in Paraguay which were based on collective ownership and asset distribution based on needs. Admired by Babeuf, Mably has often been read as a proto-communist.

Mably, like Fénelon, criticized luxury and material inequality on moral grounds. He argued that inequality of wealth and condition destroyed human sentiments and fostered humiliation and hatred.[100] Importantly, and in a straight republican spirit, Mably thought that inequality opened the possibility of widespread domination, creating a society of "tyrants and slaves."[101] By contrast, Mably concluded, we need to imagine that equality will produce the contrary: it will create feelings of benevolence and friendship. Mably's equation between inequality and commerce explains his critique of the latter. "Commerce is a kind of monster that destroys everything by itself," writes Mably.[102] In a commercial society, there is no limit to the ambition of the wealthy, needs are multiplying, and corruption is everywhere.[103] More radically than Fénelon, who had a more moderate view on commercial society, Mably's republicanism took commerce to be incompatible with a free society.

Does this mean that Mably provides us with a clear case of classical French republicanism announcing the democratic republicanism of

[98] Nelson, *The Greek Tradition in Republican Thought*, 177.
[99] Hammersley, *The English Republican Tradition and Eighteenth-Century France*, 87.
[100] Mably, *Legislation*, t. I, 49.
[101] Mably, *Observations sur les Grecs*, 23.
[102] Mably, *Droit public de l'Europe*, t. VI, 315.
[103] Mably, *Œuvres* t. VIII, 456 (*Observations sur l'Amérique*).

the revolution? Despite Constant's claim about the importance of Mably in shaping revolutionary republicanism, there are two reasons why we should downplay the importance of his writings. The first is that in one key dimension his republicanism was decisively nonrevolutionary. While he was doubtlessly an egalitarian, Mably was hardly a democrat and did not argue for popular government.[104] His writings showed a lack of trust in the people's capacity to govern themselves. In his *Observations on the United States*, Mably repeatedly noted that common men are limited in their cognitive capacity and their capacity to channel passions. Mably's republicanism was thus animated by a fundamental mistrust of the fickle and uneducated people. In his *Observations,* Mably's worry centered on the fact that in modern states, individuals did not have the virtue of the ancients.[105] He contended that the number of men capable of thinking for themselves and discussing an opinion was always very small. The rest, he thought, were a crowd of children without ideas of their own. The state ought to act like a father preventing his children from encountering dangerous and corrupting ideas.

The second reason for downplaying Mably's importance for revolutionary republicanism is that he did not believe in the possibility of implementing his plans in modern France. France could never be organized as an ancient republic, he held, precisely because modernity prevented the possibility of a government based on citizens' virtue. Mably did not think that ancient republics could be reproduced in modern times – in this sense, he shared Montesquieu's diagnostic about modernity.

Ultimately his view is that "what legislators could have done in happier times, our accumulated vices and prejudices have made them impracticable."[106] This is why he tempered his position, whenever the issue was the applicability of republicanism to the modern world. In *De l'Étude de l'histoire*, he emphasized that he did not support the violent expropriation of the rich, as "we cannot aspire today to the equality of Sparta."[107] Mably therefore proposed a less-radical solution – simply making sure that poverty and extreme opulence should not have a place in society. This also meant that no radical change could be enacted: social ranks could not in his view be eradicated, nor could the passions of the people of the lowest ranks evolve. In Mably's version, classical

104 *Observations sur le gouvernement et les loix des Etats-Unis,* 21.
105 Ibid., 128.
106 *De l'Étude de l'histoire,* 240.
107 Ibid.

republicanism was certainly not a radical call to apply the rigid rules of ancient republics to a world entirely unfit for them. Whatever Mably's influence had been, it was nowhere as radical as Rousseau's.

THE AMERICAN REPUBLIC

I have argued so far that on three key issues – imperialism, freedom, commerce – the republican tradition did not have the homogeneous and definitive views that Montesquieu ascribed to them. Rather, republicanism appeared as an eclectic tradition proposing mixed guidance to modernity. Yet republican theory was not just shaped by intellectual traditions. It was also transformed immensely by the American Revolution: a world-shattering event of a new and large nation deciding to self-organize on republican principles. The impact of the American Revolution on the fall of the French monarchy was undoubtedly considerable.[108] It may therefore come as a surprise that there is so little research on the topic of the American influence on the French Revolution.[109] The American War of Independence, supported by a costly influx of French soldiers, contributed to the immense debt of the French State, which triggered the convocation of the Estates General and the radical political changes that ensued. Yet the connections between the two revolutions were far from being only financial and material. The American Revolution spurred a formidable enthusiasm in France, especially in reformist circles and among those who aspired to shake off the monarchy. In a 1778 letter to Richard Price, Anne-Robert Turgot, the ex-controller of Finances of Louis XVI, described the American people as the "hope of the humankind" and suggested that Americans "could become the model" for future political progress in Europe by showing that "humans can be free and live in peace, and live without the chains that tyrants and charlatans of all kinds have tried to impose under the guise of the public good."[110]

In his 1786 *On the Influence of the American Revolution in Europe*, Condorcet (who referred to himself as "an obscure inhabitant of the old hemisphere") argued that the American example proved that there was hope for a republic in the modern world. After having recognized the specific horror of slavery on American soil, Condorcet nonetheless

[108] Godechot, *France and the Atlantic Revolution of the Eighteenth Century, 1770–1799*.
[109] On this point, see Bell, "Questioning the Global Turn: The Case of the French Revolution."
[110] Turgot, *Œuvres de Turgot et documents le concernant*.

maintained: "the spectacle of a great people, where the rights of man are respected, is useful to all others, despite the difference in climate, mores and constitutions."[111] Condorcet also admired the American declaration of rights. "The first declaration of rights really worthy of the name is the Virginia declaration, signed on 1 June 1776, and the author of that declaration deserves the eternal gratitude of the human race."[112] For these early commentators, the political legacy of the American states on the formation of a modern form of republicanism was invaluable. It proved that a large modern republic was possible. The American republic flamboyantly disproved the scale thesis and overcame all of the obstacles Montesquieu had warned about.

The "model" represented by the American case was pitched early as a promise for a peaceful life free from tyrannical government – that is, in *republican* terms. American state constitutions were translated very promptly into French and constituted the basis for the European discussion on the novel constitutional design appropriate for the changes they hoped to undertake in their home states.[113] The intense scrutiny of these new constitutions gave the impression, for a while, that the American "model" or "models" would dominate the French intellectual and political scene. Reformers as different as Condorcet, Turgot, Raynal, Brissot, and Mably published extensive analyses of the American Revolution and its state constitutions.[114] Echoing these intense Atlantic exchanges, historians have seen a strong affinity between the two revolutions. The thesis of the continuity between the French and the American revolutions, and the political regimes they generated – the so-called "Atlantic thesis" – became popular among American historians in the 1960s, after Palmer and Godechot's publications arguing that they formed a continuous form of democratic change.[115]

111 Condorcet, "De l'influence de la Révolution d'Amérique sur l'Europe (1786)," 13.

112 Condorcet, "On Despotism. Thoughts on Despotism (1789)," 177.

113 Appleby, "America as a Model for the Radical French Reformers of 1789."

114 Mably, *Observations sur le gouvernement et les loix des Etats-Unis d'Amérique*; Turgot, "Lettre du Docteur Price sur les constitutions américaines"; Condorcet, "De l'influence de la Révolution d'Amérique Sur l'Europe [1786]"; Raynal, *Révolution de l'Amérique*; Brissot and Clavière, *De la France et des Etats-unis ou de l'importance de la révolution d'Amérique pour le bonheur de la France.*

115 Godechot, *La Grande Nation. L'expansion révolutionnaire de la France dans le monde de 1789 à 1799*; Palmer, *The Age of the Democratic Revolution: A Political History of Europe and America. 1760–1800*. Patrice Higonnet also sees the two revolutions as parts of the same process (Higonnet, *Sister Republics. The Origin of French and American Republicanism*).

In France, the educated public had early access to the constitution of a few American states as well as to the texts of the Declaration of Independence and the Articles of Confederation, as a translation of these texts appeared in an edited volume in 1778.[116] The *Constitutions des treize Etats-unis de l'Amérique,* another edition with the full texts of the constitutions of the thirteen former colonies appeared in 1783, as Benjamin Franklin aimed to shape the public opinion and protect it against the criticisms coming from England.[117] It is sometimes incorrectly assumed in the republican scholarship that French republicans lacked interest in other forms of republicanism, including the American one.[118] The abundant comments on the American state constitutions is clear evidence that this is untrue.

The early discussion on the constitutions of the thirteen former colonies bears witness to an interesting phenomenon: the existence of a multitude of "American models." The "democratic model" of Pennsylvania was of great interest and met the approval of Turgot and Condorcet. A group that came to be known as *américanophiles* praised the American experience, though they mostly valued the democratic constitution of Pennsylvania, written under the leadership of Franklin and Paine, rather than the later federal constitution. On the other hand, the bicameral model offered by the Constitution of Massachusetts was praised by Mably, in a letter to Adams.[119] Mably clearly favored a mixed constitution, in which a body like a Senate could preserve the stability of laws and national character. Just as in Rome, the Senate in the Massachusetts constitution enabled a mix of aristocracy and democracy, which allowed them to benefit from the advantages of both without suffering the shortcomings of either. Admiration for Adams' work did not come from the *américanophiles* but from the *anglomanes* such as Jean Joseph Mounier, who thought that constitutions should be "balanced."[120] This plurality of models, however, shows the same problem as in other aspects of the republican tradition: a deep indeterminacy and unclear guidance for French republicans, who still had to choose their own path.

[116] *Recueil des loix constitutives des colonies angloises, confédérées sous la dénomination d'Etats-Unis de l'Amérique-Septentrionale.*

[117] La Rochefoucauld d'Enville and Franklin, *Constitution des treize Etats-unis de l'Amérique.*

[118] Chabal, *A Divided Republic. Nation, State and Citizenship in Contemporary France*, 11.

[119] Adams, *The Adams Papers.* Vol. 16. "Abbé Gabriel Bonnot de Mably to John Adams, 25 February 1785."

[120] Watkins, *Reclaiming the American Revolution*, xv.

Yet, soon, and maybe surprisingly, the American reference was totally eclipsed in French debates over desirable constitutional changes. After all, the United States, a new country of 4 million inhabitants still defining its laws, mores and territory, had little in common with the French state of 35 million inhabitants territorially organized around old laws, privileges, separate regional parliaments, and rooted in different and rival customs and local languages. In his 1771 *Constitution of England,* Jean-Louis De Lolme described France as a juxtaposition of different territories that slowly formed an imperfect unity.[121] This explained, according to him, why France was not capable of acquiring the kind of balanced institutions and free regime that characterized England: such a patchwork, constantly torn apart by the disputes of nobles, required a strong authoritarian regime.

One explanation for the disinterest toward American theoretical solutions may be that very early on, the thought that the American federal republic could not provide a model for France started to spread. The differences in the circumstances of the two countries were so considerable that the American solutions could not be directly applied. In his *Tableau de la situation actuelle des Etats-Unis d'Amérique* (1795), Charles Pictet, a Swiss diplomat, presented an interpretation of the American situation that became later associated with Tocqueville. The Americans, he argued, were never really oppressed, and therefore did not have to conduct an extreme revolution that would turn their society upside down.[122] In this regard, their circumstances were incommensurable with the French ones.

Another insurmountable difference was the federal dimension of the American Republic. Federalism deeply contradicted one of the few beliefs uniting French revolutionaries across the spectrum: that in a country like France, sovereignty ought not to be divided. In his *Letters from a Bourgeois of New Haven,* for instance, Condorcet criticized the American federal constitution, and its emulation of the English bicameral system. He was far from the only person to hold this conviction. Turgot also noted that the system of balances that was necessary in England to counterbalance the power of the king has "no use in republics based on the equality of all citizens."[123]

From the early nineteenth century on, the American and the French Revolutions have often been contrasted, unfavorably for the latter. Hannah

[121] De Lolme, *Constitution de l'Angleterre ou état du gouvernement anglais, comparé avec la forme républicaine & avec les autres monarchies de l'Europe.*
[122] Pictet, *Tableau de la situation actuelle des Etats-Unis d'Amérique*, 19.
[123] Turgot, "Lettre du Docteur Price sur les constitutions américaines."

Arendt famously saw a novel beginning (an "action") and the expression of freedom in the American Revolution, while she dismissed the French Revolution as embodying basic social needs, that is, as expressing bare life.[124] The two events also gave birth to two distinct republican theories, that have also been unequally assessed in the scholarship. American republicanism became hailed for being the first modern form of republicanism. It gave an institutional solution to the problem of freedom in a plural and large state by embracing checks and balances, bicameralism, and federalism. Instead of the ancient martial republic, the American adaptation privileged commercial relations, which fitted well with the development of individualism and the plurality of life modes. While the Americans provided a priceless gift to the French republicans – the hope of emancipation and the proof of its possibility – they did not offer a blueprint for France, an old, divided country with a mass of illiterate peasants.

CONCLUSION

Montesquieu's challenge largely explains why there were few republicans in France on the eve of the Revolution. All the past and existing republics presented circumstances fundamentally at odds with the situation of France. They might show that republics were theoretically possible, but they did not come with a clear guidance to set up a republican government in other situations. Republicanism, in its multiple forms across time and space, appeared essentially inapplicable in France without considerable recrafting. How could a theory made for an elite become a theory for the self-governing many? How could a theory made for the virtuous be efficient for self-interested individuals? And how would a large and diverse country be capable of being united without a king? Montesquieu's challenge appeared insurmountable.

However, the complexity and diversity of the republican tradition offered hope and a host of theoretical options. I have argued in this chapter that many of the central concepts of the tradition – glory, conquest, freedom, slavery, dependence, commerce – were not clearly defined. They thus provided possibilities of innovative interpretation. One of the theorists who seized such an opportunity was Jean-Jacques Rousseau. His influence on the fate on French republicanism cannot be overestimated, or so I will argue in Chapter 2.

124 Arendt, *On Revolution*, 59–61.

2

Rousseau's Proposal

For many French revolutionaries, Rousseau's work laid the theoretical foundation of both the Revolution and the Republic.[1] References to his ideas can be found all over constitutional debates from 1789 to 1795.[2] It was in fact obvious to everyone in the Assembly that anyone among them would have a close knowledge of Rousseau's ideas. As one representative, Jean-Baptiste Salle, puts it in the (vain) hope of stopping the flow of long-winded discourses that plagued the Convention, "please, let us stop preliminary discourses! Everybody here has ideas on the principles of government: it is enough for us to have read Rousseau's *Social Contract.*"[3] In the Fall of 1790, asking for the erection of Rousseau's statue with the words "The Free French Nation to J. J. Rousseau," one representative, Ange-Marie d'Eymar, made the case that the Assembly should honor the great man on the ground that he provided the "eternally true principles which are the immutable basis for the French Constitution."[4] While Rousseau was appropriated by revolutionaries from all across the spectrum, his work was retrospectively associated most closely with Robespierre. Despite rarely making direct references to Rousseau's name

[1] This claim prevailed during the Revolution. See Louis-Sébastien Mercier, "De Jean-Jacques Rousseau, considéré comme un des premiers auteurs de la révolution." For contemporary analysis of this idea, see Bernard Manin, "Rousseau"; Swenson, *On Jean-Jacques Rousseau, Considered as One of the First Authors of the Revolution* and Neidleman, *The General Will Is Citizenship.*

[2] Barny, *Rousseau dans la révolution. Le personnage de Jean-Jacques et les débuts du culte révolutionnaire (1778–1791)*; McNeil, "The Cult of Rousseau and the French Revolution."

[3] *AP* LXIII 384, April 26, 1793.

[4] *AP* XXI 128, November 29, 1790.

in his interventions at the Assembly, Robespierre certainly admired him, calling him a "precursor" of the revolution and a man who "by the elevation of his soul and the grandeur of his character, showed himself worthy of the position of teacher of the human race."[5] After the end of the Terror, and despite their opposition to Jacobinism, the Thermidorians concurred with Robespierre's assessment and consecrated Rousseau's status as "one of the first authors of the Revolution" by transferring his remains to the Pantheon.[6]

Notwithstanding the revolutionary cult of Rousseau, contemporary scholarship generally considers the revolutionary appropriation of his work to be a blatant misinterpretation, on the ground that the Citizen of Geneva never intended for his theory to be applied to a large and diverse country like France. On the contrary, they claim, Rousseau followed the opinion of his time in thinking that republics ought to be limited to small agrarian and homogeneous polities, in keeping with Montesquieu's "scale thesis."[7] Consider, for instance, the following diagnosis: "Rousseau offered little solace for modern corrupt societies, since his republican vision was never intended for those states where commerce, luxury, and inequality were rife. […] Rousseau's own political proposals did not constitute a possibility for modern states once beset with luxury and entrenched inequality."[8] Indeed, as another scholar concludes, "the ideal type of republican rule which [Rousseau] outlines suits only a small and Spartan society comprised of virtuous citizens."[9] According to this widespread interpretation, the ideal he proposed in the *Social Contract* was simply unrealizable in the modern circumstances of large and commercial states, a tragic fact that Rousseau himself acknowledged.

The interpretation of Rousseau as a proponent of a small Spartan-style republic is not a late invention of the twenty-first century. It became popular in liberal circles in the immediate aftermath of the French

[5] Interestingly though, he does not mention his name even in this passage. *AP* XC 137 (8 May 1794), "Rapport présenté par Robespierre au nom du Comité de Salut Public, concernant le culte à l'Etre Suprême, lors de la séance du 18 Floréal an II."

[6] See Lakanal, "Rapport sur J. J. Rousseau, fait au nom du Comité d'Instruction Publique," 29 Fructidor Year III.

[7] See for instance Hammersley, *The English Republican Tradition,* 86–87; Garsten, "From Popular Sovereignty to Civil Society in Post-Revolutionary France," 237; Kelly, "Popular Sovereignty as State Theory in the Nineteenth Century," 275; Pateman, *Participation and Democratic Theory,* 22.

[8] Douglass, *Rousseau and Hobbes,* 202.

[9] Fetscher, "Republicanism and popular sovereignty," 277.

Revolution, largely as a way of repudiating Jacobin politics.[10] Rousseau's antiquated republicanism of virtue, the argument goes, led to the fateful enterprise of the Jacobins who, in the name of virtue and abstract reason, forcefully adapted it to times unfit for them, and created the Terror as a result.[11] This postrevolutionary liberal narrative found an uptake in the revisionist interpretation of the French Revolution, which became dominant from the end of the twentieth century on in the wake of François Furet's work.[12]

The scale thesis, I contend, is inaccurate as a textual interpretation of Rousseau's work. Correcting this reading means giving back Rousseau the place he deserves in the republican tradition as a pivotal figure who proposed the main conceptual and institutional devices to adapt the old elitist ideal of republicanism to the modern and democratic circumstances of France.[13] This chapter makes two overarching arguments. The first one is that Rousseau revolutionized republicanism by aiming to adapt it to a large and modern country. In what follows, I show what this adaptation looked like, and how Rousseau responded to Montesquieu's challenge concerning the lack of virtue of modern citizens (the "motivation objection"), the lack of common identity of a large people (the "unity objection"), and the epistemic deficiency of a large and uneducated mass (the "epistemic objection").

In this process of adaptation, Rousseau offered a new vision of republicanism based on an inclusive popular sovereignty. Instead of an ancient theory relying on self-sacrifice, Rousseau's modern republicanism is based on the rational interest of each citizen to remain free. He developed a theory of republican citizenship as a shared intention toward creating and maintaining a community of free and equal beings – an inclusive theory of sharing freedom.

Importantly Rousseau intentionally used the concept of freedom in different ways.[14] Like republicans before him, he often defined freedom as non-domination, that is as not being under the arbitrary will of another (*LM* 8th letter; *OC* III.84). This is the "civil freedom" that individuals enjoy in a well-ordered republic (*SC* I.8.2), and that is the

10 Constant, *Political Writings*, 318.

11 Blum, *Rousseau and the Republic of Virtue: The Language of Politics in the French Revolution.*

12 Furet, *Penser la Révolution française.*

13 For a complementary argument to place Rousseau back in this tradition, see Dijn, "Rousseau and Republicanism."

14 Simpson, *Rousseau's Theory of Freedom*, 1.

reason why individuals want to associate in the social contract in the first place (*SC* I.6.4; *SC* I.7.8). He also endorsed a positive conception of freedom as self-government, which supposed not only a lack of domination, but also "obeying the law one has prescribed to oneself" (*SC* I.8.3). At the individual level, it is moral freedom, and at the collective level, it is a form of freedom as self-government. What will emerge in this chapter is that in Rousseau's republican project, sharing freedom as self-government among an inclusive citizenry is necessary to obtain freedom as non-domination.

The second argument concerns the new problems created by Rousseau's conceptual innovations. As readers of Rousseau like to point out, there are many paradoxes in his work. I focus here on those that are the most pertinent for the later fate of French republicans, who will inherit, and struggle with, them: the indeterminacy of the people and the lack of stability of the republic on a rational-universal basis. Together, they form the ground of the paradox of national universalism that I examine in Chapter 5.

THE POSSIBILITY OF A LARGE REPUBLIC

Let us first examine the claim that Rousseau believed republics could only exist in small agrarian and tight-knit communities. Rousseau, indeed, often makes declarations that could be interpreted this way. See, for instance, his remark in the *Social Contract*: "all things considered, I do not see that among us the Sovereign can henceforth preserve the exercise of its right unless the City is very small" (*SC* III.15.12). In the epistle to the *Second Discourse,* Rousseau similarly writes that a society can be well governed only when it has a "size confined to the range of human faculties" (*SD* 114). These remarks are not incidental: they concern central tenets of his theory that arguably make republics only fit for small communities. Take for instance Rousseau's rejection of representatives (*SC* III.15.5). How can the citizens of a republic beyond the size of a city-state physically assemble? If, as some scholars contend, Rousseau is a proponent of participatory democracy, how could this participation happen?[15]

The question seems all the more worrying in that Rousseau followed Montesquieu (sometimes to the point of near plagiarism) in arguing that the best type of government could only be thought of in terms of

[15] For the claim that Rousseau is a participatory democrat, see Pateman, *Participation and Democratic Theory*, 22–27.

the particular features of a people and a country: there needs to be a fit between government, mores, size, climate, and geography (*SC* II.11.4 and III.8).[16] Different types of circumstances therefore warrant different types of regimes, and some regimes are impossible in some circumstances (*SC* II. 11). Rousseau therefore did argue that there were important limits in terms of size for a country to remain well governed:

> Just as nature has set limits to the stature of a well-formed man, beyond which it makes only giants and dwarfs, so, too, with regard to the best constitution of a state, there are bounds to the size it can have in order not to be either too large to be well governed, or too small to be self-sustaining. (*SC* II.9.1)

Scale is one of the structural limits to a free state. There is a proportion between the centralization of executive power and the size of the territory. "The more the State expands, the more freedom contracts" (*SC* III.1.11). The larger the State, the harder it will be to avoid centralization and therefore a possible form of absolutism (*SC* III.6.4–5). The second book of the *Social Contract* argues further that in large states, either there are too many different laws that create chaos and confusion, or the same laws are imposed yet are bound not to be adapted to this diversity (*SC* II.9.3). Diversity exacerbates the complications created by a large size.

Problems unfortunately do not end there. Again, following Montesquieu, Rousseau repeatedly states that modern individuals do not have the virtue of ancient peoples. A "well-constituted state" is one in which citizens "fly to the assembly" (*SC* III.15.3). "All is lost," when citizens prefer their own business over the pursuit of the common good. Such preference mars modern states mostly, though not exclusively, due to the development of commerce and luxury. "It is the hustle and bustle of commerce and the arts, it is the avid interest in gain, it is softness and love of comforts that change personal service into money (...) Give money and soon, you will have chains" (*SC* III.15.2). As if scale was not enough of a problem, the circumstances of modernity, which include increased commercial activity, also bring about a drastic change in the moral make-up of individuals.

All the different issues with large, commercial, and diverse countries come down to difficulty in sustaining what Rousseau calls "the social bond," that is the social connection between individuals that ensures their continued willingness to live together. Because for Rousseau humans are

[16] For the description of the fitness argument, see Williams, "Political Ontology and Institutional Design in Montesquieu and Rousseau."

naturally asociable, the "social bond" is fragile and needs to be sustained by common practices. "The more the social bond stretches, the looser it grows, and in general a small state is proportionally stronger than a large one" (*SC* II.9.1). In Rousseau's organicist way of thinking, the social bond is the key element that keeps a community alive.

In his repeated remarks about the immense obstacles to freedom that the moderns face, Rousseau acknowledged the force of Montesquieu's objections. In large and commercial countries, individuals *prima facie*

(1) share no common knowledge of the common good (the epistemic objection).
(2) are self-interested and unwilling to become virtuous (the motivation objection).
(3) have no common mores and identity (the unity objection).

Yet, if it is so, what is Rousseau's point in writing the *Social Contract*, a theory which would have no possible application in the real world? In the *Letters from the Mountain* (*LM* 6; *OC* 3, 810), he claims that the reason for the condemnation of the *Social Contract* is precisely that it is not an abstract "system" that could be discarded as hopelessly utopian, "like Plato's *Republic* or [More's] *Utopia*" (*OC* 3, 810). His censors presciently attributed to Rousseau ambitions that could disturb public order maintained by France's absolute monarchy.

Let us now look at the first piece of evidence that Rousseau believed he was capable of meeting Montesquieu's challenges about the possibility of a large and modern republic. The *Social Contract,* the most "utopian" and abstract piece in Rousseau's work, insisted on the difference between the citizen in the ancient world and the modern bourgeois. The third and fourth books of the *Social Contract* are organized around the distinction between ancient and modern republics. Initially it seems that the moderns have nothing to show for themselves. For Rousseau, the Greeks had many advantages ranging from a mild climate, a language that could be heard in the public square, the use of slaves, and the love of freedom (*SC* III.15.9). The moderns do not have any of these advantages. "No longer having the same advantages," Rousseau asks, "how are we to preserve the same rights?" (*SC* III.15.9).

In response to this question, the *Social Contract* sets out to demonstrate an interesting and neglected argument: that the historical existence of a very large republic – Rome – should be considered a piece of evidence that large republics are possible, and not chimerical, as the critics of republicanism and democracy have argued. I locate this argument in a long passage in the fourth book of the *Social Contract* (*SC* IV. 4–7), four sections about the Roman Republic's institutions, that are otherwise largely left unexplained.[17] As the fourth book of the work is somewhat convoluted, many scholars have simply preferred to steer clear of it. A dominant interpretation, offered by Derathé, has been that Rousseau wrote these sections as a filler to bridge between its political principles (Book I–III) and the chapter on civil religion (IV.8).[18] This interpretation seems supported by a genetic approach: the first version of the *Social Contract,* the *Geneva Manuscript,* bears no trace of the Roman Republic Chapters, though it presents large developments from Books I–III and the largest part of the civil religion chapter. The summary of the book in *Émile* is also silent about it (*E* 458–467).[19] Yet this interpretation is unsatisfactory. It fails to explain why Rousseau would write these detailed chapters. That he did not envision them early in the writing process does not disqualify their importance. On the contrary, this addition may suggest that they were written in response to an important gap in the argument that Rousseau was making.

In my interpretation, Rousseau announces the purpose of these sections, when in Book III, he suggests a possible objection to his theory of direct popular sovereignty: that it is impossible for a large people, or a people in a large country, to assemble, implying that they would need representatives. Yet far from taking the example of the Roman Republic as a model from the past that we should try to mimic out of nostalgia, he presents it to rebut the argument that a large popular government without representatives is unrealizable. He argues, in fact, that it can be achieved: "The inference from what is to what is possible seems to me sound" (*SC* III.12.5).

Rousseau uses the Roman Republic example to argue in favor of the applicability of the *Social Contract* in modern Europe: "Let us consider

[17] Among the few exceptions, see McCormick, "Rousseau's Rome and the Repudiation of Populist Republicanism"; Williams, *Rousseau's Social Contract: An Introduction*; Arena, "The Roman Republic of Jean-Jacques Rousseau"; Oprea, "Pluralism and the General Will: The Roman and Spartan Models in Rousseau's Social Contract." I strongly disagree with McCormick, who takes these passages to demonstrate Rousseau's endorsement of oligarchic republicanism. My interpretation is closer to Arena's.

[18] See Derathé's comments in his edition of the *Social Contract,* in Rousseau, *Œuvres complètes. Tome III.*, 1494–1495 and Cousin, "JJ Rousseau, interprète des institutions romaines dans le Contrat Social."

[19] The mention of the "Roman populace" in *Émile*'s summary refers to the Book III.12 instead. The summary does not develop the specific voting system of the Roman Republic or explain why Rousseau would dwell on this case.

what can be done in light of what has been done. I shall not speak of the ancient republics of Greece but the Roman Republic was, it seems to me, a large state and the city of Rome a large city" (*SC* III.12.3).

The presentation of Rome as a large nation is not particular to the *Social Contract*. Rome's size and its status as "the capital of the world" appear in different arguments in Rousseau's corpus (*FD* 10; *OC* 3, 10). Yet, in this one passage, the gigantic Roman Republic was a particularly judicious example for Rousseau because it proved successful in realizing the most controversial aspect of his theory: that there should be no representatives of the sovereign. "It is quite striking that in Rome, where the Tribunes were so sacred, no one ever so much as imagined that they might usurp the functions of the people, and that in the midst of such a great multitude they never attempted to pass a single plebiscite on their own authority alone" (*SC* III.15.6). This interpretation supposes our agreement with Rousseau's rather strange view of the Roman Republic. For him, and in contrast to almost all the interpretive tradition, the Roman Republic was not an example of a mixed constitution: it was a simple form of government where the people was sovereign and exercised power directly, that is, a democracy.[20] Granted this condition, Rome was the ultimate historical proof that it was possible for a large country to be a republic, that is, one in which the people, and not its representatives, had legislative power.

The Roman Republic was also a great example for Rousseau as it displayed the trait that he rated the most important for a republic: that all citizens be protected against domination, that is, all citizens' freedom be guaranteed. The only reason individuals would want to enter a social compact is if they could be guaranteed to be as free as they were in the state of nature (*SC* I.7.4). In this regard, according to Rousseau, the Roman Republic surpassed all other states. Regardless of any shortcomings in their institutions and practices, "the Romans distinguished themselves above all peoples on earth by the government's regard for private individuals, and its scrupulous care to respect the inviolable rights of all members of the state" (*DPE* 18).

[20] I agree with Arena that Rousseau takes issue with the contention that republics need to have mixed constitutions. However, Arena misses the argument about the possibility of *large* republics, which is Rousseau's main point in these passages in my view. I also disagree with her claim that the Roman Republic is a "perfect model" – on the contrary, in Rousseau's narrative, Rome is distinctive for its imperfection. See Arena, "The Roman Republic of Jean-Jacques Rousseau."

That Rome exhibited both an unprecedented size and heterogeneity was incontestable for Rousseau. It came to be the capital of the world and spanned a large number of territories with peoples of different cultures, languages, mores, and religions (*SC* IV.4). Yet it was able to protect all its citizens' freedom and have a popular sovereign without representatives. Rousseau's detractors cannot argue that his theory was impractical for large modern states because it lacked historical precedent. The Romans, "the freest and most powerful people on earth" (*SC* IV.4.2), are blatant proof that a large and diverse Republic, in Rousseau's demanding sense of the government of a popular sovereign through the rule of law, *can* exist.

The argument of the *possibility* of a large and diverse republic is proved by the historical existence of Rome. A complementary argument runs through the book IV of the *Social Contract,* though it is less apparent than the possibility argument: that Rome proves not only that such a republic is possible, but it also suggests that it is *plausible* that it will return. This line of reasoning can be seen through Rousseau's insistence on the considerable obstacles encountered by Rome. The structure of the argument is thus: If even under extraordinarily unfavorable circumstances, a republic like Rome was able to thrive, then under (even marginally) more favorable circumstances, it is plausible to think another republic can also thrive.

My argument relies on Rousseau's rhetorically peculiar insistence on the imperfection of Rome as a model. The list of Rome's shortcomings and unfavorable circumstances is long, and Rousseau painstakingly presents them. The Romans proved capable of overcoming the greatest obstacles: a conspiratorial beginning as an association of thieves (*P* 181), a lack of founding genius unlike Sparta or Athens (*SC* III.10 fn), a constant state of war (*SC* IV.4), not only a diverse citizenry but a citizenry with growing diversity and inequality (*SC* IV.4.5), constantly moving borders, an incapacity to count its own citizens, and so on. The number of obstacles that Rousseau mentions, in a treatise that is ostensibly *not* about Rome, suggests what I would call an *a fortiori* strategy: if Rome was able to be a republic despite all these obstacles, surely it should be easier for countries that had better beginnings, *or* had better founders, *or* were not constantly at war, *or* had a less diverse citizenry to become republican.[21]

The *a fortiori* argument has its limits though, and the "possibility" argument may be all we can get out of the lengthy passage on Rome's

[21] For the complete presentation of the *a fortiori* argument, see Rousselière, "Rousseau and the Puzzle of the Roman Republic."

institutions. Indeed, I have not addressed the key distinction between the ancients and the moderns, which Rousseau underlines as a follower of Montesquieu: the ancients were virtuous, the moderns are not. "The [political men] of today speak to us only of manufacturing, commerce, finance, wealth and even luxury" (*SL* III.3), Montesquieu had argued. Rousseau concurred, copying almost literally this sentence in his *First Discourse*: "The ancient politicians forever spoke of morals and virtue; ours speak only of commerce and of money" (*FD* 18). Even if a large and diverse country like France might be able to avoid many obstacles that were in the way of Rome, the defining difference between the two was that modern men – eighteenth-century Frenchmen to be specific – could not be described in any way as virtuous. Their "devouring greed, unsettled spirit, intrigue, constant comings and goings, and perpetual revolutions of fortune" (*SC* IV.4.19) made them ill-suited for a republic. This conclusion may suggest that for Rousseau, the balance of advantages still tilts in favor of Rome.

THE MOTIVATION OBJECTION

If it is possible for a large republic to exist, this republic will need the kind of virtue that made Romans overcome the greatest of misfortunes, the most damaging institutional shortcomings, and the worst policy decisions. Rousseau therefore needs to answer Montesquieu's motivation objection: how can the moderns, fundamentally deficient in virtue, form a republic? At first sight, Rousseau does not seem to respond to Montesquieu in any innovative or plausible way. On the contrary, he is often thought of as an old-fashioned proponent of a classical republicanism of virtue.[22] In most of his work, he seems to reiterate the idea that citizens need to be virtuous for a republic to exist. It is nowhere as prevalent as in the *Discourse on Political Economy*: "The fatherland cannot endure without freedom, nor freedom without virtue, nor virtue without citizens; you will have everything if you form citizens; if you do not, you will have nothing but nasty slaves, beginning with the chiefs of the state" (*DPE* 20).

Throughout the *DPE*, Rousseau repeats his advice over and over in the form of an injunction: "Make virtue reign!" (*DPE* 13). The maxim of virtue (the second of the *DPE*) is necessary for the people to follow

[22] For the moral and political importance of virtue in Rousseau's work, see Reisert, *Jean-Jacques Rousseau. A Friend of Virtue*.

the first maxim of a legitimate government: "in all things to follow the general will" (*DPE* 9).

However, the *Social Contract*'s position on virtue does not immediately align with this view. In fact, and in sharp contrast with the *Discourse on Political Economy,* virtue is barely mentioned in the *Social Contract,* and never to characterize a necessary condition of the modern republic. Virtue only appears three times in the *Social Contract*: II.11 ("virtue" as characterizing Rome); III.4 ("virtue" as the principle of republics according to Montesquieu), and IV.7 ("virtuous" as characterizing a Spartiate). This should alert anyone familiar with Rousseau's thought that a significant theoretical move is occurring in this text.

Recall the contextual understanding of "virtue" that Rousseau would have inherited. Montesquieu's description of republican virtue fits the tradition that Pocock called "civic humanism," as the alternative name to classical republicanism.[23] According to Harrington, for instance, an author Montesquieu quotes in the *Spirit of the Laws,*[24] virtue is "something planted [in men] by God, which required fulfilment in the practice of self-rule."[25] "The affirmation of classical humanism," Pocock continues, "entails the affirmation that *homo* is naturally a citizen and most fully himself when living in a *vivere civile.*"[26]

Rousseau's description of the social compact contrasts radically with the "classical" vision of a political community grounded on virtue as the destination of men. It does not fit either Montesquieu's twist of the tradition with his addition of the idea of "self-sacrifice." The *Social Contract* mentions neither God-given virtue, nor society as the highest calling of men. In building a theory "uniting what right permits with what interest prescribes" (*SC* I.1.1), Rousseau pragmatically presents the device of the social contract as operating with self-interested individuals who aim to associate in a legitimate way because it is the only rational solution to their problem: how to remain free when they are forced to be in society, under the imminent threat of becoming ever more dependent on the arbitrary will of others (*SC* I.6.1).

23 Pocock, "Virtues, Rights, and Manners: A Model for Historians of Political Thought," 354. In Chapter 1, I contested the idea that there is a homogeneous category of "classical republicanism."

24 See *SL* XI.6 and XXIX. 19. On Montesquieu and Harrington, see Spector, "Harrington, James," in *Dictionnaire Montesquieu.*

25 Pocock, "Virtues, Rights, and Manners: A Model for Historians of Political Thought," 357.

26 Ibid., 355.

Rousseau thus rearticulates Montesquieu's motivation objection in terms of freedom: the question is not how individuals can be motivated to self-sacrifice in modern states, but rather how they can be motivated to remain free from dependence in circumstances that force them to forgo their natural freedom, such as the hostile economic and social conditions of modernity. If one supposes that individuals have a rational interest to be free (this is a premise, whose truth Rousseau simply posits) and that such a desire does not necessitate any supererogatory virtue (since it is self-interested), the question then becomes how to align individual self-interest with the durable pursuit of the common good that conditions the contract: "how to find a form of association that defends and protects with all the common force the person and the goods of each associate, by means of which each is united with all, obeys none but himself, and remains as free as before" (*SC* I.6.4).

Rousseau insists that there is no renunciation or sacrifice, in the social contract (*SC* II.4.10). The social contract is first and foremost an "advantageous transaction" (*échange avantageux*) (*SC* II.4.10). Therefore, the republic exists because the social contract is driven and guided by "the general will," which, however, is not created by the self-abnegating virtue of contracting agents. "By this word [republican] I understand (...) any government guided by the general will, which is the law" (*SC* II.6.9. fn).

In my interpretation, Rousseau avoids the term "virtue" because he aims to emphasize the rational dimension and the plausibility of the political project of a large and modern republic. Now it should be clear that virtue is in no way eliminated. Rather virtue is reconceptualized, distancing it from Montesquieu's polemical notion of self-abnegation. Tracking the evolution of Rousseau's theory, I would argue that this visible transformation did not occur suddenly. It was already prepared in the *Discourse on Political Economy*. See for instance: "every man is virtuous when his particular will conforms in all things to the general will" (*DPE* 15). And "virtue is nothing but this conformity of the particular will to the general will" (*DPE* 13).

It is important to note that for Rousseau, individuals always experience conflicts between their multiple interests – between their "particular" interests (personal, familial, factional, etc.) and the general interest that is theirs in so far as they are citizens. The struggle between these interests can never be entirely resolved, since "according to the natural order (...) each man is first of all himself, and then a magistrate, and then a citizen – a gradation directly opposed to that which the social order demands" (*E* 464). This internal struggle of citizens between their different wills leads to the destruction of the republic when mores and institutions are not strong enough for the "general and sovereign will [to be] the standard for all the other [wills]" (*E* 464). Rousseau's theory of *amour-propre* explains how virtue is constantly endangered by the inflation of the particular will and the demotion of the general will.[27]

While a large part of Rousseau's work emphasizes this internal struggle, and therefore the difficulty for humans to live free together, he also contends that there is a possibility for humans to align their particular will and their general will if the right conditions and institutions are maintained. The social contract is the device that operates this transformation.

THE UNITY OBJECTION

Let us provisionally accept Rousseau's reworking of virtue as self-interest well-understood (that is, an alignment of private interest and common good). Yet for moderns to be virtuous in that sense, it requires that they think of themselves as part of a community, that they share a common interest with other citizens, which it will be their own self-interest to follow. This points again to Montesquieu's unity objection: *individuals do not share a common interest in a large state, let alone a common identity*. In this section, I show how Rousseau addresses this objection at length in the *Social Contract*. I argue that he takes the device of the social contract through the formulation of a general will to *generate* a strong social bond between the members of the republic. This is possible only because the fundamental act of associating in the social contract transforms individuals into citizens, that is, individuals whose will is not only particular but also a shared intention toward being free, also known as a "general will." To make this argument, we will need to revisit Rousseau's idea of the general will.

It is beyond the scope of this chapter to solve the ambiguity of Rousseau's different statements concerning the nature of the general will. The general will, more than maybe any other concepts in his work, is multifaceted and undoubtedly serves several functions. My argument aims to show that the general will creates a sense of solidarity between citizens, because it presupposes a joint practical intent toward realizing a

[27] Neuhouser, *Rousseau's Theodicy of Self-Love: Evil, Rationality and the Drive for Recognition*, 55–152.

common goal, which is maintaining everyone's freedom. I therefore want to emphasize an often-neglected aspect of the general will rather than rebut other interpretations.

We should attend to the key dimension of the general will: that the will, *qua* will, is an intention toward an object, before it becomes an objective (objectified) result, that is, the outcome of this will. Both the French *volonté* and its English translation, *will,* contain this double dimension of the volitional act and its objectified result. We should pay attention to the nature of this volitional act, as an act engaging the individual as part of a collective. I contend that the general will is the name of a shared will, or shared intention, to preserve the freedom of each as part of the collective. It is an act that has transformative properties vis-à-vis the identity of the agent, whose will partly becomes one he shares with others.

The general will is a notoriously elusive concept.[28] Depending on the specific argument he is making, Rousseau characterizes it in different and potentially incompatible ways. The general will has been interpreted as a transcendent or substantive ideal (the general will expresses an anterior commitment to the common good)[29] as well as the procedural result of a deliberation (the general will is a procedure that generates an outcome).[30] Taken as an answer to Montesquieu's motivation and epistemic objections, I propose to interpret it in yet another way. The general will is the shared intention of individuals to adopt a common standpoint that enables them to be free both as moral beings and as citizens living under a code of laws. It is therefore not only a form of practical reason, as Kantian interpreters hold, but also a form of shared *intention* for common action, that is, of allegiance to the community.[31] The general will manifests not only the capacity of individuals to access a common standpoint from which they can assess what is fair for all, but it also marks

[28] Boyd, "Rousseau and the Vanishing Concept of the Political?," 75. For classification of traditional interpretations of the general will, see Farr and Williams, *The General Will: The Evolution of a Concept*; Bertram, "Rousseau's Legacy in Two Conceptions of the General Will: Democratic and Transcendent."

[29] Williams, *Rousseau's Platonic Enlightenment.*

[30] Sreenivasan, "What Is the General Will?"

[31] There is a long tradition of Kantian readers of Rousseau. Among them, see Cohen, *Rousseau*; Rawls, *Lectures on the History of Political Philosophy*; Cassirer, *The Question of Jean-Jacques Rousseau.* For the stakes of Kantian readings of Rousseau, see Hasan, "Rousseau on the Ground of Obligation: Reconsidering the Social Autonomy Interpretation." For the distinction between the Rousseauian and the Kantian contracts, see Williams, "Ideas and Actuality in the Social Contract: Kant and Rousseau."

the intention of common membership in abiding by and realizing this common standpoint.

In the *Social Contract,* Rousseau starts by explaining the general will as the will of the "moral" or "public person" created by the initial act of association of self-interested individuals. "At once, in place of the private person of each contracting party, this act of association produces a moral and collective body made up of as many members as the assembly has voices, and which receives by this same act its unity, its common self, its life and its will" (*SC* I.6.10).

The act of associating produces the common identity of the body politic. It creates, Rousseau writes, "a people": "As for the associates, they collectively assume the name *people*; and individually call themselves *Citizens* as participants in the sovereign authority" (*SC* I.6.10).

The idea that a voluntary association creates a people is a claim that needs to be unpacked. I will do so in the section on "The People" in this chapter. Let us note for now that Rousseau underlines this idea by calling the individuals before the act of associating a "multitude" (*SC* I.6.4). He also clearly indicates that the social contract is "the true foundation of society," as "the act by which a people is a people" (*SC* I.5).

Following Hobbes, Rousseau also describes the act of association as forming not only a people, but also a collective person. Any agent, moral or real, personal or collective, needs to have a will in order to assert its existence in the world and preserve itself. Rousseau calls this will "general" because it is the will of the collective agent to preserve the whole instead of preserving only specific parts of its body. This is something that Rousseau most clearly argues in the *Discourse on Political Economy*: "The body politic is also a moral being that has a will; and this general will (…) always tends to the preservation and the well-being of the whole and of each part" (*DPE* 6).

That the collective or moral person has a "general will" immediately poses serious problems. Indeed, having a will to X supposes, by definition, having an intent to X, which, in turn, supposes a desire or motivation to X. The will therefore has two dimensions: a cognitive one (taking an object as part of a representation), and a motivational one (being motivated to X). So, first, how can a collective person have a unitary representation? Second, how can it have a desire?

Rousseau does not consider the collective person of the Republic to be a real person. It does not have an independent existence apart from its members. "The sovereign is formed entirely of the individuals who make it up" (*SC* I.7.5) – in an important distinction with the Hobbesian sovereign.

The sovereign, for Rousseau, cannot have a will that is not the will of the individuals that compose it: the sovereign does not have a particular will (except, of course, when considered in relation to foreign nations). The fact that the sovereign cannot have a particular will is not only, so to speak, an ontological fact. It is also due to Rousseau's conception of freedom as non-domination. While Rousseau's theory of the political personification of the body politic is Hobbesian, he strongly objects to one aspect of Hobbes' theory of personification. For him, the point of the association is remaining free, and freedom requires not being under the arbitrary will of another. Now if the moral person of the sovereign were to be represented by a particular person, all individuals would be under his arbitrary will. Rousseau therefore cannot make the "general" will a particular will.

What does it mean to say that the general will of the sovereign does not exist outside of the will of all the individuals? It means that as a volitional act, it exists only as a form of individual will that each shares with other members of the collective. "Each person may, as a man, have a particular will contrary to or different from the general will he has as a citizen" (*SC* I.7.7). The general will needs to be a *shared* will, different from the particular will of individuals, yet still willed by the individuals themselves. It can be interpreted as a shared intention of individuals to participate in the association whose goal is their own freedom, that is, as a shared intention to be members of the collective person created in order for them to be free and preserve themselves (i.e., their common good).

> If then one sets aside everything that is not of the essence of the social compact, one finds that it can be reduced to the following terms: *Each of us puts his person and his full power in common under the direction of the general will; and in a body we receive each member as an indivisible part of the whole.* (*SC* I.6.9)

One advantage of this interpretation is that it becomes clear why Rousseau insists that the general will can be constituted only by the totality of all the voices and that any exclusion makes it void. The "content," or outcome, of the general will (what I call the "objectified will") may be law X or law Y, but laws X or Y, decided without the shared intention of some citizens, would not conform to the most important aspect of the general will *qua* will: that it is the shared intent of all individuals to be part of the political community and act accordingly. *There can be no exclusion from the people* – otherwise, the general will cannot be expressed, and thus the identity of the people itself is compromised.

In order for the general will to be a will at all, it supposes that all the individuals belonging to the association are capable of having a shared representation. The general will thus demands the constitution of a standpoint through which the individual sees himself[32] as a citizen, and not just as an individual with his own private interest.

The first and the most important consequences of the principles established so far is that the general will alone can direct the forces of the State according to the end of its institution, which is the common good: for while the opposition of particular interests made the establishment of societies necessary, it is the agreement of these same interests which made it possible. What these different interests have in common is what forms the social bond, and if there were not some point on which all interests agree, no society could exist. Now it is solely in terms of this common interest that society ought to be governed. (*SC* II.1.1)

In order for the shared intention to exist, individuals need to form a common standpoint, which is also the point of view of the common interest.

This leads us to an important aspect of the general will: the will is not epistemically free-floating or arbitrary. It needs to be informed by a correct assessment of the common interest. In the *Geneva Manuscript,* Rousseau defines the general will as an act of the understanding. The general will thus has a formal dimension: it is determined by what each person can ask of another and can be reciprocally asked to do. "Indeed that the general will is in each individual an act of pure understanding that reasons in the silence of passions about what man may demand of other men, and what others have the right to demand of him, nobody will deny" (*GM* I.ii; *OC* 3, 286).

The common interest is the object of all citizens' reasonings in so far as they think as citizens. The correct assessment of the common interest is made possible by the formal structure of the social pact as a pact of equality creating mutuality of benefits. It is also what forms the properly republican social bond between individuals (*SC* II.1.1).

The general will, I argue, generates solidarity between self-interested contracting agents in the social contract for three reasons:

(1) *The freedom reason*: It secures freedom, which is the goal of the members of the association. It creates beneficial interdependence in lieu of harmful dependence.[33]

32 I only use male pronouns in this chapter as Rousseau thought women did not have the capacity to be autonomous, that is, the capacity to generate their own ends as citizens do (*E* 377). Women therefore cannot be citizens in the sense implied by the social contract. For an analysis of Rousseau's views on women, see Rousselière, "Rousseau's Theory of Value and the Case of Women."

33 For the full explanation of the transformation of harmful into beneficial dependence in the social contract, see Rousselière, "Rousseau on Freedom in Commercial Society."

(2) *The mutual recognition reason:* It creates stable mutual recognition, which feeds the essential need of having one's *amour-propre* satisfied.
(3) *The fairness reason:* It secures equal treatment between members.

I contend that for Rousseau the general will, as a shared intent to secure freedom, fulfill three essential human needs: being free, being recognized by other individuals, and being treated with justice. It thus generates solidarity, or what Rousseau calls "the social bond."

Let me now spell out these three reasons so that it becomes clearer how the general will, as a device that meets essential human needs, creates a social bond between members.

(1) *The freedom reason:* The subjection to the general will is the solution to the traditional republican problem of remaining free from domination. For Rousseau, the problem of social men is that they can fall both under the subjection of other individuals (private domination), or under the tyranny of the majority or the state (public domination). It is well known that the first problem is central to Rousseau's political thought, since he develops at length the evils of dependence in society. "Being free from personal dependence" is the explicit goal of the social contract (*SC* I.7.8). But the second problem, the tyranny of the majority, is also central to his thought.[34] The traditional republican problem of the tyranny of the majority is how individuals can be free in a political setting when they are bound, at one point or another, to have to obey laws that they disagree with.

The general will frees individuals from subjection by solving both problems at the same time. For Rousseau, in order to be free, I must at the very least not depend on the arbitrary will of another. The general will, however, is not arbitrary in that it tracks the common interest of all and it is not the will of "another" since it is also *my* will. This is clear when one interprets the general will, as I have, as shared intention toward the maintenance of freedom as the common interest of all. This means that even though I happen to disagree with the general will, it is only because I fail to understand the interest of all, which is also part of my own interest as a citizen. The general will thus frees individuals from personal dependence by transforming harmful personal dependence into dependence on the law. It also frees them from dependence on the government by guaranteeing that the law will track everyone's interest, that is, it will not be arbitrary.

[34] See Dijn, "Rousseau and Republicanism."

(2) *The mutual recognition reason:* The second reason why the general will generates solidarity is that it fulfils one essential need of our moral psychology: recognition. Rousseau insists, notably in the *Second Discourse,* that human psychology is characterized by the development of *amour-propre* as soon as men enter in relation with one another (*SD* 166). Recent studies on *amour-propre* have developed the idea that it is not just a negative faculty, bringing about all the evils of social life such as envy or cruelty. Rather, Rousseau implies that *amour-propre* is also the spring of our moral and intellectual development.[35] Human psychology, however complex, is marked by one uncontroversial feature for Rousseau: we want to be recognized by others. Rousseau develops different ways in which in society – especially commercial society – *amour-propre* can never be contented, as there is no uncontroversial standard of value, and as the recognition of others is always unstable.[36]

Yet the social contract offers a stable source of recognition for the potentially unquenchable *amour-propre.* I have argued that the general will, as a shared intent toward the common good, supposes a common standpoint between individuals. This standpoint can only be attained on one condition: that individuals recognize each other as agents capable of reaching it. Another way to say this is that individuals must recognize each other as equal interpreters of the general will.[37] It is only because they recognize each other as such rational agents – epistemically capable agents – that it makes sense for them to accept failure of their own judgment and be "forced to be free" if they happen to disagree with the majoritarian interpretation of the general will (*SC* I.8.8).

We should note that this feature of the general will marks an important difference with Hobbes. In *Leviathan,* individuals surrender their judgment to the sovereign. By contrast, in *The Social Contract*, individuals do not surrender their judgment, and instead commit to recognize the validity of each other's judgment, which provides the basis for the mutual recognition of citizens.

(3) Finally, *the fairness reason.* The general will fulfils another psychological need: the desire to be treated fairly. The social contract can guarantee freedom and generate mutual recognition because it is grounded in

[35] Dent, N. J. H., *Rousseau. An Introduction to His Psychological, Social and Political Theory*, 52–56; Neuhouser, *Rousseau's Theodicy of Self-Love: Evil, Rationality and the Drive for Recognition*, 218–64.

[36] Rousselière, "Rousseau's Theory of Value and the Case of Women."

[37] They must do so despite their natural inequality. See Schwartzberg, "Political Equality among Unequals."

equality. Equality is an essential end of the association because "freedom cannot subsist without it" (*SC* II.11.1). It is the strict equality of all participants in the social contract that makes it possible for them to recognize a standpoint that they can all share: "Since each gives himself entirely, the condition is equal for all, and since the condition is equal for all, no one has any interest in making it burdensome to the rest" (*SC* I.6.6). The equal position of all in the contract guarantees the mutuality of benefits and generates the trust that each will be treated fairly: "From whatever side one traces one's way back to the principle, one always reaches the same conclusion: namely, that the social pact establishes among the Citizens an equality such that all commit themselves under the same conditions and must all enjoy the same rights" (*SC* II.4.8).

The "equality of conditions" implies that citizens think of the terms of the social contract as "just." Rousseau insists the general will tends toward justice. Justice bonds otherwise unconnected individuals to one another. I therefore take Rousseau to be arguing that justice, that is, here, equality before the law, creates a social bond between individuals. The social bond created by the three benefits reaped by participating in the general will – freedom, recognition, and equality – is what ensures the unity of the people.

THE EPISTEMIC OBJECTION

So far, I have argued that Rousseau believed in the possibility of a large and modern republic, and that the social contract provided a few conceptual innovations to bring such a large republic to life. First, agents do not need to have preexisting virtue, they just need to be interested in remaining free. Second, agents do not need to be part of an already cohesive people with a sense of the common good because the act of contracting on equal terms creates the people, the general will and a stable sense of solidarity.

Before we assess the extent to which Rousseau is successful in these arguments, we should turn to the last part of Montesquieu's challenge: the epistemic objection, that is, the idea that modern citizens, driven by different interests and lacking both common mores and the education of an elite, could not know the common good and could not govern the complex administration of a large country by themselves.

Montesquieu's argument seems initially corroborated by Rousseau's insistence that in small communities, "the common good is everywhere fully evident and requires only good sense to be perceived" (*SC* IV.1). The situation of "troops of peasants attending to affairs of State underneath an oak" (*SC* IV.1.1) is contrasted with large states where intrigues and eloquence dominate public discussions (*SC* IV.1.2).

The particular situation of a large state intensifies Rousseau's worry about the epistemic capacities of the people: "By itself the people always wills the good, but by itself it does not always see it. The general will is always upright, but the judgment that guides it is not always enlightened" (*SC* II.6).

I contend that Rousseau responds to Montesquieu's epistemic challenge with two conceptual devices. First, he lowers the epistemic burden of the people by creating a distinction between sovereignty and government. Second, he lays out the voting institutions necessary to channel right decisions in a situation of pluralism and low enlightenment that characterize large states. His two-pronged strategy is to ease the people's burden and to make it easier for them to reach the right decisions through well-designed institutions.

Let us start with the difference between the government and the sovereign, a conceptual distinction central to the third book of the *Social Contract*.[38] Indeed, we should not believe that a free government is one in which the people constantly assemble and make decisions on everything. On the contrary, Rousseau distanced himself from the model of Athenian direct democracy by conceding one central feature of modern societies: citizens will not be able to attend to public business all the time and they ought not to have to decide the administration of the state in all its complex details. "Not being idle as ancient peoples were, you cannot ceaselessly occupy yourselves with the Government as they did: but by that very fact that you can less constantly keep watch over it, it should be instituted in such a way that it might be easier for you to see its intrigues and provide for abuses" (*LM* III.483).

Rousseau clearly articulates the need to adapt classical republicanism to the specific conditions of modernity. Such an enterprise necessitates a redefinition of the concept of sovereignty. A sovereign people ought not to constantly intervene in the daily business of the state. Rather, it should simply be in charge of the fundamental laws of the state.

The distinction between government and sovereignty makes it possible for executive power to be exercised even when the sovereign is extremely

[38] As Rousseau's detractors are keen to point out, Bodin was the first to articulate the distinction between sovereignty and government in *Six Books on the Commonwealth* (1576), arguing that magistrates are only trustees or custodians of the sovereign power, and that sovereign power is by nature perpetual.

large and unwieldy (*SC* III.1).[39] If sovereignty cannot be represented, power certainly can, and even ought to be, delegated. Rousseau therefore participates in a longer history of popular sovereignty that pictures the sovereign as a "sleeping" one, that is, one that awakens only at given intervals to accept or edit the constitution.[40]

Indeed, Rousseau developed the idea that power can, and in fact should, be delegated. Delegates are not entrusted with an open mandate that makes it possible for them to will on their own.[41] They simply have an "imperative mandate" (*mandat impératif*) that commissions them to specific tasks. For instance, in the *Considerations on the Government of Poland,* Rousseau insisted that "representatives [ought] to adhere exactly to their instructions, and to render a strict account of their conduct in the Diet to their constituents" (*GP* 201). Rousseau's delegates do not have independent legislative power, yet they do most of the necessary work in a large republic. In this model, the popular sovereign is not one that is constantly gathered and deliberating, rather it is one that opines and ratifies.

The delegation of executive power only partially alleviates the epistemic objection – the mass of the people still need to be able to perceive the common good in order to set fundamental laws. How could the people's judgment not be perverted when it is hard to see the common good and when some individuals try to make their own interests take the place of the general will? Rousseau is deeply concerned with this question, which he formulates in the section of the *Social Contract* on "whether the general will can err" (*SC* II.4.3).

In this section, Rousseau presents the conditions necessary for a vote to result in the correct expression of the general will: citizens need to be "adequately informed," they should "have no communication among themselves," and there should not be "factions" or "partial society" in the state (*SC* II.3.2–4). Importantly, Rousseau adds that the interdiction of factions should be entirely reversed if the state happens to be already divided with factions, in which case the remedy is the opposite: "if there are partial societies, their number must be multiplied and inequality among them prevented, as was done by Solon, Numa and Servius" (*SC* II.3.4). This last note shows that Rousseau takes the example of the Roman Republic as providing a remedy in the necessarily flawed large state in which factions will inevitably arise.

[39] I am here in agreement with Tuck, *The Sleeping Sovereign: The Invention of Modern Democracy*, 141–2.

[40] Tuck, *The Sleeping Sovereign: The Invention of Modern Democracy*, 134–5.

[41] Urbinati, *Representative Democracy*, 60.

Rousseau eventually acknowledges that he is not able to entirely solve the epistemic deficiency of the newly founded people. The act of association does not magically boost the epistemic capacities of an ignorant mass of individuals. "How will a blind multitude, which often does not know what it wills because it rarely knows what is good for it, carry out an undertaking as great, as difficult as a system of legislation?" (*SC* II.7.10). This is where a *deus ex machina* is needed: "Hence arises the necessity of a Lawgiver" (*SC* II.7.10). Unless such a providential figure is found (and in fact, even if this providential figure is found), the republic will need to find a way of *producing* the knowledgeable citizen who was required in the first place. This is why I argue in Chapter 5 that a republican theory will have to rely on public education as a central political tool to create an educated citizenry.

THE PEOPLE

I have provided so far the general arc of what I see as Rousseau's case for a large and modern republic, with a charitable reconstruction of his responses to Montesquieu's challenges. As I show in Chapter 3, this provides the republican blueprint inherited by revolutionaries.

We need to attend to important objections that I have set aside until now for the sake of clarity. There is no dearth of paradoxes in Rousseau's work. It is important to keep in mind my narrow argumentative goal here, which is situating Rousseau's theoretical contribution within the development of French republicanism. I will therefore focus only on the considerations that directly matter for our investigation on the question of exclusion in French republicanism. Who is the people invoked in Rousseau's theory? How inclusive or exclusionary is this conception?

It is possible to argue that there is a logical problem in Rousseau's formulation of the contract. When the individual contracts, he subjects himself to the political community as a whole, yet this political community does not exist prior to the contract itself. This logical issue is internal to the social contract tradition. It might seem less concerning when we consider that the social contract sets the legitimate basis of the political association, and is not a historical act. Yet the logical puzzle remains.

This logical problem can be seen in Rousseau's dual exposition of what a "people" is. I have argued that, for Rousseau, at least in *SC* I–III, the social contract *produces* the people out of a multitude. The question immediately arises as to what the "people" means in this statement. Here a people can be defined as a collective entity created by the legal device of the social contract. Yet this is not the only meaning of "people" under Rousseau's pen. Rousseau also describes peoples as communities that are connected by social and cultural bonds arising from having grown together across time in a geographically specific area. Let us call the latter idea of the people, "people*."

While Rousseau initially presents the social contract as creating a people out of a multitude, it becomes clear – in the *Social Contract* but also in *The Second Discourse* – that it is not possible to have a community united by common interest without a group of individuals already having a form of common life with interdependent relations and interests – that is a people*. A people*, as a culturally related group of individuals historically united by social ties, needs to be already present for them to form a coherent political community out of a legitimate form of association. The idea of a random group of unrelated individuals forming an association to become a people is a complete abstraction that Rousseau never envisions.

What is at stake here is not an exegesis of Rousseau's work, or an examination of its argumentative quirks. Rather, the problem relies on the structural confusion between the *ethnos* and the *demos*, or between a historical (i.e., ethnic, cultural, territorial) foundation and a rational one.[42] It should be noted that this problem is of course not proper to republicanism. Yet, if we hold republicanism to a high standard of normative consistency, a specific shortcoming of French republicanism arises in the indistinction between the two that this theory cultivates.

What if we confuse the rational and the historical foundations? The political concerns are immediate. The people* coming out of a shared history is by definition exclusive. It is based on religious ties, particular social practices, an acquired sense of a common culture, the predominance of the majority group setting cultural rules, and possibly dominant ethnic groups. By contrast, the people coming out of the social contract is by definition egalitarian and inclusive in its aspiration, as it only demands the rational subjection to common laws applying to all equally. This initial conceptual confusion provides a constitutive indeterminacy about the boundary of the people in a republican theory if and when it does not acknowledge the existence of this ambivalence.

In the *Considerations on the Government of Poland,* Rousseau provides narratives of the people's founding that significantly differ from

[42] I agree here with Abizadeh, "On the Demos and Its Kin: Nationalism, Democracy and the Boundary Problem."

the rationalist story of the *Social Contract.* The construction of a people necessitates nationalist games, rituals, and common cultural practices because, before they exist as a people bound together within a legitimate government, they participate in imperfect and unfree political institutions with considerable obstacles that need to be overcome for them as a people* to become a people.

Take for instance the three "ancient peoples" that Rousseau describes as shaped by the "ancient lawgivers," Moses, Lycurgus, and Numa. Moses, we are told, managed to save his people from oppression by fostering unique bonds between them, to the point of creating an exclusive notion of belonging ("to keep his people from being absorbed by foreign people, he gave it morals and practices which could not be blended with those of the other nations" [*GP* 180]). Lycurgus had to "institute a people already degraded by slavery and the vices which are its effect." In turn, Numa, who was "the true founder of Rome," had to deal with the fact that the Romans were just a cabal of thieves that Romulus had gathered: he had to do nothing less than turn vicious men into citizens (*GP* 181). Being an imperfect people* with personal vices (as in Rome), institutional vices (as in Sparta), or outside circumstances of oppression (as the Jews), the rational bond offered in the social contract was not going to be enough to make them into a people. The task at hand for the ancient lawgivers was not only to create a social pact on rational grounds, but also to destroy the relations of domination of all sorts that ruled their lives until then – the people* is both a condition and an obstacle to the realization of the people.

It is noteworthy that Rousseau is far from arguing that the people* needs to be dissolved into an abstract notion of the people. Instead, the law needs to strengthen the particular connections and cultural practices of the people* to maintain a strong social bond. The law needs to deepen national character in order for the people, united by a strong common interest, to be able to express their general will. The solution to become free is to become more coherently particular as a people* (*SC* II.11), that is, to become a people* with a strong *national* character.

On the one hand, Rousseau proposes a rationalist understanding of the social bond in legitimate political communities – this is the interpretation I have proposed in the first sections of this chapter. On the other hand, he emphasizes mores, culture, and history as anchoring national sentiments and creating a deep feeling of solidarity and moral obligations toward the community. It is this "elation of the heart" that makes citizens ready to die for their fatherland.[43] See, for instance, this passage in his *Considerations on the Government of Poland*:

> No Constitution will ever be good and solid unless the law rules the citizens' hearts. So long as the legislative force does not reach that deep, the laws will invariably be evaded. But how can men's hearts be reached? (...) Dare I say it? With children's games, with institutions which appear trivial in the eyes of superficial men. (*GP* 179; *OC.* III. 956)

Is there a contradiction within Rousseau's thought? Or an oscillation between two different views, written for different occasions? In his writings on Poland, Rousseau insists on the importance of what can be called "nation-building," to adopt a vocabulary that will become central to the nineteenth century.[44] Civic festivals, public education, and marks of national unity are a central part of republican institutions: they are necessary to foster national solidarity and ensure the love of the fatherland. Rousseau's writings on Poland have sometimes been understood as pertaining to a realistic strand in his thought, which could possibly explain the difference between them and the rationalist dimension of the *Social Contract.*[45] This does not seem to me the right explanation.

In the *Social Contract,* Rousseau lays out the distinction between the "principles of political right" (announced in its subtitle), which are the theoretical foundations of a legitimate state, and the science of the lawgiver, which contains the "maxims of politics" (*SC* III.18.3) that are useful to realize these principles.[46] While the lawgiver's function can be seen as one of adaptation to, and therefore compromise with, the specific circumstances of each country (which are rather dire in the case of Poland),[47] the lawgiver's work is first and foremost to foster a strong affective relation of citizens to their political community.[48] It thus aims to develop the "most important of all law," written "in the hearts of

[43] See in particular *The Discourse on Political Economy, Letter to d'Alembert, Considerations on the Government of Poland* and the *Constitutional Project for Corsica.*

[44] Stilz, *Liberal Loyalty*, 113–36.

[45] Putterman, "Realism and Reform in Rousseau's Constitutional Projects for Poland and Corsica." Like Putterman, I do read Rousseau as a realist, but I take this realism to be already present in Rousseau's supposedly utopian texts.

[46] Hanley, "Enlightened Nation-Building: The Science of the Legislator," 224; Scott, *Rousseau's God,* 204–5.

[47] Hanley, "Enlightened Nation-Building," 223–30.

[48] Schaeffer, "Realism, Rhetoric and the Possibility of Reform in Rousseau's *Considerations on the Government of Poland,*" 380.

the Citizen, which is the States' genuine constitution": "morals, customs, and above all opinion," on which "the success of all other laws depend" (*SC* III. 12.5). More than mere adaptation, it is the continuation of the work of moral and emotional transformation that is already at play in the rational device of the social contract.

Rousseau insists on the continuity between his legislating project in the *Considerations* and the theory he proposes in the *Social Contract*:

> All of [the ancient Lawgivers] sought bonds that might attach the Citizens to the fatherland and to one another, and they found them in distinctive practices, in religious ceremonies which by their very nature were always exclusive and national (see the end of the *Social Contract*), in games which kept the Citizens frequently assembled, in exercises which increased their pride and self-esteem together with their vigor and strength, in spectacles which by reminding them of the history of their ancestors, their misfortunes, their virtues, their victories, stirred their heart, fired them with a lively spirit of emulation, and strongly attached them to the fatherland with which they were being kept constantly occupied. (*GP* 182; *OC* III. 958)

The considerations about the creation of a social bond around particular institutions are indeed an important aspect of the last book of the *Social Contract*. For instance, the elaboration of the civil religion which offers "a purely civil profession of faith the articles of which it is for the Sovereign to fix, not precisely as dogmas of religion but as sentiments of sociability, without which it is impossible to be either a good citizen or a loyal subject" (*SC* IV.8.32). I will get back to the importance of solidarity-creation in Rousseau's civil religion in Chapter 5.

At the very least, one could say Rousseau oscillates between the two stories, offering the impression that neither the rationalist nor the historico-national interpretations can be complete without the other. We are led to a paradoxical conclusion. Rousseau's *Social Contract* proposes a universalist theory offering a rationalist and inclusive way for citizens to be free together in a society of equals. Yet, if the act of contracting on rational and egalitarian terms does generate a series of motivations to act in allegiance to the republic, it does not create a sufficiently stable and enduring disposition because of the affective nature of human beings and because of the pre-existence of the people* as a national-cultural community. Hence the need for a complementary strategy: humans need exclusive practices and mores that will seal their social bond within a particular national culture and make them different from other peoples, as well as deciders on who should and should not belong to their political community. This tension underlies what I call the paradox of national universalism. While Rousseau's work develops it at length, it prefigures a recurring problem weighing on the historical development of French republicanism. I will turn to this issue in Chapter 5.

CONCLUSION

What did Rousseau achieve in his response to Montesquieu's challenge? First, I argued that he transformed earlier forms of republicanism from an elitist theory of free communities based on the mixed constitution into an inclusive theory based on popular sovereignty. This *tour de force* necessitated reworking the concept of sovereignty. Rousseau was able to do so by turning away from Montesquieu and arguing that the condition for a government to be legitimate was to be based entirely, and only, on popular sovereignty, regardless of the form of its administration. In carrying out this radical transformation of the republican doctrine, he reduced the extent of the role of the sovereign by distinguishing between government and sovereignty. In so doing, he alleviated concerns expressed in Montesquieu's "epistemic objection."

Second, Rousseau transformed the elitist theory of republicanism into an egalitarian one. One could argue that in this regard, he simply followed Montesquieu, who equated republicanism in its democratic form with the love of equality. However, such an argument would discount his real contribution. Rousseau inverts the relation between equality and virtue. Instead of virtue being the love of equality, as Montesquieu had it, Rousseau demonstrates that virtue is generated by the egalitarian terms of the contract: it is the equal sharing of freedom itself that makes individuals virtuous, by transforming them into citizens. Equality creates virtue, instead of necessitating it. In so doing, Rousseau ingenuously responds to Montesquieu's "motivation objection."

Finally, through the theory of the general will, Rousseau argues that a social bond is created between individuals and the sovereign, in their participation as equal and active members of a community of equals. While he recognizes the limits of his own theory in this regard, Rousseau imagines the unity of individuals in the republic through their shared identity as "citizens." For all these reasons, Rousseau opens the way for a transformation of the republican tradition in France into a democratic theory emphasizing the role of equality in the creation of solidarity.

Yet, Rousseau's reworked theory of republicanism had significant problems that were transmitted to revolutionaries. In response to Montesquieu's epistemic, unity, and motivation objections, Rousseau developed a notion of citizenship that initially appears thin (i.e., based on the rational self-interest of being free) but ends up being thick (based on national-cultural bonds). It therefore confounds the idea of a general will with a particular communal good. In this theory, the people is both a rational community of free and equal citizens and a particular community of individuals tied with cultural bonds. The indeterminacy of the people creates an unresolved tension about the inclusiveness of the republican political community.

3

Revolutionary Republicanisms

Republicanism was not a burning issue in 1789. Montesquieu, as we have seen in Chapter 1, had warned that a democratic republic would not work in a large country like France. In contrast to his illustrious predecessor and defying the odds, Rousseau had developed a blueprint for such a large republic based on popular sovereignty, or so I argued in Chapter 2. However, Rousseau did not explain how the transition to such a republican regime could come into being out of an existing monarchical and inegalitarian regime. In a word, he had not offered a theory of revolution, nor had he predicted that one would be imminent.[1] He was not alone. The French Revolution, which occurred a decade after Rousseau's death, took everybody by surprise. Virtually no one in 1789 imagined that such a revolution could topple the most powerful monarchy in Europe, thereby inaugurating the long course of republican history in France.

The transition from the neglect of republicanism to its political triumph occurred with astounding rapidity. It took only three years from the opening of the Estates General (May 1789) for revolutionary France to become a republic (September 1792). Surprisingly, there was little talk of republicanism among revolutionaries in the first period of the revolution (1789–1792), except for a few isolated publications authored by an active and growing group of radicals.[2] The abundant scholarship on the Revolution has much to say about its possible causes

[1] Yet some revolutionaries, in their cult of J-J. Rousseau, came to believe that he had predicted the revolution, as he wrote that "the age of revolutions was near" (*E* 194). See Lakanal, *Rapport sur J.J. Rousseau fait au nom du Comité d'Instruction Publique*, 8.

[2] Gueniffey, "Girondins and Cordeliers: A Prehistory of the Republic?"

and its troublesome devolution into the Terror. However, it has left unexplored the important question of how republicanism took off as the decisive political theory of the Revolution, a theory that not only would shape the new political experiences but would also remain, to this day, the most important in France.[3] As I argued earlier, republicanism had an illustrious past. It had been transmitted as an intellectual tradition among the elite and was the most coherent and attractive theory of emancipation available to the revolutionaries, yet it was not thought to be the best fit for the radical transformation of a large and a diverse country.

There were good reasons for thinkers to be skeptical that republicanism was a theory with a promising future. As the early events of the Revolution unfolded, obstacles initially confirmed this skepticism. The destruction of the social order of the *Ancien Régime*, together with the emergence of the people as a political actor, reinforced the urgency of Montesquieu's warnings – the problem of unity of a large and divided people (the "unity challenge") and the problem of the self-governing capacity of a largely uneducated people (the "epistemic" and "virtue" challenges) become obvious. Who, if not an educated elite, could govern this large-scale republican democracy? And how would the country remain united, if not through a strong executive or a virtuous citizenry?

This chapter presents the revolutionary proposals to transform the theory of the small-scale republic governed by an educated and virtuous elite into a theory of a large-scale democratic republic based on the sovereignty of an uneducated and divided people. I interpret this transformation process as the adaptation of the republican tradition to a situation essentially shaped by the practical irruption of popular sovereignty on the one hand and the circumstances of a large and divided country on the other.

First, the fact of the irruption of popular sovereignty, as an entrance on the political stage of an insurgent people, irremediably constrained and redirected the theorization of republicanism. The republican tradition

[3] The neglect of this question can be in part explained by the early tendency in Anglo-American political theory, following Pocock's book *The Machiavellian Moment*, to dismiss the French experience. See, however, the following studies on republicanism during the Revolution: Hammersley, *French Revolutionaries and English Republicans: The Cordeliers Club, 1790–1794*; Linton, *Choosing Terror: Virtue, Friendship and Authenticity in the French Revolution*; Sonenscher, *Sans-Culottes. An Eighteenth-Century Emblem in the French Revolution*; Spitz, *La liberté politique. Essai de généalogie conceptuelle*; Monnier, *Républicanisme, patriotisme et Révolution française*; Edelstein, *The Terror of Natural Right. Republicanism, The Cult of Nature and the French Revolution*; Baker, "Transformations of Classical Republicanism in Eighteenth-Century France."

suggested that the freedom of all was only possible in a tempered regime where government was ensured primarily by a virtuous elite. With the recurrent and forceful irruption of *sans-culotte* street actions in 1789, the demand for popular sovereignty and self-government emerged as a fact of politics, one that would need to be taken into consideration by any theory of government looking for legitimacy.[4] It was more than a tiny amendment. Republicans had to expand their account of the origin of political power to the whole of the people. However, France, a large and divided country fearing dismemberment, was not immediately able to deal with the consequences of this new situation.

The period can be seen as a laboratory of such innovative ideas across a fairly large political range, delimiting a field of possibilities for a future republican democracy. On the right, we find Sieyès' liberal-elitist and technocratic proposal. While Sieyès did not understand himself as a republican (and I should add, accurately so), his ideas were an important counterpoint to the republican imaginary. On the left, Robespierre's democratic (and finally populist proposal) defines the Jacobin vision of the Republic, one hopelessly torn between the need for a strong executive and the appeal to a virtuous people. In the center, Condorcet offered an epistemic democracy based on a decentralized view of citizens' participation. I argue that despite being often opposed on the daily political stage of revolutionary France, republican projects delimited a political space of conceptual tensions with a few central shared tenets. They agreed on the priority of citizen's protection against domination, the importance of popular sovereignty and the necessity to represent it adequately, the framing of government goals in terms of the general will, and the development of an educated and patriotic citizenry, that is, the transformation of individuals (subjects) into citizens. As for tensions, they essentially disagreed on the nature of the institutions that would best represent popular sovereignty.

The highly divided historiography on the Revolution has tended to sort out types of republicanism into two camps: ancient and modern, will-based and reason-based, Jacobin and Girondin – and finally, bad and good.[5] These categories are normatively loaded, revealing the political preferences of historians and placing them in clear-cut camps in recurrent

4 On the sans-culotte movement, see Sonenscher, *Sans-Culottes. An Eighteenth-Century Emblem in the French Revolution.*

5 Furet, *Penser la Révolution française*; Baker, "Transformations of Classical Republicanism in Eighteenth-Century France."

loops of controversy over the legacy of the Revolution. In my view, these categories unduly simplify the issues at hand.[6] For once, all republicans shared a mix of ancient references and aspiration to modernity. Furthermore, they all shared a devotion to some supposedly "modern" ideas such as rights, the will (in particular the idea of a general will), and reason.[7] I'll show some of this more nuanced picture in this chapter, though my demonstration does not primarily target this issue, which would distract us from our goal. I am more interested here in tracing the range and nature of theoretical options imagined by revolutionaries in their transformation of republicanism. Once we come to understand this diversity, we can grasp the commonality of the terms they share and determine the original external limits and internal tensions of republican theory in the making.

An important upshot of this chapter is that revolutionary republicans across the political spectrum (Girondins, Jacobins, moderate, radicals, and others) came to the same conclusion: a republic could not do without a certain kind of citizen – one who would be knowledgeable, virtuous, patriotic, and always ready to align his particular will with the general will. The premises of anterior republican forms (the republican citizen is educated, virtuous, non-dependent, patriotic) were expected in a large people even though most of the citizens at the time were clearly uneducated, divided in their interests, and plagued with personal dependence. This ideal citizen was needed and imagined to be present even if not actually there. And since this ideal citizen was not there, he would need to be invented.

This chapter first presents the initial situation in which republicanism developed. I argue that the irruption of a popular movement constrained republicans by positing an inclusive popular sovereignty as a fundamental premise. The complicated birth of the First Republic, at once extra-legal and legalized, asked how popular sovereignty ought to be represented, and what role the "people," the unruly and undefined masses, ought to play in the elaboration of a political theory aiming at freedom. I then turn to the original ideas of early republicans, a heterogeneous group aiming to adapt anterior republican ideas to solve France's predicament. I then present the theory of Sieyès, the most

[6] I agree here with Hammersley, *The English Republican Tradition and Eighteenth-Century France*, 6.

[7] Hamel, "L'esprit républicain anglais adapté à la France du XVIIIe siècle: un républicanisme classique?"

original and influential counterpoint to republicanism, followed by Robespierre and Condorcet, the two most important republican theorists of the period.

SITUATION

Consider the Revolution as a "situation." The unraveling of revolutionary events is well documented, if challenging to interpret. Historians are divided over the periodization of the Revolution, yet as far as our investigation is concerned, we can safely distinguish three phases: the first one, from the convocation of the Estates General to August 1792, was the creation of a new political order based on rights and popular sovereignty; the second one, from August 1792 until the Thermidorian Convention, the foundation of a democratic republic;[8] and the third one, from Thermidor 10 Year II (July 28, 1794, i.e., Robespierre's death) to the 18th Brumaire Year VIII (November 9, 1799, i.e., Napoleon Bonaparte's coup), the "bourgeois republic."[9] The first period was immensely rich in terms of political, legal, and social transformations, but it was a period of latency for republican theory itself. It is only after the proclamation of the First Republic in September 1792 that the theorization of new forms of republicanism became explicit.

In a few months in 1789, the old regime was completely overhauled. A new order was erected on principles aimed at alleviating inequality, eliminating domination, and giving a new political role to the people. This destruction prompted the construction of a new order, which materialized in some key declarations: the promise of a new constitution at the Tennis Court Oath (June 20, 1789); abolition of feudal privileges (August 4, 1789); Declaration of the Rights of Man and the Citizen (August 26, 1789). These transformations did not immediately mean the end of the monarchy. The King suffered a blow to his legitimacy, yet he was still proclaimed the "restorer of French freedom" (*restaurateur de la liberté française*).[10] Representatives relentlessly

[8] I agree here with the analysis of Alphonse Aulard, *Histoire politique de la révolution française. Origines et développement de la démocratie et de la république (1789–1804)*.

[9] I take the name "bourgeois republic" from John Dunn and Biancamaria Fontana. (See Dunn, "The Identity of the Bourgeois Liberal Republic.") In turn, Sophie Wahnich calls the years of the Thermidorian Convention and the Directory the "Republic without virtue nor terror" and "the Republic without revolution" (Wahnich, *La révolution française*, 119).

[10] Article 17 in *Décrets de l'Assemblée Nationale des 4, 6, 7, 8, & 11 Août 1789*.

worked on elaborating the fundamental laws for a moderate monarchy with a mixed constitution giving a veto role to the King, which was planned to come into force in September 1791. Yet in June 1791, the King fled, leaving behind a note detailing his plan to invade France with the help of the armies of foreign monarchies. The scandal was immediate, but the Assembly, put in an awkward political position, sought to protect the King by unabashedly disseminating the "fake news" that the King had been kidnapped.[11]

The path of compromise and moderation was at an end, and a different path opened up for radicalism and republicanism. On August 10, 1792, outraged by the treason of the King, the military pressure of foreign monarchies, and the complicit weakness of the Legislative Assembly, the people of Paris, organized in a "Commune," and a group of *Fédérés* (revolutionaries coming from different *régions*) stormed the Tuileries singing the Marseillaise and threatened the King who, once more, asked for the protection of the reluctant Legislative Assembly. Their insurrection enacted the end of the monarchy.[12] The regime was dissolved, and with it the possibility of a compromise between monarchy and constitutionalism. To fill this immense political void, the proclamation of a republic, once implausible, became the only way forward. Republicanism, once a theoretical impossibility, thus became a practical necessity in 1792.

A Republican assembly was promptly elected by universal male suffrage. It took the name of Convention, in clear reference to the 1787 Constitutional Convention of the United States of America. Up to this point, this historical narrative is fairly uncontroversial. More contested is the story about the foundation of this First Republic. However one may interpret the events of "August 10," I contend that the First Republic came to existence in circumstances distinct from those of its American sister: not as the result of an act of collective deliberation, or the thought-out drafting by "founding fathers," but as the institutional offshoot of the Commune's act of seizing sovereignty suddenly, violently, and decisively in the name of the people. The Republic came into being, or literally *happened* by an extra-legal act of the people, even if it was sanctioned *post hoc* by popular vote, that is, a legal act of popular sovereignty. Even though the First Republic was thereby formally brought to existence, everybody knew that it still had to be founded in law and given substantive content.

[11] Ozouf, "Varennes."

[12] Mathiez, *Le Dix-Août*; Marcel Reinhard, *10 Août 1792. La chute de la royauté.*

The terms of this legal foundation were initially uncertain. The Republic, which had no constitution, was not even properly declared by elected officials. The Convention merely stated that all laws and reports would be from then on dated in relation to September 21, 1792, the first day of the Republic. But on what basis should the republic be founded? What exactly was this republicanism, which was supposed to solve the predicaments of France? And if a republic was supposed to be based on popular sovereignty, how exactly should popular sovereignty be exercised?

The Convention had to face its own crippling doubt: was the republican assembly properly representing popular sovereignty? Did the people of Paris demonstrate popular sovereignty in overthrowing monarchy through violence? Was popular sovereignty instead the exercise of voting through universal suffrage? Or was the low turnout (the Convention had been elected by less than 20 percent of the 7 million electors) a decisive blow to the Convention's legitimacy?[13] Because of its foundation in an act of the people, interpreted as an act of collective self-emancipation, the idea of the Republic was based on the affirmation of popular sovereignty. The idea of "sovereignty," however, was itself not entirely clear. While "sovereignty" traditionally meant the supreme authority over a territory, as Bodin had defined it, popular acts hardly amounted to any stable form of supreme authority – instead, they were unpredictable irruptions of power.

Republicanism and popular sovereignty – with these two starting points, the Convention had to elaborate a new regime, though the exact meaning of both terms remained to be determined. Its central task was to write a republican constitution based on popular sovereignty. The first session of the Convention had to decide whether the constitution should be ratified by the people. The question was therefore how sovereignty would be exercised. For the Jacobins Georges Couthon and François Chabot, deputies should "all pledge allegiance to the sovereignty, the absolute sovereignty, of the people" and follow "the French nation's will (…) to set a popular government."[14] The essential task of representatives was drafting a "social contract."[15] For the prominent radical journalist

[13] Figures for the elections of the Convention are disputed among historians. They vary between lower than 10 to around 20 percent. See Edelstein, *The French Revolution and the Birth of Electoral Democracy*; Gueniffey, *Le nombre et la raison: la révolution française et les élections*; Crook, *Elections in the French Revolution. An Apprenticeship in Democracy, 1789–1799*.

[14] Chabot, in *AP* LII 70, September 21, 1792.

[15] Couthon, in *AP* LII 70, September 21, 1792.

Camille Desmoulins, elected at the Convention, "once the social contract is drafted by representatives, it should be approved by all the members of the social body as contracting parties." The Constitution therefore could not exist without the explicit consent of all the people assembled in the primary assemblies.[16]

The first parliamentary sessions of the Convention show the extent of the debt of this emerging republicanism toward Rousseau. Popular sovereignty, social contract, general will – the vocabulary and arguments of representatives bore witness to the Rousseauian path that the adaptation of republicanism to the circumstances of France had taken. There were many disagreements between representatives at the beginning of the Republic, and even deeper quarrels to come. Yet there were a few republican principles framed in Rousseauian terms that would not be disputed. Sovereignty belonged to the people, all the people, and only the people; and the social contract needed to be approved – willed – by every single member. Republicanism was here reworked as a social contract of equal and free citizens.

This basic agreement still left many problems open. The Republic had not come into existence by a social compact of the kind Rousseau imagined, but by the people's act of throwing off monarchical rule and seizing sovereignty for themselves. How could this act of self-emancipation relate to an established political tradition – the republican tradition – to which they referred? The act of emancipation posited an inclusive, if indeterminate, popular sovereignty at its foundation. Yet the republican tradition had historically endorsed a narrower citizenry. It had also taken the mixed constitution – not popular sovereignty – as a key institution needed to fight domination.

If the irruption of common people as a political actor of national importance was new, the concept of popular sovereignty was not. In the *Six livres de la République* (*Six Books of the Commonwealth*), Bodin defined sovereignty as the "absolute and perpetual power (*puissance*) in a State (*république*)" (Bk 1, Ch. VIII). He took popular sovereignty as one possible form of sovereignty (Bk 1, Ch. VIII), if, clearly, not his preferred form (Bk 6, Ch. IV).[17] Even if the identification of popular sovereignty with democracy can be said to begin with Bodin,[18] the notion of sovereignty itself circulated long before. While there is relative consensus that the idea

[16] Desmoulins, in *AP* LII 72, September 21, 1792.
[17] Lee, *Popular Sovereignty in Early Modern Constitutional Thought*, 218.
[18] Bourke, introduction to *Popular Sovereignty in Historical Perspective*, 4.

developed as characterizing the unitary power of the monarch around the sixteenth century,[19] and that "popular sovereignty" was a form of resistance to it,[20] recent scholarship has challenged this view.[21] We do not need here to take a position in this debate, though we do need to note that the republican tradition has been consistently opposed to the notion of sovereignty and remains largely so today.[22] Critics of French republicanism as a theory potentially inimical to freedom are keen to mention the continuity between Bodin and French republicanism regarding sovereignty. Such a relation could mark, in this view, a lineage of authoritarianism.

Both the people's act of seizing sovereignty and the theoretical legacy of "sovereignty" via Bodin contradicted the republican tradition as it was widely received at the time of the Revolution: a tradition of thought where freedom was preserved thanks to some balance of power and a limit to popular action. The traditional mixed constitution, for instance, was a device of the ancient and early modern republicans to avoid the tyranny of the majority, by blocking the possibility that the most numerous or most powerful group could affirm its will to the detriment of minorities. For Polybius, the mixed constitution was the institutional innovation that had made republics the only stable regime overtime: they were stable because the mixture of powers prevented one part of the population from exercising tyrannical control over the rest.[23] For Cicero, the mixed constitution was a way to ensure that the virtuous and enlightened part of the population would infuse the regime with their wisdom. The mixed constitution thus was generally taken to guarantee the dominance of virtue and prevent the tyranny of any group.[24]

Even more concerning for the French was the fact that the Americans, whose Republic they greatly admired, had sided with the ancients on this question. They decided in favor of institutional checks and balances to curb a popular sovereign. In *Federalist* n. 63, Publius (here Madison) argued for a Senate as one of these institutions:

> There are moments in public affairs, when the people stimulated by some irregular passion, or some illicit advantage, or misled by the artful misrepresentations

[19] See for instance Ober, *The Athenian Revolution: Essays on Ancient Greek Democracy and Political Theory*, 120–21, who argues that it is anachronistic to talk about sovereignty in antiquity.
[20] Morgan, *Inventing the People*.
[21] Lee, *Popular Sovereignty in Early Modern Constitutional Thought*, 10.
[22] Lovett, *The Well-Ordered Republic*, 5.
[23] Atkins, *Cicero on Politics and the Limits of Reason: The Republic and Laws*, 117.
[24] Ibid., 110.

of interested men, may call for measures which themselves will afterwards be the most ready to lament and condemn. In these critical moments, how salutary will be the interference of some temperate and respectable body of citizens, in order to check the misguided career, and to suspend the blow mediated by the people against themselves, until reason, justice and truth, can regain their authority over the public mind?[25]

For Madison, institutional checks on power like a Senate would have been of great help to early democracies like Athens. If Madison was right and the mixed constitution was a formidable tool for curbing the tyranny of the majority and the impulsive nature of the popular sovereign, French republicans were depriving themselves of a key institution to prevent domination.

With the foundation of the republic on popular sovereignty, the question arose as to whether the people would be dominating. How could a new type of republic decidedly unicameral avoid the problem of the domination by the popular sovereign? This new republic had neither the wisdom of the few as Cicero had suggested, nor the institutional structures to balance power as Polybius and Madison had proposed, nor the layers of intermediary powers of English society, given the early work of revolutionaries to uproot aristocratic power. The daunting challenge of French republicans was thus to prevent the sovereign people from dominating minorities, without dividing or limiting sovereignty. The urgency of the task was not based simply on an academic or theoretical worry. For the representatives, it was an urgent concern based on palpable threats. The pressure of the people of Paris, the *sans-culottes*, was a constant reminder of the possible excesses of an unrestricted popular force. In September 1792, just before the start of the First Republic, a series of massacres took place as mobs (les "*septembriseurs*") entered prisons and randomly killed prisoners at sight. Deeply frightened by this erratic violence, the representatives of the Convention needed to reconsider the lofty Rousseauian concept of popular sovereignty guided by a general will that cannot err.

REPUBLICANISM BEFORE THE FIRST REPUBLIC (1789–1792)

When the Estates General were slated to meet and the revolution was about to start, republican ideas were well-known among the educated elite, who translated Cicero as children with their tutors and read

[25] Hamilton, Madison, and Jay, *The Federalist*, 307.

Machiavelli, Harrington, and Montesquieu as young adults. In his *Letters on a Regicide Peace,* this is how Burke, as perceptive as he was critical, described the typical eighteenth-century French elite: "They had continually in their hands the *Observations* of Machiavel on Livy. They had Montesquieu's *Grandeur et Décadence des Romains* as a manual; and they compared, with mortification, the systematic proceedings of a Roman Senate with the fluctuations of a monarchy."[26]

What republicanism exactly meant was less precise – as I have argued in Chapter 1, the reception of the tradition was layered and multifaceted. More than a single unified tradition, different republican authors pulled the theory in diverging directions: glory vs. austerity; imperialism vs. autarky; virtue vs. commerce; democracy vs. aristocracy. The glorious past of republicanism as a political theory of freedom was admired, but its theoretical coherence was quite uncertain, and, in any case, its practical appeal for the French was rather low, as Montesquieu had forcefully taught them with the "scale thesis." The perception in Europe was that republicanism was a regime only fit for small close-knit communities, and certainly not for France, a diverse country with the strongest monarchy on the continent.

I argued in Chapter 2 that Rousseau played an important role in the reception of republican ideas during the Revolution. More than merely transmitting the tradition, Rousseau proposed a renewed understanding of republicanism based on popular sovereignty – precisely what would come to be needed under the emancipatory circumstances of the Revolution. He did not offer a theory of emancipation per se, but laid out what a republic could be for a large and modern people. Many of his readers believed him to be a proponent of the scale thesis but read him against himself as offering the blueprint for a French Republic. As many revolutionaries came to believe, "it is the Revolution itself, that, so to speak, explained the *Social Contract* to us."[27]

While the United States had given birth to an unprecedented political form – a large commercial republic – Europeans still wondered whether such a regime had not been made possible only because of the extraordinary circumstances of the large, emancipated colony on the other side of the Atlantic, a territorially large but demographically small country with ample resources and few immediate enemies. The attractiveness of the American model was irrelevant if it was not applicable to European

[26] Burke, "Letters on a Regicide Peace," 175.

[27] Lakanal, *Rapport sur J.J. Rousseau fait au nom du Comité d'Instruction Publique*, 6.

states. Montesquieu argued that, unless one were to go down the federalist route, as the Americans finally had, large and modern republics posed considerable, if not intractable, challenges to overcome.

The revolutionaries did not initially plan to fight for a non-monarchical regime, even as they decided to react against the King's insistence that the Third Estate would get only a third of votes in the General Estates despite representing around 97 percent of the population. Scholars have long noted this characteristic of the French Revolution – the reluctance of the French to get rid of their King – which can be partly explained by the state of the debate on republicanism as I presented it in Chapter 1, and partly by the strong love of the person of the King traditionally ingrained in France. The French were unhappy with their monarchy, yet their rebellion against the inequities of monarchy did not involve getting rid of the King. The *Cahiers de doléances,* that is, the "grievance notebooks" gathered in preparation of the convocation of the Estates General in March 1789, mixed their requests for social, political, and economic changes with a sentimental and deferential attachment to the King. Indeed, even in 1791, not even Robespierre could be counted as an avowed republican.[28] After the King's flight to Varennes, the necessity to do away with the monarchy transformed the intellectual scene and fostered a new kind of reflection.

Scholars often note that there were only a few republicans in 1789.[29] The number slowly increased in the following years. In the 1789–1792 period, several republican pamphlets were published: *Du peuple et des rois* (Lavicomterie), *La France libre* (Desmoulins), *Le républicanisme adapté à la France* (Robert), and *L'Acéphocratie* (Billaud-Varenne). These years were a time of experimentation as republicanism was hardly a clearly defined doctrine. Republicans were a diverse group of thinkers, journalists, and representatives who found themselves in opposition to monarchy and were animated by the quest of emancipating the people.

Who were these early republicans? They ranged from obscure to well-known figures, and while all were radical in some sense – they wanted to get rid of the King – they did not all evolve in the same direction in the course of the revolution. Among them, many were leading figures of the times: Jacques Brissot, Etienne Clavière, Nicolas de Condorcet, Sophie de Grouchy, Francois Robert, Louise de Keralio, Camille Desmoulins,

[28] Robespierre, *Œuvres* VII, 552. "I have been accused in the midst of the Assembly of being republican – too great an honor for I am not."

[29] Gueniffey, "Girondins and Cordeliers: A prehistory of the Republic?" 86.

Manon Roland, and Jacques-Nicolas Billaud-Varenne. Some of them were or became Jacobin. Desmoulins was a journalist who became famous through his journal *Révolutions de France et de Brabant.* He was a determined defender of freedom of the press until his dramatic death sentence by the Committee on Public Safety in 1794. François Robert played an important role in the development of patriotic societies in 1790 together with his wife, Louise de Keralio, and founded with her the republican journal, *Le Mercure national.* On the other hand, several early republicans were associated with the more "moderate" group of Brissotins, later known as Girondins. Brissot, Condorcet, and Grouchy founded *Le Républicain* and secured the participation of Thomas Paine. Grouchy, Condorcet's wife, was an active *salonnière* as well as the author of several republican tracts published anonymously or together with Condorcet. Republicanism cannot thus be attributed solely to one group or another on the political spectrum of the French Revolution.

The early republicans were burdened with the necessity of explaining and justifying a tradition suspected of being ill-fitted and outdated, if not obsolete. In July 1791, Condorcet's journal *Le Républicain ou le Défenseur du Gouvernment Représentatif* stated that its purpose was to enlighten spirits about republicanism "which is calumniated because people do not know what it is" (p. 5). In his initial letter in *Le Républicain*, Thomas Paine wrote against the mistaken opinion that the "republican system only fits small countries." On the contrary, he continued, republicanism, "thanks to election and representation," was the only way of "proportioning wisdom and knowledge of the government to the size of the country." For Paine, the need to understand republicanism in a new light meant that Holland, Genoa, and Venice were not in fact republics. All these governments, he argued, were "under aristocratic slavery" (p. 10). Republicanism could only be popular: the tradition had to be reinterpreted for the theory to have a modern future.

Were there common points in these diverse early pamphlets that all argued for a republic? A first element is their claim that republicanism was an old tradition that would have to be "adapted." This adaptation in fact meant a considerable restructuring to fit the unprecedented situation of the French as an emancipating people. There was a high degree of self-awareness in this period: republicans knew that they were at once heirs of a glorious tradition and pioneers of a necessary transformation. The idea of *adaptation* was central to the project of these republicans, who were walking a fine line between embracing the republican tradition and promoting change. One of the main republican tracts of the period with a fitting name, François Robert's *Republicanism Adapted to France,* started with a vibrant call to the tradition, placing his work under the patronage of Brutus and offering his spirit as the model for the new generations of patriots committed to freedom: "Your name is dear to us, O Brutus! (...) May your genius inspire us! (...) May your voice be the oracle of France; may France be a Republic; and may finally my fatherland say, looking at the glory of free Rome: *and I too, I had a few Brutus among my children*!"[30]

Yet immediately as he closed the rhetorical invocation to "the manes of Brutus," Robert retracted the possibility of a model. "One must abandon the faithful guide of history," he wrote, suggesting that in fact history does not teach us what to do. For Robert, the French needed to do their own thinking to shape their future.

Second, the reason why republicanism would have to be different from previous political forms came from a new principle: inclusive equality. The starting point of this new republicanism was equality among men – *all* men.[31] This is where the difference with antiquity is startling: "we have to see *everywhere only men, and only equal men*," Robert wrote.[32] This starting point from the equality of all is not an abstract principle but a will coming from the people: "I am talking about the people, the nation, the mass of individuals; and I answer that they all want to be free and equal."[33]

Third, these pamphlets were violently anti-monarchical. Their understanding of republicanism was strictly exclusivist, that is to say they understood the existence of a King as contrary to the freedom of the people, as well as an illegitimate force countering popular sovereignty.[34] Republicanism, they claimed, was incompatible with monarchy. It was also an affirmation of popular sovereignty: "I am a republican, and I write against kings. I am republican and I was one before I was born. Every man is by nature destined to take part in public affairs (*chose publique*). I have my share in the sovereign rights of the people. I will defend them."[35]

30 Robert, *Le républicanisme adapté à la France*, "Aux Manes de Brutus" (preface).

31 Importantly, women were not considered to be "men" for most revolutionaries. I will analyze this issue in Chapter 4.

32 Robert, *Le républicanisme adapté à la France*, 1.

33 Ibid., 5.

34 For an analysis of republican exclusivism, see Hankins, "Exclusivist Republicanism and the Non-Monarchical Republic."

35 Lavicomterie, *Du peuple et des rois*.

In turn, another tract, *De la monarchie françoise* by M. Baumier argued that "the monarchical government is contrary to the laws of nature."[36] This is what "the illustrious citizen of Geneva, a more profound thinker than Montesquieu, had taught us."[37] In *L'Acéphocratie* (literally *The Headless Power*), published after the King's flight, Billaud-Varenne took Louis XVI to be a "hollow man" (*un homme nul*). Monarchy itself feeds domination: a king is a "master," and therefore he will be surrounded by slaves.[38] "There is no free nation which has any other master than law itself."[39] Simply put, "monarchy is the grave of freedom."[40] Billaud-Varenne took up the traditional republican language of opposing freedom and slavery, freedom and monarchy.

Fourth, it is clear in both their endorsement of the tradition and their anti-monarchism that these emerging forms of republicanism followed the central idea of opposing domination in all its forms. Robert's *Républicanisme* presented the fight against domination as the foundational principle of republicanism in both its original and "adapted" form. "The French people are proud, they cannot and do not want to be dominated and today freedom is a need for them."[41] The opposition to monarchy and the fight against domination are tightly connected: in a monarchy, the people can be but "a band of slaves."[42]

Finally, they all understood republicanism as being founded in popular sovereignty and popular self-government. "What is the people?" asks Lavicomterie, "The People is everything. A King is nothing without a People, and a People is everything without a King."[43] This sovereignty had to be inclusive and absolute, because any power that would counter it would be dominating.

The five terms that we can extract from the work of these early republicans – adaptation of a tradition; inclusive equality; anti-monarchism; freedom as non-domination; and popular sovereignty – point toward the fundamental ideas that constitute French republicanism during the Revolution. The question now was how and if these ideas could be combined coherently.

[36] Baumier, *De la monarchie françoise*, 3.

[37] Ibid., 3.

[38] Billaud-Varenne, *L'acéphocratie ou le gouvernement fédératif démontré le meilleur de tous pour un grand empire, par les principes de la politique et les faits de l'histoire*, 3.

[39] Ibid., 4.

[40] Ibid., 53.

[41] Robert, *Le républicanisme adapté à la France*, 8.

[42] Ibid., 11.

[43] Lavicomterie, *Du peuple et des rois*, ch. 1.

FEAR OF DISMEMBERMENT (SIEYÈS)

A new form of republicanism was taking shape, not only characterized by its anti-monarchical impulse and its endorsement of freedom as non-domination as fits the tradition, but also its emphasis on popular sovereignty and inclusive equality. However, these anti-monarchical pamphlets were also confronted by the problem posed by Montesquieu's "unity objection." The unity objection could be formulated in simple terms: the larger a country, the more it needs a united and strong executive. History and experience showed that monarchies provide strong executives, republics not so much. More than an academic or technical problem, though, the danger of disunity of the country was associated with a deep fear that could be found everywhere in the political discourse of the time: the fear that France would be dismembered without a King because there was no real people without the person of the King to represent it.

The early work of the Assembly was dominated by this fear, when they voted to overhaul the whole administration of France and transformed all its historical regions into a homogeneous grid of departments.[44] The idea was that regional differences, customs, and unequal powers needed to be dissolved into equally constituted parts in order to prevent separatism. The idea was mocked by Burke as abstract in his scathing *Reflections on the Revolution in France*. Targeting the idea as republican even before France was a republic, Burke took the reform to kill the vitality of an organically and historically constituted political body by artificially cutting it into "eighty-three independent municipalities" that can never "be governed as one body."[45] "I believe that the present French power is the very first body of citizens who, having obtained full authority to do with their country what they pleased, have chosen to dissever it in this barbarous manner."[46]

Even before the end of the monarchy was foreseeable, the fear of dismemberment was very strong. A common feature of all French revolutionaries across the spectrum was the desire to keep France a unitary and indivisible state.[47] The desire to keep a monarchy remained strong for at least this reason. The idea of a federal state was horrifying to all. A constitutional monarchy was attractive as a regime that could guarantee freedom and reduce the risk of dismemberment.

44 Ozouf, "Départements."
45 Burke, *Reflections on the Revolution in France*, 46.
46 Ibid., 160.
47 Hont, "The Permanent Crisis of a Divided Mankind."

This fear of federalism fed a related belief. For French revolutionaries across the political spectrum, sovereignty could not be divided: the people needed to be one and indivisible if it was to be sovereign at all. That much, revolutionaries of different sensibilities had inherited from Bodin. The idea of popular sovereignty – that is, the ultimate source of authority exercised in state institutions comes from the people – was hardly new at the start of the Revolution.[48] Yet this notion supposed the anterior existence of a united people. The logical problem underlying popular sovereignty, that scholars have called the "indeterminacy of popular unification," appeared as a salient practical obstacle for the French.[49] On the eve of the revolution, and despite a slow rise of nationalism in the eighteenth century, "a widespread conviction arose that a true nation and a true *patrie* did not yet exist in France."[50] It remained unclear if and how, without a King, a united people, and therefore a popular sovereign, could exist in such a large country divided by languages, regional customs, laws, class, orders, and the rivalry between Paris and the *régions*. If the King bore the unity of the country, what or who was the French people without a King, and therefore without a certain *Ancien Régime* idea of the constitution of the people? Could the sovereignty of such an indeterminate people be represented?

On the session of September 7, 1789, in his "Dire sur la question du veto royal," Sieyès, who was at the forefront of the administrative transformation of France into departments, argued:

> France must not be an assemblage of little nations, governing themselves separately as democracies. It is not a collection of states; it is a *single whole*, composed of integral parts. These parts must not enjoy a complete and separate existence by themselves, because they are not united wholes, but parts forming but one whole together. The difference is immense; it is of vital interest to us.[51]

For Sieyès, the risk was to have a heterogeneous and unconnected collection of districts and provinces, "united solely by the ties of common force or protection." In such a situation, the idea of a general will would be lost. Sieyès forcefully argued against the idea of municipalities or provinces becoming "so many republics" that would be joined only by a simple bond of protection.[52] The specter of federalism, presented in

48 "The identification of popular sovereignty with democracy (...) begins with Bodin" (Bourke, "Introduction," in *Popular Sovereignty in Historical Perspective*, 3).
49 Ochoa Espejo, *The Time of Popular Sovereignty. Process and the Democratic State*, 7–9.
50 Bell, *The Cult of the Nation in France: Inventing Nationalism, 1680–1900*, 7.
51 Sieyès, *Ecrits politiques*, 234.
52 Ibid.

a negative vision of the United States as a loose federation of democracies, loomed large. Such a federation could never correctly express the general will because the parts would be too heterogeneous. The bond must be stronger:

> Instead of a general administration spreading from a common center and uniformly falling on the furthest reaches of the empire; instead of legislation formed out of elements given by all citizens coming together in an ascending scale that reaches up to the National Assembly, the sole interpreter of the general will; instead of this will that descends once again with all the weight of an irresistible force on the very wills that have concurred to form it – instead of all this, we will have nothing more than a kingdom bristling with every kind of barrier, a chaos of local customs, regulations and prohibitions.[53]

Fearing war between small republics,[54] Sieyès made a detailed argument in favor of a new territorial division of France a month later, in his *Observations du 2 Octobre 1789*. Provinces will always keep their "*esprit de corps,* privileges, pretensions, and jealousies," he wrote, unless their borders are radically transformed. Sieyès exhorted the representatives to be attentive to the terrible consequences of administrative inaction: "France will never be able to access this political 'adunation' so necessary to be *one* great people subjected to the same laws and the same administrative forms."[55] "Adunation" is a neologism used exclusively by Sieyès to describe the process of nation-creation in France through the integration of communes and departments into a united whole. This integration thus necessitated first a destruction of previous unities that could be separatist or think of themselves as a distinct whole and not as a member of a body.

One conclusion should be drawn: the fear of losing the authority of the King necessitated revisiting institutions and recrafting them in a way that would foster this unity. The problem thus became how such institutions should be created. Sieyès' conception of representative government became very influential after the success of his pamphlet *What is the Third Estate?* While Sieyès was neither a republican nor a democrat, his work came to embody the spirit of modern representative government after the Revolution, that is, a techno-liberal form of government.[56] I will briefly

53 Ibid.

54 Hont, "The Permanent Crisis of a Divided Mankind," 200; Forsyth, *Reason and Revolution: The Political Thought of the Abbé Sieyès*, 140.

55 Sieyès, *Écrits politiques*, 247.

56 For a different view on Sieyès' credentials as a republican, see Pasquino, *Sieyes et l'invention de la constitution en France*.

present the main ideas of Sieyès that both Robespierre and Condorcet took as counterpoints for their respective republican projects.

Sieyès' early theory of representation expresses the central ambiguity of representative government. Sieyès rarely uses the concept of "sovereignty," largely because he contests the absolutism of power associated with it. Instead, his new vocabulary of *pouvoir constituant and pouvoir constitué* makes it possible to assert the power of the people and limit the power of representatives (who act only within the constitutional frame authorized by the people) at the same time that it limits the power of the people itself by channeling it exclusively through representation.[57] This double limitation opens a liberal and constitutional way of thinking about politics.[58] Yet, despite his antiabsolutism, Sieyès gives early revolutionary credentials to the Hobbesian idea that it is the unity of the representative that guarantees the unity of the represented: "The people or the nation has only one voice, the voice of the national legislative (…) I say it again, in a country that is not a democracy (and France can not be one), the people can speak, can act only through its representatives."[59]

This conception is often considered properly modern because it is explicitly framed as a form of division of labor. In his discourse of September 7, 1789, Sieyès presents representative government as a necessary consequence of the modern character of European people, who are busy with commerce, agriculture, and industry.[60] It is not only compatible with commercial society, but it derives its conception of political activity from the idea of commercial society itself. While regular citizens can be busy pursuing their private interest, representatives can focus on the business of legislating. The task of governing is a form of professionalization.[61] Quoting Adam Smith, Sieyès endorses the idea of society as based on a division of labor and embraces the ideal of modernity: society is a cooperative venture of individuals who enjoy the freedom of *being represented* – the freedom *not* to have to govern directly, which enables them to pursue their own private goals. This system is the best fit for a commercial society composed of self-interested individuals.

57 Rubinelli, "Sieyès versus Bicameralism."

58 Rubinelli, "How to Think beyond Sovereignty: On Sieyes and Constituent Power"; Pasquino, *Sieyes et l'invention de la constitution en France.*

59 Sieyès, *Écrits politiques*, 238.

60 Ibid., 236.

61 Ibid., 262.

However, it also promotes a self-avowed antidemocratic and technocratic elitism. For Sieyès, "France cannot be a democracy."[62] There is an epistemic reason to prefer representation over direct sovereignty. Common people are less capable than the elite of governing since they have neither the instruction nor the leisure to do so: "It is for common utility that citizens choose representatives who are more capable of knowing the general interest (*intérêt général*) and of interpreting their own will than they are themselves."[63]

The representative system relieves individuals of both the work of willing and the technical task of having to interpret their own will. Representatives express their will on behalf of the people.[64] This division of labor entails the empowerment of a new caste: the "experts," who know what the people wants better than them. "One effect of representative government is to place each function in the hands of an expert."[65] Sieyès' antidemocratic thought explicitly endorses technocracy as the best expression of a well-functioning representative government.

This elitist conception of representation leads him to endorse, very early on, the distinction between active and passive citizenship in his *Préliminaire de la Constitution* (July 1789). I will come back to this issue in Chapter 4. What matters here is that while Sieyès expresses the need for the formation of a general will, he argues, in completely anti-Rousseauian fashion, that the general will does not require an inclusive and egalitarian sovereign. While individuals associate in order to remain free, they do not necessarily have to participate in the formation of the common will in order for this goal to be achieved: "All inhabitants of a country ought to enjoy the rights of passive citizenship: all have a right to the protection of their person, their property, their liberty, etc. but not all have a right to take an active part in the formation of public powers; not all of them are active citizens."[66]

Sieyès thus proposed to think of the people in inegalitarian terms. The unity of the people does not necessitate the equality of citizens. Again, it is the unity of the representative (the Assembly, which for this reason should not be divided) that expresses and ensures the unity of the nation,

[62] Ibid., 237.
[63] Ibid., 236.
[64] Sieyès, *Political Writings*, 13.
[65] Sieyès, *Des manuscrits de Sieyès*, 488.
[66] Sieyès, *Écrits politiques*, 199.

while also being better situated to express the general interest that the people is incapable of determining by itself.[67]

Sieyès rejected Rousseau's conception of unlimited sovereignty and criticized his metaphysical conception of the general will as forming a "ré-totale" rather than a republic.[68] Against Rousseau's idea of the complete alienation of all rights in the social contract, Sieyès argued that in the political association, "we put in common, under the name of public or political power, the least possible and only what is necessary to maintain each one in their rights and duties."[69] Sieyès understood Rousseau's conception of the republic as a sacrifice of individual liberty.[70] In his criticism of Rousseau, Sieyès reiterated Montesquieu's idea that classical republicanism killed personality and individual liberty, and promoted a society of self-sacrificial individuals akin to monks.[71]

Sieyès did not propose a form of republican democracy. Rather he offered a way of modernizing the country by transitioning it toward a technocratic and liberal regime. His solution to the danger of dismemberment was first an administrative transformation of the French territory to prod individuals into becoming equally French. His impact in this regard is considerable, and in this sense one can say that Sieyès greatly contributed to the French republican idea of citizenship. His second solution found fewer followers. Instead of sovereignty and popular government, he suggested to think of legitimate political power within the frame of *pouvoir constituant-constitué* and an elitist conception of representative government. This conception, however, became influential later among the Thermidorians.[72]

[67] This emphasis on the unity of the representative entails the rejection of adversarial competition in the Assembly. See Kirshner, *Legitimate Opposition*, ch. 7.

[68] Despite the influence of the concept of "ré-totale," Sieyès used this term very sparingly. We find it in the title of a 1792 manuscript "Contre la Ré-totale" (Sieyès, *Des manuscrits de Sieyès*, 455).

[69] Discourse of 2 Thermidor Year III. See also the similar statement in his political fragments: "A political society can only be a voluntary and free association. Men unite for a common interest. This does not mean that they put all interests in common. (...) They do not put in common all their wills, actions, assets, power. (...) A man whose superior labor force and efforts make him capable of producing ten times more than others, does not consent to share his work equally with others. Not everything is put in common in the act of political association. We put in common only what is necessary to reach the goal of the association" *(Des manuscrits de Sieyès,* 455).

[70] Sieyès, 470.

[71] Ibid.

[72] Jainchill, *Reimagining Politics after the Terror*, 13–14.

THE REPRESENTATION OF POPULAR SOVEREIGNTY (ROBESPIERRE)

The rise of republicanism during the Revolution is durably attached to Jacobinism, and in particular to the controversial figure of Robespierre.[73] Robespierre's importance in the history of republicanism cannot be measured by the length of his time in power, which was short and contested, but by his legacy. The afterlife of the Jacobinism he articulated is immense. It is often criticized in the French tradition for having fostered centralization and a top-down political style.[74] In liberal historiography, Jacobinism has been mostly understood as a form of classical or natural republicanism gone awry.[75] The Jacobins' appropriation of the republican discourse is of great historical consequence as they aimed to achieve something that previous republicans thought a difficult endeavor: realizing a republic in a large country.

What I argue here is that, in his attempt to answer Montesquieu's challenge, Robespierre strictly followed Rousseau in conceiving of the general will as necessarily based on an inclusive sovereign. More than anyone else during the Revolution, he fought to get rid of the elitist conception of the republican citizen. His views on the representation of sovereignty evolved considerably in the time of his life, moving from an endorsement of representative democracy to what can be called populism.[76] Jacobinism shows the instability of republican theory in these years, as it does not offer a sustainable answer to Montesquieu's challenge. I present Robespierre's transformation of the republican discourse: first, through the representation of popular sovereignty; then through his fight for an inclusive sovereign; and finally, through the question of the necessity of changing the material and social conditions of citizens for them to be able to be politically equal.

73 Hampson, *The Life and Opinions of Maximilien Robespierre*; Jaume, *Le discours jacobin et la démocratie*; Linton, "Robespierre's Political Principles"; Gauchet, *Robespierre: l'homme qui nous divise le plus*; Rudé, *Robespierre: Portrait of a Revolutionary Democrat.*

74 Rosanvallon, *Le modèle politique français. La société civile contre le jacobinisme de 1789 à nos jours*; Spitz, "La culture républicaine en question. Pierre Rosanvallon et la critique du 'jacobinisme' français."

75 De Staël, *Des circonstances actuelles qui peuvent terminer la révolution*; Constant, *Political Writings*, 308–28; Edelstein, *The Terror of Natural Right. Republicanism, The Cult of Nature and the French Revolution*; Furet, *Penser la Révolution française*; Baker, "Transformations of Classical Republicanism in Eighteenth-Century France."

76 Rousselière, "Can Popular Sovereignty Be Represented? Jacobinism from Radical Democracy to Populism."

One cannot write about Robespierre without acknowledging the passions stirred by the invocation of his name.[77] A representative of the Third Estate in the Estates General and therefore a member of the first national assembly (1789–1791), he was also elected to the Convention (1792–1294) and took part in several committees, notably the Committee on Public Safety which effectively ruled the country for a brief period. Robespierre was a statesman – and his writings should be analyzed as coming from a man in position of influencing law-making and exercising power. He was also clearly the most theoretically oriented of all the Jacobins, and his discourses were carefully crafted, often read at the Jacobin Club and edited before they made their way to the Assembly. He wrote a considerable number of discourses and letters, in which he reflected on the necessity of properly defining the people. This is what scholars have called the "boundary problem" of how to define the boundaries of the people.[78] In Robespierre's thought, this question is entangled with the problem of the *expression* of the people's will and the *representation* of its sovereignty. How can the people speak? Can it be represented without renouncing its sovereignty at the same time? The two questions hover around a pressing issue during the transition period between absolute monarchy and democracy in France: how can a large and divided people be represented without the unity of the King's body?

An early speech opposing the royal veto gives us a detailed account of his theory of representation in the early revolutionary process.[79] Perhaps surprisingly, given his repeated praise of Rousseau, Robespierre started by endorsing representative government: "As a great nation cannot exercise legislative power as a body, and as a small one ought maybe not to, it entrusts its exercise to its representatives, who become depositories of its power."

Robespierre concluded that representatives ought not to be contested by any other power: if anyone would oppose the Law, which is the result of the representatives' deliberation, it would mean that "the will of one is above the will of all. It says that the nation is

[77] Scurr, *Fatal Purity. Robespierre and the French Revolution*; Gauchet, *Robespierre: l'homme qui nous divise le plus*.

[78] Nässtrom, "The Legitimacy of the People"; Abizadeh, "On the Demos and Its Kin: Nationalism, Democracy and the Boundary Problem"; Frank, "Populism and Praxis."

[79] See "Discours non prononcé lors de la séance du 21 septembre 1789, par M. Robespierre, sur la sanction royale." *AP* IX 79–83, September 21, 1789.

nothing, and a single man is everything." In this period, Robespierre endorsed what I call a "weak theory of representation," in the style of Rousseau.

Can we attribute a weak theory of representation to Rousseau? Rousseau had explicitly rejected the representation of the will (*SC* II.2.1; *SC* III.15.5), a position that revolutionaries were aware of, and frankly quite embarrassed by, since direct democracy did not seem a viable option in a large country. However, Rousseau had also developed the idea that power could be delegated, even though sovereignty could not be represented. For instance, in the *Considerations on the Government of Poland* – a text that was read and often mentioned by revolutionaries, Rousseau insisted that "representatives [ought] to adhere exactly to their instructions, and to provide a strict account of their conduct in the Diet to their constituents"(*GP* 201). In his model, delegates have a mandate that commissions them to specific tasks. This weak conception of representation as delegation matched the idea of "*mandat impératif*" that representatives in the Constituent Assembly discussed.

Robespierre's views on the representation of sovereignty considerably evolved between the Constituent Assembly and the end of his life, at the height of the Terror. His central problem was how to deal with the persistent interventions of the *sans-culottes,* a power that had not been legally constituted, yet whose legitimacy appeared to him incontestable since they were perceived as the origin of their collective emancipation. He did not want to repudiate the action of the people for fear of usurping their sovereignty. Nor did he want to contest the legitimacy of the National Assembly (or later the Convention). This oscillation was hardly a sustainable position as it left sovereignty undetermined.

By the time of the proclamation of the First Republic, Robespierre had shifted from a weak theory of representation as delegation to a mixed theory of direct democracy in which both the Assembly and the people could make legislative acts. In doing so, he developed the idea that the unity of the people depended not on the unity of their representative (as Sieyès argued), but rather on their direct capacity to express the general will. From 1789 to 1792, while he moved from weak representation as delegation to the idea of the direct participation of the people, Robespierre did not waver on this crucial thesis for the revolutionary problem of the unity of the nation. He refused the Hobbesian thesis that the people would require a representative to form a person, that is, to have an indivisible unity. The people itself exists in the act of forming a general will; this is the essence of Rousseau's social contract. But recall that for Rousseau, the unity of the people depends on the inclusiveness of the will itself: for the general will to exist, no one ought to be excluded (*SC* I.6.9). Following Rousseau in this regard, Robespierre developed an inclusive understanding of "the people."

In a series of interventions at the National Assembly, Robespierre fought for universal male suffrage. He argued against the law of the "silver marc" that restricted active citizenship to those who could prove they had sufficient financial resources.[80] He also argued against the exclusion of parts of the population – the Jews, and the actors in theater companies – on the ground of their dependence: for Robespierre, a socially constituted state of dependence could not be a valid reason to be excluded from being part of the sovereign.[81] He also argued in favor of the claims of the free "people of color" from the colonies who were asking to be recognized as active citizens. I will return to these questions of citizenship in Chapter 4.

As he argued for an inclusive citizenship, Robespierre also inverted the idea of citizenship as attached to landownership. Instead, he developed the idea of taxation as "a share of the goods of citizens that is put in common,"[82] which depends on the paying capacity of each citizen. "What makes us citizens is not taxes: the quality of citizen only obliges us to contribute to the common expense of the State, according to our capacities (*facultés*)."[83] What is *common* to society is what should be used to lift destitute citizens out of their situation: instead of poverty being the mark of an exclusion, poverty should be the sign that society as a whole ought to act to bring these citizens into the condition where they can fully be equal members of the sovereign.

Scholarship on Robespierre's economic thinking is divided. For some, he is a liberal; for others, he is a dangerous radical.[84] It is clear that Robespierre did not repudiate market freedom, which, on the contrary, he deemed necessary for the benefit of all. But market freedom should stop whenever basic needs are at stake. "Freedom of trade is necessary up to the point where homicidal greed starts to abuse it."[85]

[80] Robespierre, *Robespierre. Virtue and Terror*, 5–19.
[81] Ibid., 4.
[82] Robespierre, *Œuvres Complètes* VI, 65.
[83] "Discours lu aux Cordeliers le 20 Avril 1791," *Œuvres Complètes* VII, 162. (Discours sur le marc d'argent.)
[84] Bosc, "Robespierre libéral."
[85] Robespierre, *Robespierre. Virtue and Terror*, 50.

Robespierre proposes to subordinate property rights to the right to existence:

> What is the first object of society? It is to maintain the imprescriptible rights of man. What is the first of those rights? The right to life.
>
> The first social law is therefore the one that guarantees all members of society the means to live; all the others are subordinate to that one; property was only instituted and guaranteed to consolidate it; it is primarily to live that people have property. It is not true that property can ever be in opposition to human subsistence.[86]

Robespierre here inverts the traditional republican conception of property as foundation of citizenship. He takes society to owe citizens the basic means of life. This share given by society to all the citizens is due to them in virtue of their belonging to society: "The food necessary to man is as sacred as life itself. Everything essential to conserve life is property common to the whole of society."[87]

For Robespierre, the republic owes its citizens the material conditions necessary for them to exercise their citizenship. Robespierre never goes as far as arguing for material equality, nor for an especially high level of material conditions. However, he utterly rejects the idea of a political hierarchy between citizens along the lines of knowledge or property. For him, popular sovereignty cannot be represented if all citizens do not equally participate.

Robespierre navigated the republican injunction of extending the sovereign by simply declaring this extension. One may wonder, however, how he responds to Montesquieu's epistemic and motivational challenges: how is this mass of indigent people able to know the common good? Why would they be motivated to act for the common good?

Robespierre's discourses borrow a Rousseauian trope: the people, in particular the lowest members of the people, are *naturally* virtuous. Virtues are in the class of "the poorest people."[88] "Virtues are simple, modest, poor, often ignorant, sometimes rough; they are the prerogatives of the unfortunate and the heritage of the people."[89] Robespierre thus attributes virtue to the whole people, with the exception of the rulers who tend to be corrupt. But if "virtue is natural to the people," we

86 Ibid., 51.

87 Ibid.

88 Ibid., 11.

89 Ibid., 103.

may wonder why terror is necessary.[90] The arc of Robespierre's speeches shows that his call to virtue of the people takes the form of wish fulfillment. While citizens are asked to display virtue, the enemies of the republic multiply so that only terror can steer the revolutionary government.

Robespierre invoked the virtuous citizen as an existing reality. Yet the policies of the revolutionary government show that the Jacobins thought of the virtuous citizen as a reality to be created – by festivals, education, and violently, if need be, by terror.

THE EPISTEMIC PLAN (CONDORCET)

The other remarkable republican theory of the period comes from Condorcet. Contrary to Robespierre, Condorcet had no role in the Terror, and his association with revolutionary violence is as a victim rather than as a perpetrator. His republican legacy is thus immediately easier to embrace, as the Third Republic's Condorcet cult revealed. Today vastly preferred to Robespierre by republicans, Condorcet has been praised for imagining the structure of the first democratic republican government.[91] I argue here that he responded to Montesquieu's unity challenge by addressing the epistemic part of his challenge. Yet, as in the case of Robespierre, Condorcet ended up needing to create the citizen necessary for his theory to work.

Recall that Montesquieu had asked how a large nation of ignorant individuals could be capable of determining the common good. Condorcet responded that, though a crucial problem, it was nonetheless only a technical one and could therefore be answered by designing proper institutions. Condorcet devised an institutional mechanism to draw the general will out of an inclusive, adequately represented, sovereign people. I call his solution "the epistemic plan."

In the first year of the Republic, two main constitutional plans were drafted – first the so-called Girondin plan (Condorcet's) and the Montagnard's plan (in part Robespierre's). While Condorcet was not the only author of the Girondin constitutional draft, scholars attribute a major role to him.[92] Condorcet's proposal was presented to the National

90 Ibid., 115.

91 Urbinati, "Condorcet's Democratic Theory of Representative Government," 56.

92 Contributors include Thomas Paine, David Williams, Sieyès, and Barère (see Badinter and Badinter, *Condorcet: un intellectuel en politique*, 604).

Assembly in February 1793, a rather disastrous moment given the recent trial of the King, the fights between Girondins and Montagnards, social unrest, and the acceleration of wars with neighboring nations. Furthermore, the vote on a new constitution would mean the elections of a new assembly, which the Jacobins, wary of the vote of the countryside suspected to be conservative (i.e., not in their favor), did not wish. Everything conspired to make this constitution unviable. It still remains an important document to understand one republican path that was not taken.

Like the other republicans previously mentioned, Condorcet presented the problem of drafting a constitution as the problem of making republicanism suitable to a large country:

> To form, for a territory of 27,000 square leagues inhabited by 25 million persons, a constitution founded wholly on the principles of reason and justice and securing each citizen in the enjoyments of their rights; to integrate the various parts of this constitution in such a way that the necessity for obedience to the law, and for the submission of individual wills to the general will, shall leave popular sovereignty, civic equality, and the exercise of natural freedom unimpaired: this is the problem we were given to solve.[93]

Creating a new constitution for a large country is an art of balancing opposed forces. Contrary to other revolutionaries, Condorcet did not constantly refer to Rousseau. Yet he used the concept of the general will to describe his constitutional goal: the submission of individual wills to the general will, which ensures both the existence of popular sovereignty and individual freedom.

Condorcet, however, proposed his own version of the social contract. In apparent rejection of Rousseau's theory, Condorcet embraced representative government as necessary in a large country. If sovereignty can be represented, Condorcet thought that it was still in danger of being distorted. The problem with representation is that it ought not to be a way of confiscating the sovereignty of the people. As Rosanvallon notes, Condorcet aimed to lay out a form of representative government that does not limit or distort the sovereignty of the people.[94] Deeply aware of the fear of dismemberment obsessing his contemporaries, Condorcet took the question of the representation of popular sovereignty to be at the same time the question of the unity

93 Condorcet, "On the Principle of the Constitutional Plan Presented to the National Convention (1793)," 143.

94 Rosanvallon, *La démocratie inachevée: histoire de la souveraineté du peuple en France*, 65.

of the people in the absence of a King. The first goal of Condorcet's plan was unity, and his first gesture was to deny that this unity could be best found in the person of one man. "Unity and vigor can be the result of an organization of powers simply and wisely contrived."[95] The solution had to be institutional.

Most scholars have insisted, and rightly so, on Condorcet's careful constitutional design for sovereignty to be exercised as fully as possible.[96] The exercise of sovereignty cannot be restricted to merely voting for representatives: it ought to be extended by allowing the people the possibility to propose laws, contest them, keep the representatives accountable, and oversee them. Condorcet thus imagined a complex system in which ordinary citizens would be able to control the making of the laws and their application, though not directly. This complex system relied on a periodic check on laws, a delegation of sovereignty, and a possibility of censoring the laws. Condorcet, in a sense, "multiplied" the sovereignty of the people.[97]

Representation, Condorcet argued, should rely on a system of "primary assemblies" in which every man over twenty-one who has been a resident for more than one year would be able to participate actively as a voting member (Title II Article I). The role of these assemblies was to elect delegates (Title III. Section II. Article 1), play a direct role in accepting or refusing constitutional changes and vote directly on important questions that concerned the Republic as a whole (Title III. Section II. Article 2). The executive power was a council made up of seven ministers and one secretary (Title 5. Section 1. Article 1). The presidency of this council would alternate every other week (Title 5. Section 1. Article 3). The numerous members of the executive and their short terms in office indicate Condorcet's refusal to give anyone concentrated or lasting power.

In this plan, and in conformity with his goal of inclusive and decentralized sovereignty, primary assemblies are a central device to express the general will and prevent the tyranny of private interests. This is an idea that he had already conceived in his earlier *Essai sur les Assemblées*:

95 Condorcet, "On the Principle of the Constitutional Plan Presented to the National Convention (1793)," 144.

96 Urbinati, "Condorcet's Democratic Theory of Representative Government"; Ghins, "Representative Democracy versus Government by Opinion."

97 Rosanvallon, *La démocratie inachevée: histoire de la souveraineté du peuple en France*, 67.

"In short, it is the primary assemblies which truly represent a body of citizens large enough to make all sectional or local interests fade before the general interests of humanity."[98]

Condorcet's innovation offers at least a partial answer to Montesquieu's epistemic challenge. Montesquieu had claimed that there could be no large republic since individuals would not be knowledgeable enough to know the common good. Condorcet responds by crafting institutions that would make the epistemically correct decision more likely to come out of the voting process, even if the members of the assemblies were not members of the elite, that is to say, even if the republic was a democracy.

Importantly, in Condorcet's view, popular participation is not meant to reflect particular *interest*. Rather it is a voting system in which individuals can express what they see as the true answer to the question at hand. When voting, individuals are not asked: what is your interest? The question is: what is the right answer? That is to say: what will best serve the general will? Each assembly should not express particular interests but be set so that it is capable of having its particular will align with the general will.[99] For the general will to be expressed out of such a large assemblage of separate assemblies, there needs to be no variation in the way the questions are posed to them or the deliberation is organized.[100]

Condorcet's plan, while vastly different, if not opposed, to Sieyès' institutional views, still retains one important similarity: in any decision, vote or election taken as member of the sovereign, the region or department expresses itself *as the nation* and not a particular region or department. For Condorcet's epistemic plan to work, the citizens need to be detached in intention from their particular territorial origin: the knowledge that is at play is not a situated one, but a universal one, one that can be shared by all.[101] Condorcet insists on the fact that these primary assemblies are not meant to decide on territorial basis.

While Condorcet endorsed the vision of political truth being expressed through adequate institutions, he was also wary of the danger of the tyranny of the majority, or the domination of rulers accumulating power.

[98] Condorcet, *Essai sur la Constitution et les fonctions des Assemblées Provinciales*, VIII, 186.

[99] Condorcet, "On the Principle of the Constitutional Plan Presented to the National Convention (1793)," 149.

[100] Ibid., 150.

[101] Ibid., 151.

He took seriously the fear that an unlimited sovereign could wreak havoc on individual freedom in all its forms. This preoccupation antedates the *Plan.* In a short 1791 pamphlet, *De la république ou un roi est-il nécessaire à la conservation de la liberté?,*[102] Condorcet takes up one of the most important objections made by the opponents of republicanism: that a republic would be incapable of limiting absolute popular sovereignty. His response echoes Madison's argument in *The Federalist Papers*, n. 10, that the very size of a large republic would help rather than impede the control of the tyranny of the majority. "The size of France, more favorable than contrary to a republican government should not make us fear that the idol of the capital could become the tyrant of the nation."[103] For the scale of the Republic to be an advantage to fight a possible unlimited sovereign, it would be necessary to multiply administrative divisions.

However, in contrast with Madison's *Federalist Paper,* n. 63, Condorcet refuses the idea that an excellent safeguard against domination would be to have a bicameral government and create a Senate. Condorcet's hostility to bicameral government appears in several essays across the years.[104] The idea of an indivisible republic means that there can be only one house of representatives. "Those constitutions founded on a balance of powers suppose, or lead to, the existence of two parties, and one of the most pressing needs of the French republic is to be wholly free of party."[105] A bicameral system is based on the idea of preventing action, which comes from countries in which old prejudices of the ruling class push them to want to preserve the status quo. A bicameral system does not prevent domination. Instead, it entrenches the dominating power of the elite.

Condorcet argues not only against a king but against any charismatic leader. Worried about the influence that parts of the people accrue by their agitating power in the street,[106] he sees the danger coming from a populist government or a Caesarist figures – dangers that indeed will recur

[102] Text published in the "première annexe" to the session of the National Assembly of July 15, 1791, *AP* XXVIII 336–38.

[103] Condorcet, "De la république ou un roi est-il nécessaire à la conservation de la liberté?"

[104] Condorcet, *Examen sur cette question: est-il utile de diviser une assemblée nationale en plusieurs chambres?*; Condorcet, *Réflexions sur la révolution de 1688 et sur celle du 10 août 1792.*

[105] Condorcet, "On the Principle of the Constitutional Plan Presented to the National Convention (1793)," 156. On this point, see Kirshner, *Legitimate Opposition,* Ch. 7.

[106] Ibid., 153.

after the Revolution.[107] The fascination for populist leaders, he writes, is a form of "intoxication" coming from a deficit of judgment.

The solution offered by the *Plan* is to think of the people as constantly overseeing their government.[108] It proposes a system in which any citizen can ask for a law to be re-examined. "A single citizen may propose to his primary assembly that it demand the re-examination of a law, or that it express the desire for a new law to remedy a disorder which he regards as a matter of importance."[109] The judgment of the people is therefore not made only once in a voting act but is renewed on a regular basis.

Ultimately, Condorcet's epistemic plan relies on an idea held by the Jacobins too: the basis for the stability of a republic is the equality that exists between citizens as lawmakers. In his 1791 pamphlet *De la république,* this is how Condorcet concluded his thoughts about the stability of the Republic: "When equality reigns, there is very little force needed to make individuals obey, and the interest of all the parts of the empire is that no part can get away with the execution of the law that others have recognized."[110] Equality is the essential condition that enables the building of a stable republican constitution that provides freedom for all: "I have always thought that a republican constitution, having equality at its basis, was the only one that conforms to nature, reason and justice; the only one which could maintain the freedom of citizens and the dignity of human species."[111] Equality is also crucial in the creation of the constitutional voting system for Condorcet, since otherwise the general will cannot be correctly expressed. "The most scrupulous observation of equality between the parts of a whole is commanded by the law of nature, justice, the common good, and the general prosperity."[112]

The efficiency of the political machines relies on two pillars: well-designed institutions and rational citizens that can be trusted to make correct judgments. One may wonder, however, how Condorcet answers another part of Montesquieu's challenge: the lack of virtue in modern

[107] Ibid., 144.
[108] Urbinati, "Condorcet's Democratic Theory of Representative Government," 56.
[109] Condorcet, "On the Principle of the Constitutional Plan Presented to the National Convention (1793)," 153.
[110] Condorcet, "De la république ou un roi est-il nécessaire à la conservation de la liberté?"
[111] Condorcet, "Ce que les citoyens ont le droit d'attendre de leurs représentants," 424. I will explain further in Chapter 4 the limits of this claim.
[112] Condorcet, "On the Principle of the Constitutional Plan Presented to the National Convention (1793)," 153.

citizens. What would make them motivated to act rightly and align their private will to the general will?

Condorcet did not find this question worrying. Contrary to Rousseau, he thought that moral and political progress would follow from the progress of knowledge. This belief remains unabated throughout his writings. The moral disposition of citizens would take care of itself as long as they were educated. In his *Reception Speech at the French Academy*, he expressed the idea that informs all his thought:

> Remember that enlightenment makes virtue easy. One might even say that love of the general good, and the courage to devote oneself to it, is the habitual state of the enlightened man. In the ignorant man, justice is only a passion perhaps incompatible with gentleness. In the educated man, it is but humanity itself, subjected to the laws of reason. The project of rendering all men virtuous is chimerical; but why shouldn't one day see enlightenment combine with genius to create for the benefit of happier generations a method of education and a system of laws that would render the courage of virtue almost useless?[113]

The solution to virtually all moral and political problems was therefore epistemic, that is, depended on educating judgment and having the proper voting system. Condorcet's plan devised a system of laws that would render superfluous the extreme effort of voluntary virtue that Montesquieu had imagined as necessary in republics:

> Governed by these salutary institutions man would need only to listen to the voice of his heart and to that of his reason, to fulfill by natural inclination the same duties that today cost him effort and sacrifice – just as a worker without intelligence and without skill now executes with the help of machines the marvel of genius in the arts, the masterpieces that human forces abandoned to its own forces would never have equaled![114]

We can see here how Condorcet answers Montesquieu's motivation challenge. Just as modern science demonstrates the possibility of machines that minimize physical effort and multiply human forces, social science can imagine social machines that make virtue effortless. Thanks to this progress, virtue does not need to be cultivated for itself; it will occur so to speak mechanically when enlightened citizens make decisions within well-designed institutions.

Yet Condorcet's epistemic plan does not answer all of Montesquieu's challenge just by itself. The whole idea of a machine that can solve political issues, such as the truth of political decision-making, relies on his program of social mathematics, that is, the application of calculus to "the

[113] *Reception Speech at the French Academy*, in Baker, *Condorcet. Selected Writings*, 8.
[114] Ibid.

political and moral sciences," announced in his 1793 *Tableau général de la science qui a pour objet l'application du calcul aux sciences politiques et morales* (General survey of science concerning the application of the calculus of probabilities to the political and social sciences). The application of mathematics to voting procedures was already the focus of his landmark work *Essai sur l'application de l'analyse à la probabilité des décisions rendues à la pluralité des voix (1785)*. "Among the great number of important matters to which mathematical calculation can be applied," writes Condorcet, "I have chosen to examine the probability of decisions taken by majority vote."[115] Even before the Revolution, Condorcet thought that his scientific discoveries were of middling importance unless they could be applied to issues that impacted the freedom and happiness of people.

Condorcet took political decisions to be akin to decisions about the truth of propositions that have a political content. This was not, however, how political decision-making was understood in premodern times. He noted that "when the practice of subjecting all individuals to the will of the greatest number was introduced into society, and men agreed to regard the decision of the majority as the common will of all, they did not adopt this method as a means of avoiding error and acting according to decisions based on truth." Rather the idea was to subject the will of the lesser number to "allow themselves to be led by a single will."[116] Condorcet took one of the great advances of modernity to be the ability to think about political decisions in terms not of the prevalence of the will, but in terms of the truth of propositions. This is something he found in the notion of trials by jury: "they all seem to indicate efforts to obtain decisions *in conformity with reason*."[117]

The famous Jury Theorem is formulated as follows:

> One finds that if the probable truth of the vote of each voter is greater than ½, that is to say it is more probable than not that he will decide in conformity with the truth, the more the number of voters increases, the greater the probability of the truth of the decision. (...) If on the contrary, the probability of the judgment of each voter is below ½ (i.e., it is more probable than not that he will be mistaken), then the more the number of voters increases, the more the probability of the truth of the decision diminishes.[118]

[115] "Essay on the Application of Mathematics to the Theory of Decision-Making" in Baker, *Condorcet. Selected Writings*, 34. The title is freely translated by Baker, but it is the same text.

[116] Ibid., 34–35.

[117] Ibid., 35. My emphasis

[118] Ibid., 48–49.

Condorcet's Jury Theorem is widely used by epistemic democrats to demonstrate the superiority of democracy, as a type of regime more likely to lead to just political decisions.[119] Condorcet's remark on this fact is however not reassuring: "It is clear that it can be dangerous to give a democratic constitution to an unenlightened people. A pure democracy, indeed, would only be appropriate to a people much more enlightened, much freer from prejudices than any of those known to history."[120]

This statement should not be interpreted as a rejection of democracy, but rather as the argument that a certain number of conditions are necessary for democracy to be well-functioning. The jury theorem does not consecrate any democratic decision, or even the superiority of democracy, but rather provides the conditions that make democratic decisions likely to be better than other types of political arrangements.[121]

In his *Plan,* Condorcet considered that the people would express their will, but in such a way that they would aim at truth rather than the expression of particular interests. Condorcet's democratic plan supposes that common people are sufficiently enlightened to make such judgments. However, Condorcet insists, for them to have a reasonable chance to make the right decision, they would need to have a basic education that would allow them to properly assess the question and the facts at hand. The republican citizen of antiquity was part of an educated elite; the citizen of revolutionary France was not. The French Republic thus required a complementary plan to its constitution: the creation of a nation of educated citizens. Condorcet worked on a project of public education with the same ardor as he worked on his constitutional draft. We will look at this project in Chapter 5.

CONCLUSION

I'd like to pause here to situate my interpretation. Scholarship on the period converges in thinking of republicanism as being divided between a classical and a modern form. In an influential study, the historian Keith Baker argues that there were two kinds of republicanism that arose during the French Revolution – the ancient republicanism of virtue, and

119 List and Goodin, "Epistemic Democracy: Generalizing the Condorcet Jury Theorem."

120 *Essay on the Application of Mathematics*, in Baker, *Condorcet. Selected Writings*, 49.

121 Roussin, "La démocratie épistémique: une perspective condorcétienne," 66.

the modern republicanism of reason.[122] The former, influenced by the ancients, held a language of collective will, virtue, and participation. The latter was characterized by the language of rights, reason, representation, commerce, social progress, Enlightenment, and rational administration. On the one hand, Robespierre and the group of the Cordeliers. On the other, Condorcet and Paine.

My reading converges with a minimal version of Baker's claim. Baker is certainly right that there were tendencies pulling in different directions and that there were a range of proposals with different priorities of virtue and reason. What this tells us, in my view, is that we need to look at French republicanism not as one unitary doctrine, but as a range of possibilities. From the elitist project of Sieyès to the democratic populist plan of Robespierre through the decentralized constitution of Condorcet, we see the demarcation of a space of possibilities for republican democracy during the Revolution. Republicanism does not become a unified theory in this period but rather carries a range of possible, though not all compatible, solutions to the historical problems created by the rise of the popular sovereign and the dismantling of the old regime.

Baker, however, holds much more than a thin thesis about poles creating a field of tension. His main distinction, in my view, does not hold as many of the features of the so-called "classical republicanism" are also part of "modern republicanism." While there are indeed important differences between those who later came to be known as the Girondins and the group of the Cordeliers Club, this distinction is a simplification. For once, both groups abundantly refer to antiquity and both refer to (modern) English republicanism. They also both ground their discourse on the importance of a constitution, the rule of law, and rights. The distinction between "classical" and "modern" republicanism, polemically used after the Revolution and endorsed by liberal historiography is imprecise, perhaps tactically so.[123] I hope to have also demonstrated that reason and will are present in all proposals as they interpret the Rousseauian idea of the general will, as both an act of judgment and an act of the will.

I also disagree with Baker's suggestion that we should condemn one as obsolete and praise the other as modern – these different solutions are all modern, even as they point toward different resolutions. What I

[122] Baker, "Transformations of Classical Republicanism in Eighteenth-Century France."

[123] I agree with Hammersley on this point. See Hammersley, *The English Republican Tradition and Eighteenth-Century France*, 6.

suggest is to come to terms with an important outcome: that revolutionary republicans across the political spectrum have a core agreement on a few ideas of what needs to be done for France to become a republic, and they are pulled apart by internal tensions in processes that would allow them to do so.

All the republicans, whether Girondins or Jacobins, agreed that, however one thought about the best way to adapt republicanism to the circumstances of France, it always came down to one idea. Freedom in the republic – freedom from private and public domination – depends on the general will being expressed correctly. And this can happen only if all inhabitants think of themselves first of all as citizens and not as particular individuals with private and separate interests. The preservation of the freedom of all depends on their capacity to identify as one people and to identify with the general will they have as citizens. This also meant they had to be morally upright and cognizant citizens – the necessary conditions for the general will to be correctly expressed. The agreement is straightforward: the Republic needs to create a certain kind of citizen, the kind capable and willing to subject their individual wills to the general will. Building citizenship would thus become the center of any republican project.

4

The Paradox of Republican Emancipation

On the day the Convention declared the abolition of slavery in the French colonies (February 4, 1794), Danton exclaimed: "Today we proclaim it to the universe, and generations to come will find their glory in this decree; we proclaim universal liberty."[1] The following day, Robespierre announced he wanted France to "fulfill the destiny of mankind" and hoped for the whole world to follow its example by "calling all men to equality and the plenitude of citizens' rights."[2] In his *Sketch for a Historical Picture of the Progress of the Human Mind,* written in hiding in the last moments of his life, Condorcet stated that "the time will come when the sun will shine only on free men who know no other master but their reason."[3] If gaining access to political freedom amounts to emancipation, universal emancipation was doubtlessly an explicit and central goal of republican revolutionaries.

From the very start, however, it became clear that the process of emancipation did not work as smoothly as republicans had planned and that it did not achieve the universality they had hoped. Take two large groups at distinct levels of subordination: the slaves in the colonies (around one million)[4] and free (i.e., nonslave) women in metropolitan France (around thirteen million). While the situation of both groups evolved in the

[1] *AP* LXXXIV 284. For the controversy around Danton's discourse, see Piquet, "Le discours abolitionniste de Danton (16 Pluviôse an II)."

[2] Discourse of February 5, 1794/18 Pluviôse Year II ("Sur les principes de morale politique qui doivent guider la Convention nationale dans l'administration intérieure de la République,") *Œuvres* X, 350–66; Robespierre, *Virtue and Terror,* 110.

[3] Condorcet, *Condorcet: Political Writings*, 130.

[4] Gisler, *L'esclavage aux Antilles françaises (XVII–XIXe siècles)*, 34.

revolutionary period, this evolution was slow and intermittent. Slavery was only abolished in 1794, with a decree that was partially implemented and soon revoked.[5] The situation of lower-class women improved together with that of lower-class men, thanks to the abolition of feudal privileges on August 4, 1789. All women gained some civil rights during the Revolution: they acquired the rights to sign contracts and get married without parental authorization. A series of laws on inheritance (April 8, 1791; March 7, 1793; and January 6, 1794) provided equality between sons and daughters. Yet women did not gain political rights and remained subordinated on many levels.[6] The complete overhaul of society during the Revolution benefited a large group of already free men but did not eradicate all domination.

This chapter's point of departure is a puzzle about emancipation: why were some parts of the population not emancipated, or very slowly emancipated, despite having vocal advocates?[7] The puzzle here is not about the material obstacles to this emancipation, which have been studied at length and are not particularly mysterious, but rather about the justifications that were given by those who believed in universalizing freedom. Why did republicans justify the dominated status of these groups even though their subordination went against republican allegiance to universalizing freedom? If republican freedom is thought of as non-domination, the puzzle cannot be answered, unless we attribute to the revolutionaries racist or misogynist beliefs, or what some neo-republicans have called "unreflective obliviousness."[8] Indeed what would be the argument against extending a robust protection against domination to the most vulnerable and the most oppressed, unless one either benefited in their oppression or believed in their inferior status?

A more fruitful approach, I contend, is to start with the ambivalence of the conceptions of freedom that the revolutionaries inherited from

[5] The abolition decree was not applied in Martinique, Ile de la Réunion and Ile de France. Slavery was reestablished by Napoleon on May 20, 1802 (decree of 30 Floréal Year X).

[6] Women started to lose rights as early as 1793 when their revolutionary activities became feared as disruptive of authority. Women's clubs were forbidden on 9 Brumaire Year II (October 30, 1793) and on May 23, 1794, women could not be admitted to sections' assemblies. On this question, see Verjus, *Le cens de la famille. Les femmes et le vote, 1789–1848*.

[7] There were many abolitionists during the revolutionary era, as I will note later. The advocates of women were considerably sparser. Women, however, proved to be their own advocates as they participated in revolutionary activities in great number (see Godineau, *Citoyennes tricoteuses*).

[8] Lovett, *The Well-Ordered Republic*, 5.

the republican traditions. As I showed in Chapter 1, this ambivalence is noticeable in several branches of the canonical republican corpus before the Revolution. Analyzing the conceptual difficulties that the republicans faced can help us understand their ethical and political conundrums in front of unprecedented challenges. While republicans endorsed the fight against domination on behalf of all, and therefore thought of freedom as a status of guaranteed protection against domination, they also mixed this idea with the closely related one of capacity for self-government: free persons are capable of self-government, that is, they can make their own choices by themselves; they are self-reliant and cognitively independent.

Once we see freedom as an ambivalent concept, emancipation, defined as the acquisition of political freedom, becomes a paradox. This is made clear when we consider the following premises:

Premise 1 (normative injunction): Political freedom ought to be universalized.
Premise 2 (definition): Freedom is both the guaranteed security against domination and self-government.
Premise 3 (definition): Self-government requires conditions, in particular epistemic, moral, and psychological independence and material assets.

Taken together, these premises create a paradox, which can be expressed as follows:

Paradox of Republican Emancipation: Only those who are not dependent, that is, those who are already free, are eligible to be emancipated.

The paradox shows an undesirable situation in which a large part of the population cannot be emancipated. Only those who are not in a situation of dependence can acquire additional political freedom.

The paradox of republican emancipation can be overcome in three different ways.

Solution 1: *Elitism.* Not everyone can be politically free (negation of premise 1). Everyone can be free in the sense of being protected against political domination, but not everyone can be self-governing.
Solution 2: *Progressivism.* Everyone will be progressively freed until universalization is realized in an indeterminate future. Everyone will need to be raised to the conditions required for self-government. In the meantime, two different statuses remain between those who are capable of self-government (the free) and those who are not (the provisionally unfree).

Solution 3: *Radicalism*. Everyone is immediately declared free regardless of conditions (negation of premise 3). Only then are measures taken to equalize everyone's conditions and make the dependent independent.

In sum, either society is split into tiers of citizenship corresponding to the difference between protection and self-government (these are the elitist and progressive routes) or a radical transformation of economic and social relations is necessary (this is the radical route). French republicans, I argue here, experimented with all three possibilities to deal with the complex challenge of the emancipation of the many.

In this chapter, I present first the discussion over degrees of citizenship and the paradox of republican emancipation. I then explore how the revolutionaries dealt with the complexity of the republican intellectual legacy on freedom and dependence. I analyze Condorcet's fastidious plan to free slaves, and then wonder with a representative to the National Assembly, Pierre Guyomar, whether the dependence of women places them in a separate category from a republican point of view. Finally, I sketch out the original ideas of Grouchy to think of republicanism anew as a theory that ought to be based on the existential dependence we all share as human beings.

THE DEBATE ON ACTIVE AND PASSIVE CITIZENSHIP

In the Fall of 1789, as I argued in Chapter 3, there were few self-avowed republicans. Yet many republican ideas circulated on the benches of the Constituent Assembly, first among them the importance of guaranteeing the status of free citizen to all. The end of the feudal status of persons, with the abolition of privileges on August 4, 1789, required the Assembly to lay out a new definition of citizenship and determine who belonged in the popular sovereign. The debate on citizenship revealed the difficulty of incorporating the ambivalent and at times varying conceptions of citizenship inherited from the republican tradition with the new goal of universal popular sovereignty in a large country.

The debate started on October 29 and continued until the law of December 22, 1789, defining the new conditions of citizenship, was passed. This law distinguished two categories of citizens, passive and active, and different levels of financial thresholds to be eligible for election to public functions. Only those who could pay the value of three days of work were considered active citizens, that is, could participate at the level of primary assemblies. This represented roughly 4.3 million active citizens out of seven million male individuals who were old enough to vote.[9] But only those who could pay the equivalent of ten days of work could participate in the election of deputies and judges. Finally, only those who could pay one silver mark could be elected deputies. Numbers are disputed, but this last group represented around 5 percent of the group of active citizens, that is slightly more than 200,000 citizens. Hence, while there were two official categories of citizens (passive and active), citizenship was in fact a gradual scale with different levels of membership indexed to gender and wealth.[10]

Sieyès was the most vocal advocate of the distinction between active and passive citizens. Such a position may initially be surprising from the author of *What is the Third Estate,* the bold pamphlet arguing for the immediate political emancipation of the Third Estate. Sieyès stated that the Third Estate was "everything" because it performed all the necessary activities for the nation "to survive and prosper."[11] The pamphlet was an argument against the political status of nobles (and to a lesser extent the clergy) who did not bring anything to the nation, yet received privileges, protection against domination as well as a higher share in governing.[12] Sieyès described the Third Estate as "Everything; but an everything that is fettered and oppressed. What would it be without the privileged order? Everything, but an everything that would be free and flourishing."[13] At the same time, Sieyès argued that "freedom does not derive from privilege but from the rights of the citizens, rights which belong to all."[14] He also defined the nation as all the working people. At face value, a citizen for Sieyès was anyone who contributed to the collectivity with his labor, regardless of his wealth, education, or other distinctions.

Yet Sieyès stated in the same pamphlet that "freedom and rights can never be unlimited," and that "like civil liberty, political liberty has its limits," suggesting that "those entitled to be electors and to be elected" are not

9 Godechot, *Les institutions de la France sous la Révolution et l'Empire*; Crook, *Elections in the French Revolution. An Apprenticeship in Democracy, 1789–1799*, 38. Numbers here are taken from *AP XXVI* 532–33.

10 See Le Cour Grandmaison, *Les citoyennetés en révolution (1789–1794)*.

11 Sieyès, *Political Writings*, 94.

12 As the clergy performed religious offices, they could be considered workers with a specific social function. By contrast, nobles performed no services that could be seen as socially valuable labor. The clergy could therefore be part of the nation, but not the nobles *qua* nobles.

13 Sieyès, *Political Writings*, 96.

14 Ibid., 99.

the whole nation, but a subset determined by the law.[15] To this he added that certain categories of the population cannot be given "people's trust," such as "beggars," and that "domestic servants or anyone dependent on a master, or non-naturalized foreigners are never to be found among the representatives of a nation." A dependent individual is part of the nation – he or she works – but cannot be a full citizen.[16] Citizens and nationals, the political sovereign and the nation, were two distinct groups for Sieyès.

The distinction between active and passive citizenship can be interpreted as separating the status of a free man into two different levels: security against domination (passive citizenship) and self-government (active citizenship). Passive citizens get protection from the law. Active citizens are in charge of decision-making and controlling the government in order for the protection of all to be secured. In Sieyès' way of thinking, this distribution of roles was a rational allocation of tasks, following a beneficial division of labor, rather than an abridgment of rights.[17]

Just as in *What is the Third Estate,* Sieyès' later reasoning about citizenship relied on the republican status of freedom as not being dependent on the arbitrary will of another. This status supposed private property as a necessary condition for independence. On August 27, 1789, during a debate on the compensation of the loss of feudal rights, he declared: "Free men, and those who want to be, are those who must be the most attached to legally acquired property. Legitimate property guarantees independence. He is a slave who depends on someone else's property."[18]

Sieyès here echoes the long tradition that equates being propertyless with being a slave. I have argued in Chapter 1 that this was a trope of English republicans, and that more generally, property was commonly seen as a condition for self-government before the Atlantic Revolutions. The republican conception of citizenship as based on independence given by property was also apparent in other currents in the Constituent Assembly. Dupont de Nemours, for instance, argued in favor of a monetary threshold to be elector, and equated citizenship with land ownership: "to be an elector, one must have property, one must have a manor (*manoir*)" concluding with an elliptic sentence that "people without property do not really belong to society; instead, society owns them."[19] For

[15] Ibid., 107.
[16] Ibid.
[17] Baker, "Political languages of the revolution," 640.
[18] *AP* VIII 503, annexe.
[19] *AP* IX 479, October 28, 1789.

Dupont de Nemours, having no property meant that you were *owned* by the state, that you were yourself, so to speak, the collective property of the state, that is a slave of society as a whole.

In the *Observations sur le rapport du comité de constitution concernant la nouvelle organisation de la France (October 2, 1789)*, Sieyès further explored the relation between active citizenship and dependence. In conformity with the English republicans, Sieyès thought that anyone who was subjected to the arbitrary will of a master, like a house servant, or who did not have a fixed residency, could not be a citizen: "Should we consider as citizens beggars, voluntary vagrants or the homeless; those whose servile dependence keep them attached not to a job but to the arbitrary will of a master?"[20] This was one of the key conditions to access active citizenship: "not being in a servile condition."[21]

Interestingly, the five conditions of participation in the primary assemblies did not entail being male ("being French," "being adult," "being a resident in the district (*canton*) for one year," "paying a contribution equal to three days of work," "not being in a servile state or condition").[22] However, Sieyès started the article III of his *Observations* by excluding women from active citizenship, justifying his gesture by mentioning "a prejudice which does not authorize any doubt." We can suppose here that this prejudice refers to the incapacity of women to be socially, economically, and psychologically independent. Despite this supposed lack of doubt, Sieyès introduced a question about the rationality of this denial of women's citizenship. He mentioned that it contradicted the historical fact that some women were queens and that it was odd to think that women could not have a useful public role, as history shows that they sometimes had. This hesitation can also be found in *What is the Third Estate*, where he attributed women's disenfranchisement to a fact that may or may not be justifiable: "Everywhere too, women are deemed, *for better or worse*, to be ineligible for this kind of mandate."[23]

For Sieyès, citizenship is one area where some guidance could be gleaned from the ancients. The status of the citizen in antiquity mirrored

[20] Sieyès, *Observations sur le rapport du comité de constitution concernant la nouvelle organisation de la France*, 20.

[21] Ibid., 23.

[22] Ibid.

[23] Sieyès, *Political Writings*, 107. My emphasis.

the active/passive distinction by being deliberately exclusive. The ancients had an approach that made the free classes "so to speak, purer."[24] A "pure" free class for Sieyès is a homogeneous one, in which every member would be *capable* of free government, and not a class where some individuals would be free in theory but not really "capable of exercising their political rights."[25] For Sieyès, the moderns should be proud to have extended the basis of the association and made everyone "equal with regard to the protection of the law, which is good politics."[26] However, because modern free states like France accept everybody as citizens, they do not benefit from the important separation between conventional and real freedom.

> However, as civiciat [sic][27] or the order of citizens comprise all the levels of the social order, the lower classes and indigent men, due to their intelligence and sentiments, are more foreign to the interest of the association than were the least esteemed members of the ancient free states. There is thus among us a class of men, citizens in right, which are never so in fact.[28]

The poor cannot be part of a collective enterprise in self-government of the sort the revolutionaries had in mind when transforming the French state and grounding it on popular sovereignty. Sieyès argues that the proclamation of their equal citizenship is an artificial convention that is not based on the reality of their capacity. The poor suffer from a double shortcoming: their lack of intelligence, which makes them incapable of self-government, and their "sentiments" which make them "foreign to the interest of the association." In the same paragraph, Sieyès insists that the poor are "foreign to any social idea." As "foreigners from within," they should not take part in the sovereign.

Sieyès continues by proposing what he sees as the obvious solution: reducing this last class to the smallest possible number and making sure they have no part in governing the country, given that they are totally unfit for it. Sieyès shies away from erecting a device to sort out capable and incapable citizens on an individual basis, which would be too much of a direct deviation from the principle of universal rights. He nonetheless asks tauntingly: "who would dare find it bad to keep them away,

[24] Sieyès, *Observations sur le rapport du comité de constitution concernant la nouvelle organisation de la France*, 20.

[25] Ibid.

[26] Ibid.

[27] I suppose Sieyès meant *civitas*, but this is the spelling in the original published version.

[28] Sieyès, *Observations sur le rapport du comité de constitution concernant la nouvelle organisation de la France*, 21.

so to speak, not from legal protection and public welfare, but from the exercise of political rights?"[29]

While Sieyès mobilizes some new tropes (such as the idea of the poor as internal foreigners), he relies on the old notion that social and economic dependence is incompatible with the status of citizen, that is, the status of free man. Simply put, and quite obviously for Sieyès, being in a situation of dependence prevents individuals from being capable of self-government. His argument is not only based on the guidance of the republican tradition, but also on simple observation:

> Among the poor people doomed to painful work, producers of the happiness of others, and receiving barely enough to sustain their aching and needy bodies, in this immense crowd of *bipedal tools,* without freedom, without morality, without intellect, owning only these barely profitable hands and this preoccupied soul, which only gives them suffering ... can you call them men?[30]

The conclusion is clear: levels of humanity can be assigned to existing levels of dependence.

Sieyès' argument goes beyond the simple association of citizenship with property. It also extends the idea of dependence to the situation of poverty in which men do not have the resources to develop their intellect or morality. Being a "man" rather than a "bipedal tool" depends on meeting these threshold conditions. A bipedal tool is necessarily dependent on a host of different people for his survival, even though he (or she) is the one "producing the happiness" of others. Bipedal tools cannot be emancipated and become active citizens because they are not even men. This reasoning leads to the dehumanization and exclusion of the poorest part of the population.

In contrast with Sieyès, Robespierre found the idea that there should be conditions for being part of the sovereign utterly revolting. Following Rousseau's demonstration that dependence was socially constituted, Robespierre took dependence to reflect one's (largely inherited) position in society, not one's intrinsic humanity. Robespierre's starting point in this debate on citizenship was *not* who was fully human, or who was capable of citizenship. The correct normative starting point in his view lay in the definition of sovereignty itself, not in a putative idea of humanity. Following Rousseau, Robespierre argued that a government cannot be legitimate if it is not grounded on popular sovereignty, and it cannot be grounded on popular sovereignty if it is not based on the consent of all.

[29] *Rapport du 2 octobre 1789*, 21.
[30] Sieyès, *Écrits politiques*, 81. My emphasis.

In the discourse of April 1791, commonly referred to as the "discourse on the silver mark" (*Discours du marc d'argent*), Robespierre started his reasoning from two premises accepted by both the Constituent and the National Assemblies: "Sovereignty resides essentially in the nation" and "The law is the expression of the general will. All citizens have the right to contribute to its formation, either in person or through their freely elected representatives."[31] From these premises, Robespierre aimed to demonstrate the necessity of instituting universal male suffrage. He contested the provision by the National Assembly to restrict voting rights to wealthy individuals (i.e., those who had at least a silver mark of assets): "Is the law the expression of the general will, when the greater number of those for whom it is made cannot contribute to its formation in any way? No."[32]

This conviction led Robespierre to wage a legislative battle to integrate the lower class of individuals into the body of citizens. He presented and rebutted the conception articulated by Sieyès:

> Through a strange abuse of words, [the rich, the powerful] have restricted the general idea of property to certain objects only; they have called themselves property owners; they have claimed that only property owners were worthy of the name *citizen*; they have named their own particular interest the general interest and to ensure the success of that claim, they have seized all social power.[33]

It is easy to hear the accent of Rousseau's *Discourse on the Origins of Inequality* in Robespierre's discourse: the wealthy tricked the poor into believing that the protection of wealth benefits all and they then transformed the possession of wealth into political power (*SD* 173). Dependent individuals do not happen to be so by nature, according to both Rousseau and Robespierre. Rather they were duped by the rich into believing that it was in the general interest to protect private property – a property that only some of them had and which was precisely the basis for the domination of the wealthy over the poor. Dependence was caused by an unjust social state; how could a social fact be used to condemn the very victims of injustice?

As he actively pushed for the integration of lower-class citizens into the popular sovereign, Robespierre also argued in favor of the inclusion of other excluded classes into the class of citizens. On December 23,

[31] Robespierre, *Robespierre. Virtue and Terror*, 5–19.

[32] Ibid., 6.

[33] Robespierre was severely criticized for his egalitarian views. A famous example is Necker's *Réflexions philosophiques sur l'égalité*, which condemns the Jacobin egalitarian view as a main cause of revolutionary chaos.

1789, the Constituent Assembly discussed whether non-Catholics could be eligible to perform all municipal, provincial, civil, and military functions.[34] The group of "non-Catholics" in fact comprised not only religious minorities but also two professional groups that were also denied this right, actors, and executioners.

Robespierre intervened in the Constituent Assembly in favor of the right of Jews and actors to hold office. His argument was based on "imprescriptible human rights": "How could the social interest be based on a violation of the eternal principles of justice and reason that are the foundations of every human society?"[35] It may seem strange, retrospectively, to think of a discussion that would group together the rights of Jews and the rights of actors, as they seem to be two groups of an entirely different nature. The accusation against the Jews (formulated on December 23, 1789 by the Abbé Maury) was that they were an "unsociable people." The accusation against the actors and executioners was that their profession was "infamous."[36] Speaking just before Robespierre, the Comte de Clermont-Tonnerre illuminated the relation between these groups. The Jews having no landed property were dependent on the use of monetary assets and therefore engaged in usury. Executioners were subjected to the "infamy" associated with their jobs despite its legality. And actors were in "an absolute dependence on public opinion" both for earning their subsistence and for being deemed corrupt and frivolous.[37] Clermont-Tonnerre expressed the missing link between these otherwise unrelated groups: they were victims of a *de facto* dependence created by law and social convention, that public opinion declared to be their own fault.

Robespierre agreed with Clermont-Tonnerre on the nature of this dependence. His reasoning against the dual status of citizenship also relied on his Rousseauvian understanding of sovereignty. If some members of the sovereign were denied citizenship, nobody could be free: the people would be dominated by the wealthy who hoarded the rights of citizenship. It is thus in the name of the freedom of all (i.e., the common good) that the citizenship of the poor could not be denied:

> What would the nation be? Enslaved; for liberty consists in obeying laws voluntarily adopted, and servitude in being forced to submit to an outside will. What would your constitution be? A true aristocracy. For aristocracy is the state in

[34] *AP* X 754–58, December 23, 1789.
[35] Robespierre, *Robespierre. Virtue and Terror*, 4.
[36] *AP* X 756, December 23, 1789.
[37] Ibid., 754.

which one portion of the citizens is sovereign and the rest subjects. And what an aristocracy! The most unbearable of all, that of the rich.

For Robespierre, the distinction between active and passive citizenship was thus a rhetorical ruse. Not being able to entirely deny citizenship to many French nationals, the wealthy imagined the passive-active distinction as an alternative to exclusion, but one that would be rhetorically less obvious. Thinking they are still citizens, the poor and minorities would not think they have a legitimate ground to complain about being excluded from active citizenship.

With Robespierre, we see one possible modern republican standpoint following the "radical" route I mentioned in the introduction: refuting the distinction between active and passive citizenship and claiming that everyone ought to be a full member of the sovereign in order to be considered free. Comparing him to another prominent republican voice, Condorcet's, can give us a sense of the complexity of interpreting the republican tradition concerning freedom. Condorcet did not participate in the debates on citizenship with Sieyès, Clermont-Tonnerre, and Robespierre. He had not been elected as delegate to the Estates General, which meant that he was not a representative in the Constituent Assembly that came out of the Estates General. Yet he wrote extensively on this question, which was central to his political plans, and we can therefore refer to his published writings of the time.

In his *Essai sur la Constitution des Assemblées Provinciales* (1788), Condorcet touched upon active citizenship, which he called "*droit de cité.*" In the first chapter, he endorsed the common practice (present everywhere in the world, according to him) to only give part of the population the "*droit de cité*," that is the right to participate in political rule.[38] For Condorcet, only landowners (*propriétaires*) could be citizens. Those who were not landowners, he stated, were allowed to stay in the country only in so far as landowners agreed to let them stay on their property. "The right to make laws can only belong to those who own the land on which these rules can be applied."[39] Condorcet insisted that this was not an "arbitrary power" given to some to make laws, but rather a right to make laws following reason and justice.

Condorcet provided a long list of all those who should be excluded from the right to political rule. Some were "natural" exclusions: "minors,

[38] *Œuvres de Condorcet,* Tome VIII, "Essai sur la constitution et les fonctions des assemblées provinciales," 127–28.

[39] Ibid., 129.

monks, domestics, criminals, those who do not have an enlightened will or their own will or those who can legitimately be suspected to have a corrupted will."[40] His argument for the exclusion of the propertyless was the same as Sieyès: just like "foreigners and travelers," they have only "an uncertain, partial and momentary interest in common prosperity."[41]

For Condorcet, the conditions under which citizens should enjoy the *droit de cité* were that "the citizen be capable of having a reasonable, free, uncorrupted will and that he has a personal right to a part of the territory that is under the law."[42] The same reasoning can be found in the letters that Condorcet wrote to influence the drafting of the US Constitution, the *Letters from a New Haven Bourgeois to a Citizen of Virginia*.[43] Only those who have property above a certain value should have the right to be electors. In this text, however, Condorcet aimed to respond to the objection that this exclusion contradicts the principle of equality. Condorcet had two rebuttals: first, he imagined that landowners below the financial threshold should be given the right to associate with one another until they raise the necessary value, at which point they would be given the right to elect one representative together as their collective elector.[44] Second, Condorcet claimed that this system gave a voice to all the small landowners, which counterbalanced the voices of the wealthy. He further claimed that this system was more egalitarian than one where all the poor could vote because in the latter, "the influence of the rich would be greater."[45] There is no explanation as to why this would be the case, but one can surmise that this is because the poor are deemed to be easy to influence as they are not capable of making independent decisions.

Yet Condorcet's position is importantly distinct from Sieyès'. Instead of wealth, Condorcet considered that the most important condition for the common good was a voting procedure that would privilege the decision-making of an *enlightened* electorate. The "interest" of the voting member was not the important factor: what mattered was whether he would be likely to take the *right* or *correct* decision when voting. For

[40] Ibid., 130.
[41] Ibid.
[42] Ibid., 132.
[43] The New Haven bourgeois is Condorcet himself, who had been made "freeman" of New Haven in 1785. The Citizen of Virginia was Filippo Mazzei, a representative for Virginia who had become friend with Condorcet during his visit to Paris.
[44] *Lettre d'un bourgeois*, in *Œuvres de Condorcet*, Tome IX, 11.
[45] Ibid., 12.

Condorcet, laws should not be considered "the expression of the arbitrary will (...) but rather truths rationally deducted from the principles of natural right and adopted as such by the plurality."[46]

In contrast with Rousseau and Robespierre, Condorcet did not take the participation of all as the most important dimension of sovereignty. In his 1785 preliminary to the *Essay on the Application of Mathematics to the Theory of Decision-Making*, the so-called jury theorem proposed to demonstrate that the probability of a decision being right grew as the number of people voting grew, so long as voting members had a sufficiently good capacity for judgment, that is, so long as their probability to be right would be greater than 50 percent.[47] Two important consequences ensued. First, a large assembly of enlightened citizens was preferable than the judgment of one person, say, a king, however enlightened. Condorcet's jury theorem could be used to justify a democracy of enlightened citizens. Second, democracy could be justified on the basis of the jury theorem, but *only in so far as* the voting members were indeed enlightened. If voting members had a probability of less than ½ to make the right decision, the consequences would be dire for the democracy in question.

On this basis, we can better understand why Condorcet would prefer an assembly of elite voting members more likely to make the right decision because they are more enlightened, that is what contemporary theorists call an epistocracy. On the other hand, Condorcet later concluded that it was crucial to enlighten the mass of the people in such a way that "as a result of the progress of enlightenment, there was a great equality between minds, as to the soundness of their judgments and the truth of the principles according to which they govern their conduct."[48] This program is presented in his work on education, to which I return in Chapter 5.[49]

The positions of Sieyès, Robespierre, and Condorcet illustrate the three possible ways of evading the paradox of republican emancipation – the elitist, the radical, and the progressive paths, respectively. For Sieyès, elitism was the only way to ensure the freedom of the whole. For

[46] *Vie de Turgot*, in *Œuvres de Condorcet*, Tome V, 211.

[47] *Essay on the Application of Mathematics to the Theory of Decision-Making*, in Baker, *Condorcet. Selected Writings*, 48–49.

[48] Ibid., 50.

[49] Condorcet, *Cinq mémoires sur l'instruction publique*. For the connection between Condorcet's jury theorem and his theory of education, see Roussin, "La démocratie épistémique: une perspective condorcétienne."

Robespierre, nothing less than radicalism would ensure the inclusive sovereignty necessary for the general will. And for Condorcet, a progressive path would be necessary to reconcile the exigency of an enlightened citizenry with the goal of an inclusive citizenry.

WHAT IS DEPENDENCE?

To understand the paradox of republican emancipation, we must further analyze the definition of dependence. I argued in Chapter 1 that the republican tradition had an ambivalent understanding of what "being one's own master" meant, defining it with a mixture of epistemic, moral and psychological capacities as well as the possession of economic assets. In any case "being one's own master" implies "being independent" and therefore protected from domination. In turn, the definition of dependence was a complicated matter for republicans.[50] I argue here that in the revolutionary period, the use of the concept of "dependence" suffered from inconsistency. We can sort out three different meanings often confused in arguments:

(1) *Coerced dependence*: The coerced subjection to another's will.
(2) *Material dependence*: The material reliance on someone else's property for one's subsistence.
(3) *Psychological dependence*: The psychological incapacity to act without someone else's approval.

Coerced dependence equates dependence with legal servitude. Slavery enters this first category as an extreme case of servitude, in which the entire person is being owned by another and entirely under their domination. Less stringent or less absolute forms of coerced dependence include serfdom, indentured servitude, or marriage in some legal systems. In this sense, the dependent cannot disobey orders or displease the master, lest they face grave consequences. Here, dependence supposes a legal structure actively or passively supporting coercion. It does not suppose any need or desire from the coerced to be or remain subjected.

[50] Later republicans also encountered the difficulty. See for instance Kant conceding that "It is, I admit, somewhat difficult to determine what is required in order to be able to claim the rank of a human being who is his own master" (*Theory and Practice*, fn, 8:296 in Kant, *Practical Philosophy*). Kant resorted to technical Latin terms to give an aura of scientific rigor to his classification (*Doctrine of Right* 6:315, 458 in Kant, *The Metaphysics of Morals*).

If anything, the master is the one who needs and desires the dependent, servant, wife or slave's subjection.

The second meaning, *material dependence*, does not involve physical or legal coercion but supposes the willing subordination of the dependent who is looking to fulfil primary material needs. Dependence here entails the incapacity of a person to rely on their own property (economic assets) to provide for themselves or their family. If it were not for this incapacity, the person would not willingly subject themselves to a master. This second meaning does not directly imply domination, but a situation in which the person, who is not materially independent, places themselves in a position vulnerable to domination in order to survive or improve one's condition. This form of dependence can characterize for instance the situation of the domestic, the wageworker, and, again, marriage in some circumstances.

The third meaning, *psychological dependence*, refers to the psychological need of the agent to rely on someone else for their own survival or well-being. Psychological dependence may arise in conjunction with coercion or material dependence or may be independent of them. One could be psychologically dependent on someone else despite having the material conditions to be self-reliant and not objectively needing to be subjected to this person. Yet, they could also develop psychological dependence as an effect of their being dominated and internalizing their domination as an essential aspect of their identity or life. This meaning of dependence could characterize the situation of the servant who "feels" they could not do without their master, the poor who accept paternalism as legitimate, and also, again, wives. This form of dependence, however, could also apply to the wealthy, the husbands, and to masters of all sorts. While material dependence is asymmetrical, psychological (moral and emotional) dependence is not. The worker needs the wages from his employer more than the employer needs the labor of a specific worker: the inequality in their level of material independence means that their dependence to one another is not equal in intensity and urgency. Psychological dependence is different: a husband for instance may be as emotionally dependent on his wife than she is on him. This is Rousseau's insight: masters and slaves are both enslaved even though their material dependence is asymmetrical.

The confusion between these three senses amplifies the problem of dependence itself. Those who are under legal domination, or those who fail to provide for themselves are accused of being *servile,* that is, psychologically dependent. The wealthy or powerful who are psychologically dependent on their subordinates are instead called "needy" or "entitled." Importantly, the relation between these three sorts of dependence is obscure in the discourse of those who put dependence at the center of the problem of emancipation.

These three senses of dependence in republican texts are intertwined in ways that may raise doubts about the coherence and depth of the republican emancipatory project. I would like here to turn to one author who weaved these different meanings of dependence together and who more than anyone else thought that dependence was at the center of all the evils of modern life – Rousseau. Throughout his work, Rousseau describes dependence as a psychological and material phenomenon, insidiously present in modern society in all aspects of social life. Dependence for him is the direct gateway to domination.[51]

As Rousseau's writings were extensively quoted by revolutionaries and later republicans, the ambiguities of his thought on dependence and domination are worth exploring. I will here focus on three common interpretations of Rousseau's stance on dependence that, upon examination, may be less straightforward than it seems.

First, Rousseau is often taken to be an uncompromising opponent of slavery. This seems *prima facie* true when we read his straightforward rejection of slavery at the beginning of the *Social Contract* (*SC* I.4). His position does not leave open the possibility of legitimate slavery, as Locke and Grotius do.[52] His condemnation of slavery is absolute and has no restrictive clauses. Recall Rousseau's concluding paragraph in his demonstration about the impossibility of legitimate slavery:

> From whatever angle one looks at things, the right to slavery is null, not only because it is illegitimate, but because it is absurd and meaningless. These words *slavery* and *right* are contradictory. Either between one man and another, or between a man and a people, the following speech will always be equally absurd, *I make a convention with you which is entirely at your expense and entirely to my profit, which I shall observe as long as I please, and which you shall observe as long as I please.* (*SC* I.4)

Rousseau, however, rapidly moves to what seems most important to him: how a purported right to slavery has been used to justify the people's subjection to a king. What motivates the antislavery demonstration is

[51] Dent, N. J. H., *Rousseau. An Introduction to His Psychological, Social and Political Theory*, 59–64; Rasmussen, *The Problems and Promise of Commercial Society: Adam Smith's Response to Rousseau*, 30–35; Rousselière, "Rousseau on Freedom in Commercial Society."

[52] Locke *Second Treatise on Government*, IV.23; Grotius, *De Jure Belli*, III.7.1 in Grotius, *The Rights of War and Peace.*

the argument repeatedly used by the enemies of republicanism: "If, says Grotius, an individual can alienate his freedom, and enslave himself to a master, why could not a whole people alienate its freedom and subject itself to a king?" (*SC* I.4.1). The problem is the political slavery of a people: the justification of political subjection on the grounds that a right to slavery exists. From a republican point of view, the right to slavery needs to be contested for the illegitimacy of political subjection to be demonstrated.

Upon inspection, any reader could see that, throughout his work, Rousseau rarely uses the concept of slavery in the technical sense of being legally owned by another. Instead, he uses slavery to designate a situation of social, economic, and psychological dependence (or as I have called both, both "material" and "psychological" dependences). Most strikingly, Rousseau did not write a treatise to condemn chattel slavery. Slavery is central to his work, but slavery does not refer to the slave trade and chattel slavery that Europeans were employing on a large scale in the eighteenth century. Rousseau's analysis of slavery in the legal sense mostly consists in a critique of Grotius' justification of slavery as the just compensation of the winners who are defending themselves in a just war (*SC* I.4). Rousseau rarely alludes to chattel slavery.[53] Even more concerning than his silence is his apparent denial of the existence of chattel slavery in his time in a passage of the *Social Contract* aiming to show that political representation is a proof of unfreedom: "As for you, modern peoples, *you have no slaves*, but you are yourselves slaves; you pay for their freedom with your own" (*SC* III.15. My emphasis). How could Rousseau deny that the Europeans were involved in slave trade?

It makes sense that Rousseau, following the English republicans, enlarged the legal meaning of slavery to characterize the situation of men subjected to a king or a tyrant. Political slavery as subjection to a king was an immediate evil for European men. By contrast, European men did not fear chattel slavery for themselves. It is concerning, however, that Rousseau has so little to say about chattel slavery in juxtaposition to his republican anti-monarchical stance as slave trade happened on a large scale in his time. This should at least make us ponder what exactly we mean when we say that Rousseau was opposed to slavery.

[53] Passages include a few sentences in *Julie* (OC II, 414) and a longer (though highly problematic) reflection on slavery in *Émile and Sophie* (OC IV, 916–18), in which Emile is made a slave.

It should also alert us to the idiosyncratic idea of "slavery" in his texts. In his view, slavery, again used in the enlarged political sense, is not primarily a situation of coerced subjection. It necessitates a preliminary state of psychological dependence. Rousseau defined dependence as the necessary reliance on others in order to fulfil one's needs (*E* 84–85). Dependence is the condition of possibility of domination for Rousseau. Indeed, "it is impossible to subjugate a man without first having placed him in the position of being unable to do without another" (*SD* 159). Surely Rousseau could *not* have meant that the men, women and children bought in Africa were enslaved because they materially needed the Europeans nor because they psychologically needed their approval. When analyzing slavery and dependence in Rousseau, we need to disentangle their different meanings carefully.

Second, the scholarship overwhelmingly takes dependence – understood as widespread psychological reliance on others – to develop from a moral cause, which is the development of *amour-propre*. Rousseau defines *amour-propre* as "a relative sentiment, factitious and born in society, which inclines every individual to set greater store by himself than by anyone else, inspires men with all the evils they do to one another, and is the genuine source of honor" (*SD* Note XV, 218). Neuhouser, a specialist of Rousseau's work, has championed the moral interpretation and argued that "the central thesis of Rousseau's *Second Discourse* is that *amour-propre* in its 'inflamed,' or corrupted, manifestations – what earlier thinkers called pride or vanity – is the principal source of an array of evils so widespread that they can easily appear to be necessary features of the human condition: enslavement (or domination), conflict, vice, misery, and self-estrangement."[54] In this reading, a psychological (moral) phenomenon can explain the spread of universal dependence.

Yet this view discounts Rousseau's more traditional reliance on the republican view of freedom, for which material independence is a necessary condition. In the *Discourse on Inequality,* Rousseau attributes happiness and freedom to a society in which individuals (or families) are self-reliant. He dates "slavery" to the moment when a division of labor creates a material dependence on the work of others:

> The moment one man needed the help of another; as soon as it was found to be useful for one to have provisions for two, equality disappeared, property

[54] Neuhouser, *Rousseau's Theodicy of Self-Love: Evil, Rationality and the Drive for Recognition*, 8.

appeared, work became necessary, and the vast forests changed into pleasing fields that had to be watered with the sweat of men, and where slavery and misery were soon seen to sprout and grow together with the harvests. (*SD* 167)

With the end of material self-reliance, property becomes a means of production allowing the use of other people's work. Psychological dependence had appeared much earlier in Rousseau's narrative of human primitive state. Before the creation of a division of labor, psychological dependence did not perturb the golden age of mankind, the period "occupying a just mean between the indolence of the primitive state and the petulant activity of our amour propre, [which] must have been the happiest and the most lasting epoch" (*SD* 167). It is only after the transformation of private property into a mode of production implying the use of others' work that psychological dependence becomes uncontrollable.

Rousseau insists that this generalized psychological dependence is created by an economic system of material dependence that is rooted in an absence of self-reliance. There are thus two solutions for him: either cultivating this self-reliance (a solution that turns out to be unworkable, but still worth exploring in *Émile*), or completely transforming political and social institutions (as the *Social Contract* proposes).[55]

In *Émile*, the development of independence as self-reliance is presented as the proper path to freedom for the young boy. Rousseau organizes the education of the young boy around his acquisition of skills that would make him capable of being self-reliant. Just like primitive man, Émile learns how to build a shelter, sow, harvest, and make weapons (*E* 185). Later, as a young adult in civil society (Book V), Emile is shown demonstrating these skills, earning the admiration of peasants and workers for his many talents (*E* 435). At the same time, his education is organized around carefully avoiding any experience of domination, giving him no occasion to either dominate or become servile in order to get what he wants.

One may wonder to what extent education, a central republican institution, could remedy the lack of self-reliance. In *Emile,* Rousseau presents the possibility that a child could acquire all the skills necessary to become self-reliant and therefore to be free in a modern commercial society. Yet *Émile* was not meant to be applied at a large scale (and certainly could not have been), leaving open the question of whether the masses could be emancipated by education.

[55] I explore this question in Rousselière, "Rousseau on Freedom in Commercial Society."

If we follow my interpretation, we can see that Rousseau's view largely overlaps the views of pre-revolutionary republicans at large. Even the most radical republican author argued that the root of freedom is self-reliance: "to live of oneself," as Algernon Sidney put it. For Rousseau, this notion is focused on skills and control of needs rather than private property (as for Sidney and Harrington), but it still suggests that freedom depends on a set of conditions that will not be available to everyone. Émile's exclusive education under the guidance of an elite tutor, Jean-Jacques, bears testimony to this idea.

Finally, Rousseau's political thought is often deemed radical because he refuses to naturalize subjection, dependence, and social power. Recall for instance the beginning of the *Second Discourse* where he dismisses the mere suggestion that the powerful could deserve their power as "a question which may perhaps be good for slaves to debate within hearing of their Masters, but not befitting rational and free Men who seek the truth" (*SD* 131). Rousseau indeed fought against the naturalization of social hierarchy, denouncing the fake contracts that make the poor believe that they owe the rich, and the servants believe that they are less good than their masters. In many respects, Rousseau's work actively destroyed the kind of naturalized dependence that revolutionaries drew upon in their discussion on citizenship in the Fall of 1789. Rousseau's critique of dependence, however, did not include women, whose dependence he ended up naturalizing. When it comes to women, Rousseau did not follow his own principle.

In explaining why women ought to remain dependent, Rousseau drew on two different senses of dependence. "Woman and man are made for each other," he wrote in *Émile,* "but their mutual dependence is not equal: men are dependent on women because of their desires; women are dependent on men because of both their desires and their needs. We men could subsist more easily without women than they could without us" (*E* 364). While men tend to become dependent on women on a psychological level, they are self-reliant and do not need women to provide for their food and shelter. They are therefore the masters of the conditions of their lives.

By contrast, for Rousseau, women lack the capacity to be self-reliant. This places them in the situation of having to please their master, man, in order to get their subsistence:

> In order for women to have what they need to fulfill their purpose in life, we must give it to them, we must want to give it to them, we must believe them worthy; they are dependent on our feelings, on the price we place on their merit, and on the opinion we have of their charms and of their virtues. (*E* 364)

For Rousseau, however, this dependence falls within the category of natural dependence that cannot be changed. Because they need to have the approval of their master, "man," it is only normal that they strive to get it and aim to "please" men. The logical consequence follows that little girls need to be educated to be obedient and not to follow their own will. Their will must be "thwarted." They "must first be exercised in constraint, so that it never costs them anything to tame all their caprices, in order to submit them to the will of others" (*E* 369). For women, dependence is not a social fact that ought to be contested, but one that needs to be cultivated so that women can fulfill their natural duties: "To please men, to be useful to them, to make herself loved and honored by them, to raise them when young, to care for them when grown, to counsel them, to make their lives agreeable and sweet – these are the duties of women at all times and they ought to be taught from childhood" (*E* 365). Instead of arguing for the emancipation of women, Rousseau justifies their dominated state by naturalizing their dependence.

We see how Rousseau, a republican fiercely opposed to domination, ends up being silent on chattel slavery, relying on the traditional idea of independence as self-sufficiency, and claiming that women's social subordination was justified by their incapacity to be materially, morally, and cognitively self-reliant. His example thus suggests to us that while dependence is an evil for republicans, it presents a complex reality, making its eradication considerably harder than republicans would like.

SLAVES

The abolition of slavery should not have been a complicated question for republican revolutionaries. This is one area where the republican guidance, coupled with the new universal injunction, was clear. If the hallmark tenet of republicanism is that slavery is the worst evil, its abolition should be central to the type of inclusive and universal republicanism that I have been describing. Yet debates on slavery at the National Assembly (whether the Constituent, the Legislative, or the Convention) turned out to be protracted and not at all straightforward. In this section, I will address the reasons surrounding this complexity. While there were obvious financial and material interests at play, I am interested here in the conceptual obstacles that republicans kept encountering with emancipating slaves and other dependents.

The First Republic officially abolished slavery on February 4, 1794 (16 Pluviôse Year II). The center of the French empire, its most profitable colony, and the "home" of half a million slaves, was Saint-Domingue, a Caribbean Island that the French had occupied since the mid-seventeenth century. On February 4, 1794, three deputies from Saint-Domingue, Jean-Baptiste Mills (a man of color), Jean-Baptiste Belley (a black former slave), and Louis Dufay (a white man) came to the Convention to present the news that Sonthonax and Polverel, the governors of Saint-Domingue, had *de facto* pronounced the abolition of slavery on the island in August 1793. This declaration had been precipitated by a long series of slave insurrections.[56] If one thing should have been clear, it was that freedom had been gained by slaves through their emancipatory struggle rather than given to them by the Republic. This was not, however, how the abolition was understood in Paris. The representatives' reactions give us a clear view of their beliefs:

Camboulas: Since 1789, a great trial remained incomplete; the aristocracies of the sword and the Church were eliminated but an aristocracy of the skin still ruled; it has just breathed its last breath. Equality is established: a black man, a brown man, and a white man (*un noir, un jaune, un blanc*) will sit among you on behalf of the free citizens of Saint-Domingue. (The deputies applaud.)[57]

Another deputy, Levasseur, noted that the abolition of slavery was faithful to the Declaration of the Rights of Man and the Citizen. To which Danton added, as we saw earlier, that "today we are proclaiming universal liberty."[58]

The reactions of representatives at the National Convention started what later became a common republican narrative. In this narrative, the insurrection of slaves was inspired by revolutionary ideas and realized the republican ideal of universal freedom. The rebellion in Saint-Domingue was an offshoot of their own universal principles under their paternalist guidance. Ultimately, the story goes, the French Republic *gave* freedom to the slaves, achieving the emancipation it had promised to all.

56 For the description and analysis of the slave uprisings that led to the Sonthonax decision, see Chapters 6 and 7 in Dubois, *Avengers of the New World: The Story of the Haitian Revolution.*

57 *Reimpressions de l'Ancien Moniteur, depuis la réunion des Etats-Généraux jusqu'au consulat* (mai 1789-novembre 1799), volume 19, Paris: Bureau Central, 1841, 385–87.

58 Ibid., 388.

The scholarship has often presented the Haitian Revolution as part of the movement of realization of universal rights.[59] It has been described as the little sister of the world-making American and French revolutions, under the general label of Atlantic Revolutions. As suggested by the title of his ground-breaking book on Saint-Domingue's insurrection, *The Black Jacobins*, C. L. R. James portrays Toussaint Louverture, who led the Haitian revolution, as a republican revolutionary in the vein of a Robespierre. "The man into which the French Revolution had made him," writes James, "demanded that the relation with the France of liberty, equality, fraternity and the abolition of slavery without a debate, should be maintained."[60] The assumption that the Haitian Revolution had been granted by the French Revolution runs deep in the scholarship. See for instance Haiti historian Laurent Dubois's assessment: "[The abolition of slavery] was a truly radical change, *the most dramatic of the many inaugurated by the French Revolution*. It took individuals who had been stripped of all human rights and made them members of a democratic republic."[61] According to this account, rather than liberating themselves, the slaves had been liberated by the republic.

This narrative has been contested as a form of colonial appropriation of the Haitian Revolution. Reducing the slaves' fights to an application of French universal principles feeds the narrative of the realization of these ideals by subalterns, as if those who had been excluded were the ones who could redeem the ideal and push it to its completion. For political theorist Adom Getachew, the frame of "exclusion" is not the right one but should be replaced by "domination."[62] It is only with this change of frame that we can come to grips with the true originality of what the slaves were doing, which was positing their own universal ideal and not realizing an imperfect one left to them by the French settlers.

I share with Getachew a great suspicion about the French gesture of recuperating the slaves' revolt as a realization of their own universal

[59] Dubois, *Avengers of the New World: The Story of the Haitian Revolution*; Blackburn, *The American Crucible: Slavery, Emancipation and Human Rights*; Buck-Morss, *Hegel, Haiti and Universal History*; Nesbitt, *Universal Emancipation: The Haitian Revolution and the Radical Enlightenment*.

[60] James, *The Black Jacobins: Toussaint L'Ouverture and the San Domingo Revolution*, 290.

[61] Dubois, *Avengers of the New World: The Story of the Haitian Revolution*, 170.

[62] Getachew, "Universalism after the Post-Colonial Turn: Interpreting the Haitian Revolution," 828.

ideal. This form of interpretation falls into what I called the republican narrative of unfulfilled promises in the Introduction. With Césaire and Getachew, I agree that the Haitian Revolution should not be primarily framed as a chapter of the French Revolution.[63] Where my analysis diverges from theirs is on the nature of the idea of exclusion. As I have argued so far, the exclusion created by French universalist republicanism is essentially due to its intrinsic relation with ideas of domination and dependence. Exclusion and domination, in my argument, are not two different frames in the case of French republicanism: the excluded are those who are dominated and whose domination remains unsolvable even in the eyes of those who would like to extend freedom to them.

While the Constituent Assembly was working on drafting a new constitution for metropolitan France, the law in application in the colonies was still the ordinance written by Colbert's son, the Marquis de Seigneley, and promulgated by Louis XIV in 1685, which later became known as the Black Code (*Code Noir*).[64] The Black Code regulated relations between settlers and slaves, proselytized Catholicism, legitimized slavery in the colonies, authorized violent corporeal punishments, and dehumanized slaves.

Slavery, however, was not a priority for the representatives. For once, slavery was not authorized on French soil. According to the "Freedom Principle," appearing as early as 1571 as an offshoot of Frankish law, slavery had been prohibited. All the kings of France had accepted and applied this law. The Freedom Principle held that any slave who set foot on French soil became free. As the default law, the Freedom Principle was upheld with remarkable consistency by the *Parlement de Paris*. Between the sixteenth and the late eighteenth century, domestic slaves who were accompanying their masters on their trip to France could petition to gain their freedom as soon as they stepped in France – and they gained it, again, with remarkable consistency.[65]

The question of slavery for revolutionaries was thus never framed in a direct way such as: does slavery contradict French law? It was a matter of

[63] Césaire, *Toussaint-Louverture, la révolution française et le problème colonial.*

[64] The name "Code Noir" also came to designate the other ordinances on the colonies added in 1723–4. On the Black Code, see Sala-Molins, *Le Code Noir ou le calvaire de Canaan.*

[65] On the many cases of slaves suing for their freedom in the *Ancien Régime*, see Peabody, *"There Are No Slaves in France": The Political Culture of Race and Slavery in the Ancien Régime.* The Edict of 1716, passed under the pressure of slaveowners, made it harder for slaves to obtain their freedom as masters could be granted exception to the Freedom Principle if they registered them ahead of time.

course that it did. Because monarchical rule had honored the interdiction of slavery on French metropolitan soil, it was not a new problem that revolutionaries had to face in the context of their new regime based on popular sovereignty and universal rights. For the representatives of the Constituent Assembly, whose main goal was drafting a Constitution for France, slavery could not be central because it did not concern the French constitution: slavery had already been made an extra-constitutional issue by the monarchy.

The question for representatives was rather the extra-constitutional status of colonies, which had been legislated by special codes and decrees under the monarchy. Many arguments in favor of keeping slavery in the colonies were presented at the National Assembly in March 1790. For example, Antoine Barnave, a prominent member of the Jacobins (until he left to join the *Feuillants* in 1791), made a case for the defense of the special status of colonies and the maintenance of slavery. One of his reasons was simply financial. "The interest of the French nation to support its commerce, to keep its colonies, to foster its prosperity by all means compatible with the metropole have seemed unquestionable to us under any perspective."[66] Recall here that the near-bankruptcy of the French State had been crucial in the advent of the Revolution, if only because it precipitated the convocation of the Estates-General. The connection between financial stability and the very existence of the revolution could not be neglected.[67] Barnave maintained that keeping the colonies was in the interest of the revolution itself because the revolution needed to be financed. The revolution could not give France "glory and prosperity," Barnave wrote, if it were not to survive, and, he added, its financial situation would not outlive the loss of colonies.[68]

The argument that slavery was necessary for the financial survival of the Revolution itself was doubtlessly the most enduring one. Until 1794, and after it was reinstated by Napoleon, slavery was justified in terms of financial utility, and financial utility in terms of political survival.[69] More than a year later, a representative to the Legislative, La Rochefoucault-Liancourt would continue to argue that the end of slavery would create the complete ruin of "our commerce" and the misery of the population

[66] *AP* XII 68, March 8, 1790.
[67] Sonenscher, *Before the Deluge: Public Debt, Inequality and the Intellectual Origins of the French Revolution.*
[68] *AP* XII 69, March 8, 1790.
[69] Le Cour Grandmaison, *Les citoyennetés en révolution (1789–1794)*, 196.

that lives on the labor of colonial goods. Losing the colonies ("abandoning the colonies") would mean accepting to lose the game of competition with other nations, the game created by "the jealousy of trade."[70]

Defending colonization and slavery thus depended on finding a way around the notion of universalism so central to the first months of the Revolution. Barnave therefore argued that colonies should keep their exceptional status and should not be subjected to the general laws that applied to the French territory. If one looked at their particularity, one would realize that "the rigorous and universal application of general principles would not fit them."[71] The reason came down to their differences in terms of mores, climate, and productions, a general principle of fit that the illustrious Montesquieu had endorsed. For Barnave, colonies warranted exception to the general law because they were unlike French provinces: "Relations of interest and position between France and its colonies are not of the same nature as those that connect French provinces with either the national body or provinces between them. Political relations between them have to differ, and we therefore have not believed that colonies could be part of the constitution decreed for the kingdom."[72]

While some republicans joined the proslavery camp, most of them were affiliated with the abolitionist movement. The influence of the English in this regard was not negligible. The abolitionist movement in England, which was more powerful than the one in France, published a series of books denouncing slavery that were circulated in France.[73] The *Société des Amis des Noirs* (Society of the Friends of the Blacks) under the leadership of Brissot was at the forefront of the abolitionist cause. The great republican theorist, Condorcet, became involved with the abolitionist movement early on, in particular in the *Société*, which he presided from January to March 1788. Entangled in the paradox of republican emancipation, Condorcet's position illustrates the difficulty of

[70] *AP* XXXI 292, September 24, 1791. The phrase "jealousy of trade" comes from David Hume's influential essay "Of the jealousy of trade" (1758) in which he criticized the following belief he found both erroneous and widespread: "Nothing is more usual, among states which have made some advances in commerce, than to look at the progress of their neighbours with a suspicious eye, to consider all trading states as rivals, and to suppose that it is impossible for any of them to flourish but at their expence" (Hume, *Political Essays*, 150).

[71] *AP* XII 71, March 9, 1790.

[72] Ibid.

[73] For instance, Ramsey, *An Essay on the Treatment and Conversion of African Slaves in the British Sugar Colonies* (1784); Clarkson, *Essay on the Slavery and Commerce of the Human Species, Particularly the African* (1785).

a straightforward republican endorsement of abolition. With Condorcet, I contend, we find a gradualist plan for abolition, one that falls within what I earlier called "progressivism."

In 1781, Condorcet wrote an abolitionist treatise *Reflections on the Slavery of Negroes,* under the pseudonym of M. Schwartz, pastor of Saint-Evangile in Bienne, a city in the Swiss mountains.[74] The treatise is remarkable because it requires not only an abolition of the slave trade, as he would argue later in his 1788 preamble to the rules for the Society of the Friends of the Blacks, but also because it asked for the abolition of slavery itself.[75] In this treatise, Condorcet unambiguously judged slavery a "crime."[76] In the first sections, he proceeded to methodically rebuke the usual arguments legitimating some forms of slavery (in the vein of Locke and Grotius),[77] the justification of slavery on economic grounds[78] and the claim that voluntary servitude was possible.[79] For Condorcet, who followed much of Rousseau's rationale in his arguments, slavery was contrary to natural right.

Yet the 1781 *Reflections* bears surprises in comparison with the 1788 preamble. In Section VIII of his treatise, after having declared that the principles of justice demand the abolition of slavery, Condorcet set out to demonstrate why the immediate and total abolition of slavery was neither possible nor desirable. One would have expected Condorcet to be in favor of immediate abolition. But instead, he argued for what can be called a *gradualist* position. Abolition should occur, but it should be a long and gradual process, one necessary to bring the unequal to equality. Freedom could not simply be declared to be universalizable immediately.

Condorcet's plan is puzzling. On the one hand, he is clearly committed to abolitionism. The treatise describes the horrors of slavery – violence, torture, murders – in graphic details, mentioning whips, torn flesh, and ovens to hide corpses.[80] The preamble shows the same awareness regarding the material reality of the middle passage: "Once on the ship to

74 Condorcet, *Réflexions sur l'esclavage des nègres.*

75 The preamble is translated under the title "On Slavery. Rules for the *Society of the Friends of the Negroes* (1788)" in Condorcet, *Condorcet: Political Writings*, 148–55. It is unclear to me why the Society of the Friends of the Blacks is given a different name in this translation.

76 *Réflexions*, 1.

77 Ibid., Section II, 3–8.

78 Ibid., Section III, 9–10.

79 Ibid., Section IV, 10–12.

80 Ibid., 27. See also the mention of torture and burning slaves as practices, 54–55.

be transported, each person is squashed into the smallest possible space and surrounded by chains. At the slightest protest, his chains are made heavier; at the slightest groan, he is whipped; and any sign of anger or despair is punished by death."[81] On the other hand, in the *Reflections,* Condorcet proposes the following: slaves (including newborns) were to remain thirty-five additional years in their condition, so that it would take seventy years to abolish slavery entirely. In his words: "We are proposing not to free negroes at the moment of their birth but to leave masters the freedom to raise them and use them as slaves, under the condition that they would be freed at the age of thirty-five years old."[82] In doing so, he presents to the reader the unbearable image of humans who, despite being tortured and wronged, would have to suffer their plight for several decades. Condorcet's text thus presents the core of the paradox of republican emancipation: a discourse that aims to universalize freedom, and yet argues for the continuation of enslavement.

A large part of the treatise is devoted to pragmatic issues justifying gradualism: how to deal with the violence that would likely arise from an immediate liberation of the slaves, the disruption of labor, and the retaliation of slave owners. Yet Condorcet's arguments for gradualism do not ultimately rely on pragmatism, realism, or a trade-off between ethics and the economic interests of the French. Rather he struggles with the idea that the dependent could be immediately free, since freedom requires conditions: epistemic and moral capacities as well as economic self-reliance, which can only be developed over time. For Condorcet, slaves objectively have none of these qualities and can attain them only through a period of tutelage and education.

The core of the case for gradualism thus revolves around the idea that dependents are incapable of self-government. "Stultified" by their lack of education and the burdens of slavery, and "corrupt" by the immoral example of slave owners, slaves are incapable of being free agents to the extent expected from a republican citizen. Denying them citizenship rights is therefore logical and not punitive or exclusionary. The suspension of rights of epistemically incompetent individuals is justifiable, and even rationally commendable. Rights can be "suspended," Condorcet adds, in the case of young children, cognitively challenged individuals ("*imbéciles*"), and the "mad" ("*les fous*"). The slaves fall in the same large group of incompetent dependents.

[81] Condorcet, *Condorcet: Political Writings*, 150.

[82] *Réflexions*, Section IX, 44.

Epistemic incapacity is connected to moral deficiency, Condorcet claims. Former slaves are incapable of self-direction; they are not worthy (*digne*) of freedom. Those who have been in situation of extreme dependence cannot be freed without risking a situation of chaos and extreme disorder. The consideration here is clearly one of "public order," that is, the fear that freed slaves would be incapable of behaving according to the basic laws of society. The anger of freed slaves, though, is here likened to moral deficiency instead of the legitimate expression of resistance to oppression.

Because slaves do not possess any of the qualities required to be free, they need to be *protected.* The necessity of protecting those who cannot self-govern sends us back to the dichotomy between freedom as protection against domination and freedom as self-government. Quite disturbingly, Condorcet suggests that slaves are better taken care of in slavery than they could take care of themselves. It is in their own interest to be under the protection of the free—here the French—rather than liberated. What the free owe the dependent, Condorcet adds, is not the enjoyment of rights but their well-being.

His reasoning unfolds along these lines. Granting rights to dependent individuals would make them lose the basic guarantee they have that their needs will be met by their masters.[83] In this case, the argument goes, the legislator ought to compromise between (the long game of) rights and the (urgent) safety of basic shelter and food. Slaves have their food and shelter needs provided by their master, Condorcet asserts without seeming to see how preposterous it is to claim that slaves' basic needs were met. If emancipated all at once, Condorcet argues, slaves would lose food and shelter and be therefore in a position of great vulnerability that they could not overcome through their own means. They are thus better off not being immediately emancipated.

One of the many problems in Condorcet's reasoning pertains to his confusion about the notion of dependence. Slaves are described as dependent and morally corrupt. Yet in fact, masters are the ones who are dependent on the labor of their slaves, and they are the ones who are morally corrupt, as Condorcet repeatedly notes. Agreeing with Rousseau, Condorcet argues that the condition of slavery creates the very vices that slave owners attribute to the nature of their slaves. However, while he states that the corruption of slaves is a reason to deny them freedom, he does not argue that slave owners should be deprived of citizenship rights due to their own corruption. If emancipated slaves are incapable of being

[83] Ibid., 16.

free because of their corrupt character, why are slave owners, who have proven to be corrupt beyond all measure by the very fact that they are slave owners, not deemed incapable of being free?

The problem of slavery veils the intricate problem of dependence: slaves have been made into dependents, and dependents are not immediately eligible to be free. It is easy for a republican to argue that slavery should be abolished but not so easy to know how to get rid of the dependence that muddies the emancipatory process.

WOMEN, "THE HELOTS OF THE REPUBLIC"

Contrary to the question of slavery, the emancipation of women was not discussed at the Assembly. There was no debate on the vote of women in France before the republican socialist Pierre Leroux's proposal in 1851.[84] Free women posed a distinct problem. In terms of sheer number, they were the most important group to be denied the rights to voting and holding office. On the one hand, the situation of the free women was not legally as dire as that of the slaves: they were dependent and deprived of many rights; but they were not legally owned by others. They could not be killed or tortured at will – at least not as openly as slaves could.[85] They could own property themselves.[86] But on the other hand, their dependence was barely questioned at all,[87] in sharp distinction with slaves, who had powerful and vocal advocates. Women in a sense were the utmost dependents, whose status could not be questioned because it was both so evident and assumed to be immutable.

Many arguments have been proposed to explain the subjection of women, as well as the limited success of their fights during emancipatory periods such as the Revolution. Scholarship on the role of women in the French Revolution has flourished since the bicentenary of the Revolution (1989).[88]

[84] On this question, see Mazeau and Plumauzille, "Penser avec le genre: trouble dans la citoyenneté révolutionnaire."

[85] I do not mean to deny the existence of violence (especially domestic violence) against women, but rather want to emphasize that this violence could not be committed as openly as the violence against slaves for reasons of both law and public opinion.

[86] The decree of March 15–18, 1790, gave equal rights of inheritance to children regardless of their gender.

[87] See for instance the decree of September 28, 1791, which affirmed that husbands are legally responsible for the criminal actions of their wives.

[88] Godineau, *Citoyennes tricoteuses*; Outram, *The Body and the French Revolution: Sex, Class and Political Culture*; Landes, *Women and the Public Sphere in the Age of French Revolution*; Fraisse, *Muse de la raison. Démocratie et exclusion des femmes en France*.

My goal here is not to ascribe the exclusion of women to prejudices or the slowly evolving mentality, a common perspective in historiography.[89] These explanations may be partially true, but they do not explain what is of interest to us here, that is, why republicans, who have long defended the emancipation of large groups of people, have failed to fight for the emancipation of other groups, such as women.

I argue here that, as in the case of slaves, the republicans' confused understanding of dependence made them incapable of grasping the legitimacy of the emancipatory demands of women. Women were understood as naturally dependent on men, which precluded the possibility of their emancipation. They were the quintessential example of the paradox of republican emancipation: they were recognizably unfree yet not eligible for emancipation. I track the reasoning of Condorcet and Guyomar, two republicans in favor of women's emancipation, who were still subjected to this logic.

We should first note that if they lacked male advocates at the Assembly, women were ostensibly their own advocates during the revolutionary period, as abundant scholarship on the participation of women in revolutionary activities has demonstrated.[90] Beyond the much-noted women's marches to protest the price of bread, it is now well established that they actively fought for the accession to full citizenship and voting rights.[91] Many of the societies leading the movement for women's emancipation were explicitly republican, such as the *Cercle Social,* in which Olympe de Gouges participated, and the *Société des républicaines révolutionnaires* (Society of revolutionary republican women), founded by Pauline Léon and Claire Lacombe.[92]

Precisely because of their participation in the Revolution, women were deemed dangerous and potentially hostile to the course of the Revolution as men saw it. At regular intervals, representatives at the Assembly worried about the danger constituted by the revolutionary activity of women. See for instance the Montagnard representative Fabre d'Eglantine arguing that "it is infinitely dangerous to put weapons in the hands of women who do not know how to use them and that ill-intentioned men could only benefit from."[93]

[89] Vovelle, *La mentalité révolutionnaire: société et mentalités sous la révolution française*, 285.

[90] Godineau, *Citoyennes tricoteuses*; Hunt, *The Family Romance of the French Revolution*; Landes, *Women and the Public Sphere in the Age of French Revolution*; Scott, *Only Paradoxes to Offer: French Feminists and the Rights of Man.*

[91] Godineau, *Citoyennes tricoteuses.*

[92] Guillon, "Pauline Léon, une républicaine révolutionnaire"; Kates, *The Cercle Social, the Girondins, and the French Revolution.*

[93] *AP* LXXVIII 34, October 29, 1793.

Just as with slaves, women needed to be protected against their desires to act when they do not have the knowledge necessary to act autonomously. Fabre d'Eglantine continued:

> I noticed that these female citizens who are at the head of these institutions or coalitions known as women's popular societies (*sociétés populaires de femmes*) are not mothers and family women, but female soldiers (*grenadiers femelles*), wandering knights (*chevaliers errants*), emancipated girls (*filles emancipées*). These same women who wanted to force other citizens to wear a red hat yesterday, will soon ask to wear a pistol at their belt.[94]

The failure of women's emancipation during the Revolution is most often explained by an intrinsic failure of universalism: the incapacity of revolutionaries to recognize difference. American historians and political theorists in particular have questioned the universalism of the Revolution by pointing that revolutionaries constituted a brotherly community of equal male citizens that excluded women.[95] The paradoxical dimension of republican universalism is best observed through the question of gender, and in the exclusion of women.[96] As the historian Joan Scott has argued, "their arguments were paradoxical: in order to protest women's exclusion, they had to act on behalf of women, and so invoked the very difference they sought to deny."[97]

In her famous *Declaration of the Rights of Woman and the Citizen,* Olympe de Gouges best presents the paradoxical image that Scott invokes. Mimicking the Declaration of the Rights of Man and the Citizen, Gouges asked for the universality of rights to be applied to women by presenting the *particular* case of women's rights. Gouges was adept at pointing out the relation between the *exclusion* of women from the universal and their *oppression*. In article 4, she writes that "women's exercise of her natural rights is only limited by the perpetual *tyranny* that man opposes to her." While Gouges can hardly be called a republican (she had strong sympathy for monarchy and she called for the protection of Marie-Antoinette), she used the republican idea of resistance to oppression to assert her case for women. Later, in the postface, addressing her female readers, she wrote: "Man, when enslaved, has multiplied his forces and had to use

94 Ibid.

95 Joan Scott, *Only Paradoxes to Offer: French Feminists and the Rights of Man*, 19–56. For the classical statement of the social contract as a hidden sexual contract, see Pateman, *The Sexual Contract*.

96 Mazeau and Plumauzille, "Penser avec le genre: trouble dans la citoyenneté révolutionnaire."

97 Scott, *Only Paradoxes to Offer: French Feminists and the Rights of Man*, x.

yours in order to break his shackles. Once free, he became unfair towards his female companion."

Gouges thus presented the idea of a mutual yet asymmetrical dependence between men and the women who helped them to become free. She noted a glitch in the emancipatory process: to emancipate themselves men (male human beings) relied on the work and the help of women, yet afterward were unwilling to help emancipate them in turn, *on the very grounds that women showed their subordinate status in assistant roles.* Male freedom had required the domination of women, and they were then unwilling to help emancipate the ones who made their freedom possible.[98]

It is precisely this issue of dependence that Condorcet addressed in his 1790 pamphlet on the *Emancipation of Women,* presented at the Cercle Social. Condorcet purported to argue that denying the right of citizenship to women was a tyrannical act of domination. In this short treatise, Condorcet debunked the most common arguments used for this denial – their fragile constitution, their "indispositions," their supposed lower intelligence, and so on. Condorcet's first argumentative move was to show that the entire class of women was no less diverse than that of men, and that the arguments used to disqualify them could be used to disqualify a large part of men (the poor, the ignorant, the sick, etc.). His second move was to refuse the naturalization of women's qualities in their current state: differences between men and women were socially constituted rather than natural. Condorcet was particularly concerned with the naturalization of dependence: "We cannot justify their exclusion by saying that women are dependent on their husbands, because we could destroy this tyrannical civil law at the same time. One injustice must never become a reason to commit another."[99] Condorcet's pamphlet did not resonate widely: most republican men chose to remain silent and Condorcet, picking his battles, did not push this issue much further.

In 1793, however, Pierre Guyomar took up the cause of women's emancipation, writing a short text called "The partisan of political equality between individuals, or very important problem of equality in rights and inequality in fact."[100] Contrary to what the wordplay in the title may suggest,

[98] See Landes, *Women and the Public Sphere in the Age of French Revolution.*

[99] Condorcet, *Condorcet: Political Writings*, 160. Translation modified.

[100] *Le partisan de l'égalité politique entre les individus, ou Problème très important de l'égalité en droits et de l'inégalité en fait* (1793). The wordplay is between droit/fait (theory/practice) and droits/fait (rights/fact).

Guyomar was not known for his rhetorical talents at the Convention, nor was he a particularly influential revolutionary.[101] His reasoning is important to us, though, in showing a possible path for republican feminism at the time. A representative from the Côtes du Nord at the National Convention, Guyomar's political group affiliation during the Revolution evolved, though he was mostly associated with the Girondin faction. Throughout his life, he described himself as a proponent of republican democracy.[102] Guyomar's defense focused on the notion of dependence as the key concept used to deny women full citizenship.

Guyomar argued that there was an obvious and straightforward contradiction between the universalism of the Declaration of the Rights of Man and the Citizen and the exclusion of women from the right to vote. He drew on the abolition of slavery to argue that his contemporaries should realize that there was no more difference between a white and a black man, than between a man and a woman:[103] "What! The French who abolished privileges, proclaimed everyone's opportunity to all positions according to each individual's talents, could, without the most monstruous inconsistency, set up an insulting exclusion for women?"[104]

Interestingly, Guyomar proposed a certain number of arguments that later feminists would commonly use. First is the parallel between racist and sexist exclusions. Guyomar argued that the color of skin was no more an argument for slavery than sex is an argument for exclusion of political rights. The second was a reflection on the implicit neutrality of the concept of "man" which in fact imposed the male gender on the pretension of universality. Guyomar initially noted that the mention of "homme" (man) was confusing because it does not only mean "homo" in Latin, as in "human," but also only male (as "vir" in Latin). This is why, he wrote, he preferred to use the word "individu" (*individual*), which unambiguously meant all humans.

Guyomar's reasoning stood on Rousseauian ground and showed that the relevant concept distinguishing men and women in their current social state was "dependence" rather than "difference." Relying on Rousseau's implicit authority, Guyomar stated that in the state of nature, both men and women were equal and independent. In such a state, encounters were

[101] Gainot, "Pierre Guyomar et la revendication démocratique dans les débats autour de la constitution de l'an III."

[102] Ibid.

[103] Guyomar, *Le Partisan*, 3.

[104] Ibid., 10.

random and not durable, which meant that no dependence could exist between men and women. Recall Rousseau's argument in the *Discourse on the Origin of Inequality*. In the state of nature, "inequality is scarcely perceptible and its influence there is almost nil" (*SD* 159). The absence of domination can be explained by the absence of material and psychological dependence. Ties of servitude between men and women can only exist if they have "reciprocal needs that unite them" (*SD* 159).

In the social state, however, men and women create a whole, that is to say, they have to lose their "natural independence" by subjecting themselves to "laws that guarantee equality and liberty to all individuals in the association." It is only in the social state that women became dependent on men.[105] If so, it is out of social convention and not out of biological necessity that women remain dependent. The substitution of natural independence for mutually beneficial dependence in the social contract supposes an equality that has hitherto been denied to women. The mutual dependence that is created in the social state requires equal participation in the law, that is, an equal participation in the sovereign. Women thus need to be part of the sovereign. From a republican point of view, Guyomar continues, if women do not take part in the sovereign, they are relieved from any obligation to obey its laws.[106] "Republicans obey laws that they have made themselves."[107]

In the republican tradition, as we have seen, the opposite of the free man is the slave. For Guyomar, this polarity neglects another state of unfreedom: the helot. This is, he argues, the position of women, who are the "helots of the republic": neither slave, nor free.[108]

> The era of the new order of things will keep women in the old one, and they will date from this day their name of helots of the republic; they will be unpaid servants, placed in the same rank as indentured servants of yesterday. Indeed, they have no city (*cité*); and they don't have the right to vote in primary assemblies; they are not members of the sovereign. These are two vain words for them. I observe, as a sidenote, that the name of female citizen (*citoyenne*) is thus ridiculous and should be deleted from our language.[109]

Even as he argues for women's suffrage, Guyomar takes the place of women to be within the household and in sedentary positions such as

[105] *Le Partisan*, 3 and Rousseau, *Second Discourse*, 164.
[106] *Le Partisan*, 4.
[107] Ibid., 6.
[108] Ibid., 3.
[109] Ibid., 11.

taking care of the ill in hospitals. "Woman's task is to feed and nurture young children; she takes care of the 'inside' business, while man takes care of the outside business."[110] Tasks are thus sorted out between women, who take care of the private, and men, who take care of the public.[111] Guyomar concludes: "The lifestyle of women, married or not, is and ought to be sedentary; the lifestyle of men is more active. Without inconvenience."[112]

This *difference*, however, does not impact their relative importance as members of the sovereign. It is not a difference that ought to create a dominated status: "Can there be, for a republican, more important business (*affaires*) than that of the city's (*cité*)?" Both men and women need to attend to their political duty. "The great family has to trump the smaller family of each individual; otherwise, private interest would undermine general interest."[113]

Yet Guyomar ultimately expressed doubts about the capacity of women to self-govern. Like many republicans, he was worried that newly emancipated women would not be ready for freedom. In primary assemblies, he argued, all citizens, including women, ought to deliberate and vote. However, men and women should be separated into two distinct sections. This would be, he wrote, to the advantage of women because they would be able to show men what they are capable of: they could show men that women would vote *in the same way as men did.* In the end, Guyomar took this disposition to be a security measure: "[in case of disagreement between the assembly of men and that of women], which way would the balance tilt? On the side of the section that a better education and a broader experience of public affairs have made worthy of predominance."[114] The vote of women would therefore not have equal value as men's. The role of women would be to confirm men's vote. Guyomar nonetheless concluded with an injunction: "Founders of a Republic, let's provide to the peoples of the universe the model of the purest democracy without helots."[115] Once again, fervent republicans struggled with the issue of dependence even as they intended to share freedom universally.

[110] Ibid., 12.
[111] Ibid., 13.
[112] Ibid., 12.
[113] Ibid.
[114] Ibid., 19.
[115] Ibid., 20.

GROUCHY'S FEMINIST PROPOSAL

Dependence needed to be fought – this much was certain for republicans as I have argued. Yet republicans were largely at a loss about how to proceed in response to the paradox of republican emancipation. Here I would like to suggest one avenue that has been largely unexplored: the work of Sophie de Grouchy, who addressed this problem of dependence with an original perspective. Grouchy traced the contours of what can be called a republicanism of care.[116]

Sophie de Grouchy is still not a well-known author and has been long neglected,[117] despite recent scholarship that presented and translated her work for a broad audience.[118] She is usually referred to as Condorcet's wife. A republican thinker and activist, she started the newspaper *Le Républicain* with Condorcet and Paine in July 1791. Most importantly, she wrote a book-length commentary on Smith's *Letters on Sympathy,* in which she endeavored to criticize him as well as develop political consequences for her revised understanding of sympathy.[119] In particular, she asked: what is the cause of sympathy? How can a social bond be created between citizens? Starting with an apparently moral question, she elaborated political ideas.

I argue here that in the course of her analysis of sympathy, Grouchy offered an original response to the republican paradox of emancipation. Instead of asking how the dependent can be raised to the level of independent people, she started with a different and more egalitarian premise: we all start dependent on the people who care for and raise us. Rousseau had argued that dependence should be fought as a fundamental evil. Yet, for Grouchy, dependence was not a regretful condition affecting only some of us: dependence was the basic premise of everyone's existence. She therefore reversed the republican logic. Instead of trying to make all citizens immune to dependence, she argued that we need to recognize that

[116] I agree here with Bergès. See Bergès, "Is Motherhood Compatible with Political Participation? Sophie de Grouchy's Cared-Based Republicanism."

[117] For instance, she is not part of the history of feminism (*Histoire du féminisme*) by Riot-Sarcey.

[118] Bergès, "Sophie de Grouchy and the Cost of Domination in 'The Letters on Sympathy' and Two Anonymous Articles in 'Le Républicain'"; Bergès, "Is Motherhood Compatible with Political Participation? Sophie de Grouchy's Care-Based Republicanism"; Douglass, "Egalitarian Sympathies? Adam Smith and Sophie de Grouchy on Inequality and Social Order"; Schliesser, "Sophie de Grouchy: The Tradition(s) of Two Liberties, and the Missing Mother(s) of Liberalism."

[119] Grouchy, *Letters on Sympathy*. See Bergès and Schliesser's introduction to their new translation.

we are all vulnerable and in need of gaining the conditions of our freedom and independence. Nobody, she said, is born a sovereign individual immune from dependence. The vulnerability of dependence was a universal human condition. To be born is to be dependent.

Grouchy's argument took Smith's *Theory of Moral Sentiments* as its point of departure. Like Smith, she argued that sympathy, "the disposition we have to feel in a way similar to others,"[120] to experience their pain and happiness, was universal. Contrary to Smith, however, she wondered what the origin of this fellow feeling was. Indeed, this feeling did not just occur randomly. By understanding how it was formed, one could understand why it took different intensities and focused on different objects. For Grouchy, if the capacity for this feeling was universal, its unequal presence among social classes and genders proved that it had a socially constituted origin.[121] Understanding its origin meant being able to use it for critical purposes.

Contrary to Smith, Grouchy found the origin of this feeling in the foundational experience of *being taken care of*. Since individuals learn sympathy through their relations with others (Grouchy agreed with Smith on this point), we should go back to the original experience of care. We learn sympathy from the care that we experienced from the person who fed us as a baby – a mother or a wet nurse. For Grouchy, the value that we give to this care comes from an existential and universally experienced situation: the immense dependence of the baby to its caregiver. "This particular dependence on a few individuals begins in the crib," Grouchy wrote, "it is the first tie binding us to our fellow creatures."

Reflecting on the existential dependence we share at birth, Grouchy concluded that sympathy, the "disposition we have to feel in a way similar to others," was a by-product of experiencing the emotions of others as vital to our own life: "Each person finds herself, for all necessities – her well-being and life's comforts – in a particular dependence on many others. This dependence, in truth more widespread and noticeable in childhood, persists to a certain degree with age and retains more or less strength depending on how one's moral development precludes it or allows it to subsist."[122] As babies, we intensely train in caring for the emotions of our caregivers, who are central to our survival and well-being. Being able to identify and empathize with the emotions of our caregivers is crucial to our own survival. From this original experience, sympathy grows to incorporate

[120] Grouchy, 59.
[121] Ibid., 58.
[122] Ibid., 70.

increasingly large circles of individuals. The origin of this faculty is sensitive, but its development is due to reflection. "If we observe man himself, we will recognize more easily still how he owes the greatest part of his humanity to the faculty of reflection. Indeed, one is human to the extent that one is sensitive and reflective."[123] Cognitive development is thus closely associated with the development of sympathy.

There are, however, a few conditions for the feeling of sympathy to develop, which may not be equally present for all humans. First, material existence must not be so hard in toil that it makes individuals incapable of experiencing the most basic sentiment that underlies sociability. Those whose occupations "do not leave time for reflection" will not develop compassion and their moral development will be thwarted. While the very poor initially develop sympathy, their limited cognitive development impedes their emotional development. This limitation has crucial political consequences for Grouchy:

> One of the principal aims of laws should therefore be to create and maintain equality of fortune among citizens, bringing to each without exception a degree of ease such that the anxiety caused by the constant awareness of life's necessities and whether they can be met does not render them incapable of such degree of reflection as is necessity for the perfection of all natural sentiments, and particularly that of humanity.[124]

Grouchy argued for a sufficiency threshold that would relieve caretakers from the anxiety of their own subsistence. Interestingly, she was not concerned only with the direct effect of poverty (limited time to develop cognition) but by the psychological affect that intensifies it: anxiety. Circumstances such as poverty exacerbate the deterioration of natural dependence into a detrimental and corrupting type of dependence. Grouchy perceived the devastation caused by anxiety, which directly creates a lack of self-reliance. When one has to be constantly struggling to find subsistence, one cannot acquire the kind of sensitivity that allows for the development of morality. While she did not develop the point further, Grouchy seemed to be arguing for a threshold of material resources that would allay anxiety. By connecting anxiety to the lack of self-reliance, Grouchy provided a missing link between material dependence and psychological dependence. She understood a hidden phenomenon that elitist republicans could not see.

[123] Ibid., 68. Translation modified.
[124] Ibid., 70.

Second, in addition to a subsistence threshold, she argued for a form of social equality that would reduce the economic difference between individuals. In order to feel sympathy toward others, we need to perceive them as fellow humans, whose pain we may experience ourselves. For Grouchy, we can develop sympathy only when we think we are likely to experience similar suffering as it depends on our capacity to identify with such an experience.[125] Yet the rich do not believe that they would experience the plight of the poor: they believe they literally form a different species.[126] This is a type of argument that we encounter in another feminist republican also in Paris during the Revolution: Mary Wollstonecraft. While Wollstonecraft took the rich to be pitiable as they cannot develop their moral sense due to their corrupting wealth, Grouchy took them to have a completely dulled sense of sympathy, exclaiming: "How great your need [to be educated at the school of pain and adversity], you the rich and powerful, whose health, egoism and customary power are an insuperable barrier between you and the very idea of misery and pain!"[127] The poor cannot identify with the rich either, which creates a lasting social gulf between them.[128] For the rich and the poor to feel that they belong to the same species, extensive political and economic reforms are needed.[129]

However, Grouchy did not believe that the poor would develop the sentiment of inferiority that the rich attribute to them: "In the midst of the shock of so many passions oppressing the weak and fending off the unfortunate, humanity secretly pleads for them from the depths of its heart, and seeks revenge against the injustice of fate by awaking the sentiment of natural equality in us."[130] Even if the poor do not get the sympathy of the rich, they can still enjoy the sympathy of their own caregivers, family and friends, fostering the sense of "natural equality." This belief in natural equality is the seed of the political changes that ought to occur. While Grouchy predicted these transformations, she did not offer a blueprint of the revolution.

Grouchy's understanding of dependence did not gain much traction in a context where men's reasoning took precedence. However, it is worth looking at her proposal as an untrodden path of republicanism that was articulated in this revolutionary moment. If dependence is a universal

[125] Ibid., 89.
[126] Ibid., 69.
[127] Ibid., 62. Translation modified.
[128] Ibid., 90. Grouchy's argument here differs significantly from Smith's.
[129] Ibid., Letter VIII.
[130] Ibid., 66.

state, it is not to be looked down as a lower position of mankind in which only inferior beings would find themselves. Dependence shapes us as social beings because we were all dependents until the care we received allowed us to build skills and tools of independence. This self-reliance, however, is based on the care provided by the most dependent individuals but also, arguably, the most reliable ones: women as mothers and caregivers.

CONCLUSION

Dependence, I have argued, was a central obstacle to the universalization of republican freedom. Dependents – slaves, servants, the colonized, women – were not seen fit to be free, their state of dependence being *prima facie* evidence that their claim for emancipation was illegitimate. A slippery concept, dependence was seamlessly transformed from legal subjection to lack of self-reliance, from a position of subordinated victimhood to natural incapacity. As individuals without agency, dependents embodied the paradox of republican emancipation: that only those who were already freed from social and economic dependence could be eligible to be politically free. That is: only the already free could emancipate themselves.

The attitude of republicans when faced with dependence shows the temptation to naturalize the social forces at play in creating dependence, which makes the socially constructed outcome of domination seem unavoidable and necessary. When faced with dependence, republicans wondered: should they ignore the relations of dependence and simply declare that individuals ought to be declared free regardless of the social relations in which they were entangled? This decision, however, would be only half a solution, as dependents would still be left vulnerable and only free nominally. Or should they bite the bullet, embrace elitism, and admit that only some people can be free because the condition of free citizen is a demanding one and maybe, the subordination of many is the price of the freedom of the few? Or, alternatively, should they conclude that freedom for all can exist only when these relations of dependence are eradicated, which cannot only be a legal decision, but would require a complete overhaul of social and economic relations with uncertain and formidable consequences? As this chapter has shown, French revolutionary republicans explored all three paths.

5

The Paradox of National Universalism

Since Edmund Burke's *Reflections on the Revolution in France*, French political thought has often been characterized as universalist and abstract by both admirers and detractors.[1] Burke was not among the admirers. The French revolutionary embrace of universalism, he argued in 1790, was nothing less than lunatic. Refusing to congratulate the French for their newly acquired freedom, Burke claimed that it was nonsense to "praise or blame" what "stands stripped of every relation, in all the nakedness and solitude of metaphysical abstraction."[2] The Declaration of the Rights of Man and the Citizen neatly fell in this category. "Is it because liberty in the abstract may be classed amongst the blessings of mankind, that I am seriously to felicitate a madman, who has escaped from the protecting restraint and wholesome darkness of his cell on his restoration to the enjoyment of light and liberty?"[3] Burke loathed the abstraction characterizing the French revolutionary impulse, but he was also repulsed by the founding narrative that the French chose for themselves: "Respecting your forefathers, you would have been taught to respect yourselves. You would not have chosen to consider the French as a people of yesterday, as a *nation of low-born servile wretches* until the emancipating year of 1789."[4]

[1] Jennings, "Citizenship, Republicanism and Multiculturalism in Contemporary France"; Jennings, *Revolution and the Republic. A History of Political Thought in France since the Eighteenth-Century*; Scott, *Only Paradoxes to Offer: French Feminists and the Rights of Man*; Schnapper, "L'universel républicain revisité"; Chabal, *A Divided Republic. Nation, State and Citizenship in Contemporary France.*

[2] Burke, *Reflections on the Revolution in France*, 7.

[3] Ibid.

[4] Ibid., 31. My emphasis.

Burke inaugurated the long-standing narrative of a French people in rupture with their past, a rupture which led them to a mad endorsement of abstract freedom, an irrational embrace of universalism, and a despicable identification with the low origins of their peasants. I have argued in Chapter 3 that revolutionary republicanism did not emerge from a desire to negate the past, as Burke contended, but as an attempt at adapting a rich conceptual heritage to unprecedented circumstances and demands. Abstraction and universalism were part of the response to a particular problem: expanding to all – those whom Burke calls the "low-born servile wretches" – a kind of freedom that had been initially conceptualized to fit the situation of the few. Abstraction and universalism were thus two powerful tools used by the French in their revolutionary attempt at sharing freedom.

In all his contempt for the Revolution, Burke rightly pinpointed a worrying issue haunting the French Republic to this day: the superimposition of a universal political association on an already existing nation. "You chose to act as if you had never been molded into civil society and had everything to being anew," Burke wrote.[5] But surely, Burke insisted, there was a civil society that preexisted the act of stating a new rational and contractual beginning. The act of *declaring* an absolute beginning could not magically negate the persisting presence of a historical nation, whose roots resisted the abstract will of revolutionaries.

While the circumstances of the French Revolution were highly particular, Burke's situated criticism tracked a structural problem that Rousseau had already identified. The *Social Contract* is often taken to instantiate the republican paradox of founding – how a group of individuals could become a people through an act that would require them to already have been citizens motivated to create a political community. Rousseau explicitly proposed to examine how a people is constituted: "Before examining the act by which a people elects a king, it would be well to examine the act by which a people is a people. For this act, being necessarily prior to the other, is the true foundation of society" (*SC* I.5.2).

Rousseau described how the people was produced by the social pact. The action of association, he wrote, "produces a moral and collective body." The associates "collectively assume the name of *people* and individually call themselves *Citizens* as participants in the sovereign authority" (*SC* I.6.10). Rousseau was clear that this political body had no life, no will, and no self before it was produced by the act of association.

[5] Ibid.

There are many descriptions of the paradox of founding, either as a contradictory act or a vicious circle.[6] I argued in Chapter 2 that an epistemic question was at the heart of this paradox: "how will a blind multitude, which often does not know what it wills because it rarely knows what is good for it, carry out an undertaking as great, as difficult as a system of legislation?" (*SC* II.6.10). The lawgiver was summoned by Rousseau to solve this epistemic problem, yet he appeared as an *ad hoc* fantastic solution, not an analytical response to solve the paradox.

The representatives in the 1789 French National Assembly were precisely placed in this extraordinary situation of instituting a people by drafting a constitution – a role which, it should be noted, they took for themselves as they had *not* been elected to the Estates General for that purpose. The delegates self-appointed as constitutional assembly, thereby short-circuiting the logical circle of foundation.

The main issue lay in the doubling of the people as two separate entities – a civil society with shared culture and history on the one hand, and a politically organized collective sovereign on the other. For Rousseau, the people was both the pre-existing group of individuals and the collective sovereign created by the social pact.[7] In Chapter 2 I called the former people*: a group of individuals, or rather families, connected by mores, language, territorial proximity, commerce, and other historical bonds. For Rousseau, a people united by the social pact could *only* be constituted on the basis of a pre-existing people*, a group of individuals and families connected by social bonds: "What people, then, is fit for legislation?" Rousseau asked, "One which, while finding itself already bound together by some union of origin, interest, or convention, has not yet borne the true yoke of laws" (*SC* II.10.5). Only some kinds of people* were plausible candidates to form the people of a republic.

Rousseau provided many examples of a people* as a condition of possibility for a people to be instituted. Not all peoples* are an adequate basis to create a people: they need to be youthful and docile, and not too set in their ways or corrupted beyond repair. Let us mention the Arcadians

6 Balibar, "Ce qui fait qu'un peuple est un peuple. Rousseau et Kant"; Abizadeh, "On the Demos and Its Kin: Nationalism, Democracy and the Boundary Problem"; Honig, "Between Decision and Deliberation: Political Paradox in Democratic Theory."

7 There is unfortunately no clear distinction between "people" and "nation" in Rousseau's work. Rousseau uses both terms more or less interchangeably, though he tends to use "nation" most commonly to refer to historical civil society. See for instance *SC* II.4, II.7, II.9, III.8, III.13, IV.7, IV.8 and *DPE* 6, 12, 22, 26, 28, 38.

and the Cyrenians, to whom "Plato refused to give laws" because "both peoples were rich and could not tolerate equality" (*SC* II.8.1).[8] Looking at the situation in 1789, the subjects of the King of France were a strange people*, if a people* at all. Many doubted that the different subjects in the kingdom of France were an actual nation (people*). I'll get to this point in the first section.

In this chapter, I analyze the tension caused by the conjunction, or co-development, of two phenomena: the existence (or supposition) of a historical nation, and the declaration of universalism on which the revolution based itself. The central claim of this chapter is that this tension leads to a series of exclusionary practices, that are triggered by what I call "the paradox of national universalism."

I first argue that, in the revolutionary period, nationalism and a novel form of republicanism develop at the same time. I then show how universalism gets entangled with the nationalist impulse, producing what I call national universalist logic. I further demonstrate how the three forms of universalism commonly invoked by republicans (cosmopolitanism, exemplariness, and generalization) turned into forms of exclusionary practices (respectively xenophobia, conquest, and homogenization). In order to illustrate the paradox of national universalism, I finally develop two main public policies with a long afterlife in the French republican tradition: education and civil religion.

THE BIRTH OF NATIONALISM

Situating the birth of nationalism during the Revolution is controversial, if only because it connects the rise of a highly criticized political phenomenon like nationalism with the glorious foundation myth of the French Republic. Historians of the French Revolution have been keener to see a peak of "patriotism" rather than a form of nationalism in the revolutionary period.[9] There are good reasons for this tendency. For once, patriotism is a hallmark of the republican tradition, whereas nationalism is associated with right-wing ideologies centered on protecting a homogeneous people.

Scholars specialized in the republican tradition insist on the difference between patriotism and nationalism. For Maurizio Viroli, for instance,

[8] See also *SC* II.7, II.8.2, and II.8.5.

[9] An important exception is David Bell's *The Cult of the Nation in France: Inventing Nationalism, 1680–1900*. See also Hazareesingh, *Political Traditions in Modern France*, 125.

republicans are necessarily patriots, but not nationalists.[10] A patriot celebrates "the love of the political institutions and the way of life that sustain the common liberty of a people, that is love of the republic," whereas nationalism "defends or reinforces the cultural, linguistic, and ethnic oneness and homogeneity of a people."[11] Maurice Agulhon, the canonical historian on the French republican tradition, defines nationalism as the theory that places one's own country (*la patrie*, the fatherland) as the highest political value. In this regard, patriots are not nationalists since a patriot will also value justice, right, or the interest of mankind and will not put the defense of the fatherland above them.[12] For Agulhon, nationalism precludes criticizing one's own country, whereas a patriot would criticize it if it errs away from justice. According to this view, nationalism is a form of patriotism that has lost its ethical compass.

Scholars specialized in the study of nationalism tend to see things differently. For Gellner, nationalism is "primarily the political principle, which holds that the political and national unit should be congruent."[13] Nationalism is not possible without a rise in the consciousness of an imaginary notion of "nation" that coincides with a moment of state-building. This results in the idea of "nation-state." For Gellner, these two movements (creation of the "nation" and creation of a state with the same boundaries) are also accompanied with the idea that the people in power should match the identity of the nation.

For this to happen, Gellner holds, there must be a mass of individuals who think of themselves as a "nation," supposing conditions of technology and means of communication sufficient for this widespread awareness to exist. This is why simply thinking of one's country as the best, or as the highest political value is insufficient to talk about "nationalism" per se. Scholarship around nationalism widely shares "an assumption which long went unchallenged (...) that nationalism only emerged hand-in-hand with an industrialist, capitalist 'modernity.'"[14]

Scholars of nationalism mostly converge to think of the concept of "nation" as a construct created by nationalists themselves, "stressing the element of artefact, invention and social engineering which enters into the making of nations."[15] According to this line of thought, "Nations do

10 Viroli, *For Love of Country: An Essay on Patriotism and Nationality.*

11 Ibid., 1.

12 Agulhon, "Aspects du nationalisme français," 59.

13 Gellner, *Nations and Nationalism*, 1.

14 Bell, *The Cult of the Nation in France*, 9.

15 Hobsbawm, *Nations and Nationalism since 1780*, 10.

not make states and nationalisms but the other way around."[16] Periods of intense formation of the concept of nation, and its diffusion among the people, would then mark the rise of nationalist thinking.

For these reasons, historians and political theorists tend to situate the rise of nationalism in Europe in the nineteenth century, when the technological conditions of modernity made it possible for a self-aware nation to exist. In France, at the end of the nineteenth century, nationalism took the shape of an opposition to perceived enemies of the nation from within and without, respectively the Jews and the foreigners from neighboring nations. French nationalism found its expression in "Boulangism," in the spirit of revenge against Germany and in acute antisemitism, as the Dreyfus Affair made visible.[17]

However we conceptualize nationalism – as a form of patriotism that lost its moral compass, or as the congruence of the nation and the political unit – I argue that the revolutionary period exhibited nationalist tendencies. The idea of "nation" took center stage in the discourses of revolutionaries in conjunction with the project of building a state in which this nation would be sovereign.

On June 17, 1789, the Third Estate self-declared itself "National" assembly. The discussions leading to this decision showed an oscillation between the concept of people (*peuple*) or nation. Sieyès lobbied for the awkward title of "Assembly of the known and verified representatives of the French nation," while Mirabeau and Rabaud Saint-Étienne insisted on the denomination "representatives of the French people."[18] The concepts of "nation" and "people" seemed interchangeable in this period, just like they were in Rousseau's work. Yet we can see how some thinkers, such as Sieyès, insisted on the idea of the constitution of the nation as a transposition from a historical entity into a political reality.

The idea that the French constituted a nation was certainly not born with the Revolution. We find plenty of invocations of "nations" in the eighteenth century, for instance in the writings of Montesquieu.[19] The

[16] Ibid.

[17] Agulhon, "Aspects du nationalisme français," 66.

[18] *AP* VIII 109–14, June 15, 1789.

[19] Montesquieu abundantly uses the term "nation" without defining it, as if its definition should be obvious to his readers. This is an interesting difference from other terms that he carefully defines. "Nation" seems to refer to a group of people tightly connected by mores, history and laws, though they may or not form an independent country. See for instance *SL* Preface, I.3, X.15. Montesquieu seems to use nation and people (*peuple*) interchangeably (see all of book XIV, for instance XIV.10).

word was used in a multitude of ways, often only to mean a group of individuals bound by some common local identity or common interest. Robespierre, for instance, wrote an early tract to the "Artesian nation," thereby calling the people of the northern region of Artois a "nation."[20] For many historians, there is a "national history of France before 1789,"[21] even though the idea of "nation" was not central to the self-perception of the French. Instead before the Revolution, the French felt allegiance mostly to the figure of the King, which held them all by sentiments of mutual obligations.[22] There was a French kingdom, and the French were subjects of the King, but they were not self-conscious members of a nation. Due to the connection of the people to the King, rather than to each other, the idea was widespread at the time that the French nation was not truly constituted but needed to be constructed.[23]

With the contestation of the power of the King, the political creation of the people as nation appeared a necessity in 1789.[24] In his pamphlet *What is the Third Estate?*, Sieyès defined the nation as the origin of all political powers: "The nation exists prior to everything; it is the origin of everything. Its will is always legal. It is the law itself."[25] The nation is thus at the foundation of political power and takes all the attributes of the sovereign monarch.

Sieyès was far from the only one using the concept of "nation" to give shape to the new body: the sovereign people. The dissensions created by the reunion of the Estates General showed that there was nothing obvious about *what* the nation was. In publications of the period, the undefined term "nation," having immediate political stakes, came under scrutiny. For Toussaint Guiraudet, the author of *Qu'est-ce que la nation et qu'est-ce que la France?* (1789), the French nation ought to be understood beyond divisions as "a society of about twenty-five million individuals under a constitution, or system of laws, that it gave itself, and in a space of twenty-nine thousand square *lieues*."[26] Instead of an analytical definition, Guiraudet asserted what became central to all in this

20 Anonymous [Robespierre], *A la nation artésienne. Sur la nécessité de réformer les états d'Artois*.
21 Agulhon, "Aspects du nationalisme francais," 61.
22 Wahnich, *L'impossible citoyen. L'étranger dans le discours de la révolution française*, 56.
23 Bell, *The Cult of the Nation in France*, 9.
24 I converge here with Rosanvallon's analysis in *Le sacre du citoyen: histoire du suffrage universel en France*.
25 Sieyès, *Political Writings*, 136.
26 Guiraudet, *Qu'est-ce que la nation et qu'est-ce que la France?*, 9.

period: the congruence of the French nation with its territorial limits and its state – that is, the fact that France was already a nation-state, whether or not its inhabitants were aware of it.

Yet *What is the Third Estate*'s central task was to show that the nation was not what it was taken to be – the alliance of the three estates – but that it was what it should always have been: only the productive people, that is, the third estate, the mass of peasants and workers.

> The Third Estate is a Complete Nation. What does a nation need to survive and prosper? It needs *private* employment and *public* services (...).[27] The Third Estate thus encompasses everything pertaining to the Nation, and everyone outside the Third Estate cannot be considered to be a member of the Nation. What is the Third Estate? EVERYTHING.[28]

Sieyès rewrote history to wipe out a traditional conception of the historical nation as constituted by the members of the three estates. To counteract this historical understanding, he advanced an understanding of the nation that was economic and functionalist, thereby excluding unproductive people. Yet at the same time he also defined the nation in *legal* terms: "What is a nation? It is a body of associates living under a *common* law, represented by the same *legislature*, etc."[29] The nobles were never part of the nation because, in addition to being unproductive, they held privileges and were never subjected to common law. The members of the real nation had a specific type of occupation in the economy of production; however, the concept of nation could not be a purely economic one, since it defined the agent of politics. What made the unity of the nation was its equal subjection to the law and its being a "constituent power," that is, the fundamental agent of politics: "As has been said, a nation is made *one* by virtue of a common system of law and a common representation."[30]

Sieyès therefore proposed two concurrent definitions of the nation, one as a political unit characterized by equal subjection to the common law, a unified will and a common representation on the one hand and one as an economic unit, made up of productive members on the other. Both these conceptions were exclusionary, though not on the same ground, and they both excluded the nobility.

[27] Sieyès, *Political Writings*, 94.
[28] Ibid., 98.
[29] Ibid., 97.
[30] Ibid., 99.

For revolutionaries, the question was how the historical nation inhabiting the Kingdom of France could become a people. It was not so much a theoretical question as a pragmatic one: how does one achieve such a transformation? In the years 1789–1790, the institution of the French people took the form of a transformation of their territorial organization with the distinctive goal of turning a diverse and unequal people* into a sovereign capable of governing a republic. The territorial transformation was seen as the means of achieving this goal. By getting rid of old regional institutions, the new division of territorial administration would channel the diversity of regional identities into a coherent people of free and equal citizens. In the Summer and Fall of 1789, the constitution of citizenship and the creation of new territorial circumscriptions were understood as one and the same act – shaping a nation-state.

It should be noted that the idea of redrawing the territory was not a quirk of the revolutionaries, but an older unfulfilled republican project. It is noticeable than even on this point, there is a continuity between French revolutionary republicanism and the older republican tradition. Even before the Revolution, French Republicans had assumed that the transformation of a diverse country into a republic would suppose a reorganization of its territory – a national reorganization on a universal rational basis. To mention but a few precursors of the members of the Constituent Assembly, Marquis d'Argenson had argued in favor of the division of the kingdom into departments in his work *Considérations sur le gouvernement ancien et présent de la France, comparé avec celui des autres Etats,* published in 1764.[31] Condorcet had suggested drawing rational and balanced boundaries to districts for different levels of local and regional assemblies in his 1788 *Essay on the Constitution and Function of Provincial Assemblies.*[32]

Different factors rendered a territorial revamping necessary even to those who were not committed to the republican cause. In the words of Charles de Calonnes, General Controller to Louis XVI in 1783:

> France is a kingdom composed of regions with their own assemblies (*pays d'Etats*) and regions with mixed administration (*pays d'administration mixte*), where provinces are foreign to one another, where multiple internal barriers separate

[31] *D'Argenson, Considérations sur le gouvernement. A Critical Edition, with Other Political Texts.*

[32] Condorcet, Essai sur la constitution et les fonctions des Assemblées provinciales, 33–41 (Article II "Des différents ordres d'assemblées").

and divide the subjects of the same sovereign, where some counties are exempt from the taxes that others bear to their full extent, where the wealthiest class contributes the least, where privileges break all balance, where it is impossible to have any constant rule nor common wish. It is a very imperfect kingdom, full of abuses, that it is impossible to govern well.[33]

No wonder then that revolutionaries prioritized the "new division of the kingdom" from the summer of 1789 till the spring of 1790. The Girondin Jacques Guillaume Thouret took the head of the Committee in charge of drafting a proposal for this new division. For Thouret, the task of setting the constitution amounted to "reconstructing and regenerating the State."[34] This task demanded for each representative to think of themselves as "a part of the whole, the nation as a whole" and not as the representative of one particular village or province or particular interest.[35]

In order to have a rational electoral system, with an equal number of electors in different departments, it was important to have a well-balanced division in contrast with the huge disparities of territorial size and population in the *Ancien Régime*. The so-called "provincial spirit" was standing in the way of the realization of a new people. The regeneration of the State demanded the shaping of new citizens devoid of particular affiliations, the creation of a nation without local allegiances.[36]

THE NATIONAL UNIVERSALIST LOGIC

In Chapter 3 I argued that universalizing freedom had been a central concern of the revolutionaries. Universalism was, however, a highly ambiguous project, with different and sometimes incompatible injunctions. I illustrate here the three types of universalism that I see at play in republican discourses: cosmopolitanism, exemplariness, and generalization. I show how each of these universalisms led to a specific form of exclusion (respectively, xenophobia, conquest, and homogenization) as it combined with the development of nationalism in the period. I call the consolidation of nationalism through a universalist discourse the "national universalist logic." I then propose to look at the 1789 Declaration of the Rights

[33] Quoted in Brette, *Les limites et les divisions territoriales de la France en 1789*, 59–60.

[34] *AP* IX 654, November 3, 1789.

[35] Ibid.

[36] On the importance of the project of regeneration, see Ozouf's article on "Régénération" and Duong, "The People as a Natural Disaster: Redemptive Violence in Jacobin Political Thought."

of Man and such Citizen as an example of the national universalist logic. I argue that universalism served, within the discourse of human rights, as a means to lend legitimacy to the constitution of the French nation.

From Cosmopolitanism to the Exclusion of Foreigners and Minorities

Among the dimensions of republican universalism, the most striking, though not the most widespread, was cosmopolitanism.[37] Anarchasis Cloots, a Prussian radical who had been naturalized in 1792 and elected to the Convention, defended the idea of a universal republic, that is, a republic that would span the whole globe, and rely on "the sovereignty of the human race."[38] Cloots defended his project in a long-winded discourse at the Convention in April 1793.[39] To rebut the suspicion that he was encouraging the annexation of the rest of the world by the French army, he suggested to get rid of the name "French" and call the republic "universal" (*république universelle*). The role of the French was only to open the road to freedom. In good republican fashion, he invoked a comparison with the Romans, yet, this time, in favor of the French: "The Roman people strived to perpetuate the slavery of the universe; the French people will take care of the means to perpetuate universal freedom."[40] Cloots was explicitly trying to find a solution to the military instability of small republics (which Montesquieu had already noted): contrary to a small state, a universal republic would be at peace by necessity. As a universal republic, France would not continue the republican tradition of incessant war; it would inaugurate a political world in which universal freedom would encounter universal peace.

Yet, if we look at Cloots' speech in its context as transcribed in the Parliamentary Archives, Cloots' isolation becomes obvious. During his presentation he was taunted and mocked by other representatives, who asked whether he wanted to connect the Earth to the Moon,[41] repeatedly wondered whether the universal republic could be voted up and urged him to shut up.[42] Cloots' version of cosmopolitanism was perceived as neither realistic nor desirable by his peers.

[37] Di Lorenzo and Ferradou, "The Early Republic of France as a Cosmopolitan Moment."

[38] *AP* LXIII 390. In 1790, Jean-Baptiste Cloots got rid of his Christian surname to take a Greek one. See Soboul, "Anarchasis Cloots, l'orateur du genre humain."

[39] *AP* LXIII 389, April 26, 1793.

[40] Ibid.

[41] *AP* LXIII 393.

[42] *AP* LXIII 397.

A less divisive cosmopolitan project was to offer French citizenship to foreigners who had distinguished themselves as freedom fighters. On August 24, 1792, the representative Marie-Joseph Chénier proposed such a motion:

> When the National Convention will elevate the French Constitution to the level of the Declaration of Rights, all those who, across the world, have cultivated human reason and paved the way of freedom must be considered allies of the French people (...). Let us give to virtues, talents and love of freedom an illustrious and worthy reward and let us proclaim the benefactors of mankind French citizens.[43]

For Chénier, this motion would imitate the Romans who gave citizenship to their worthy allies. It should be noted that the session of the Assembly did not go entirely smoothly that day. Two other representatives, Chabot and Lasource, were swift to remind everyone that the Romans "lost their freedom for having been too generous in giving citizenship to neighboring peoples." The example of the Romans served as a warning against an expanding republic more than a model of stability.

On August 26, 1792, the Legislative Assembly declared that "since men who have served the cause of freedom by their written works and their courage and prepared the emancipation of peoples cannot be considered foreigners (*étrangers)* by a nation made free by its own light and courage," they "grant the French citizenship" to illustrious freedom fighters, including "Joseph Priestley, Thomas Payne (sic), Jérémie Bentham, William Wilberforce, Thomas Clarkson, Jacques Mackintosh, David Williams, N. Gorani, Anarchasis Cloots, Corneille Paw, Joachim-Henry Campe, N. Pestalozzi, Georges Washington, Jean Hamilton, N. Madison (sic), H. Klopstock and Thadée Kosciuzko."[44]

The decision to grant these naturalizations was certainly self-aggrandizing. As in the case of the emancipation of slaves in Saint-Domingue, French representatives sought to appropriate successful fights for freedom all over the world. The logic of these naturalizations was however more than a quest for glory. It relied on a specific definition of citizenship as grounded in the will. Freedom fighters could not be considered foreigners, the argument goes, because their private will aligned with the general will, that is, the defense of freedom. The logic here was one of indefinite inclusion overcoming the boundaries of the historical nationhood.

[43] *AP* XLVIII 689, August 24, 1792.

[44] *AP* XLIX 10, August 26, 1792. All the spellings are original.

Cosmopolitanism appeared inclusive – *whoever is a republican by will is part of the nation (i.e., regardless of their place of birth, race, kinship, culture, birth tongue)*. Yet the reverse applied, and this is where the inclusive logic turned into exclusion: *whoever is not a republican cannot be part of the nation (regardless of their place of birth, race, kinship, culture or mother tongue)*. All those whose private will did not align with the general will, as understood by revolutionaries, were denied belonging to the nation – regardless of their previous belonging to the historical nation. Consider the following statement by Robespierre: "Social protection is due only to peaceful citizens; there are no citizens but republicans in the Republic. Royalists and conspirators are foreign to it, or rather they are enemies."[45]

The friend/enemy logic inhabited the violent movement of a Republic at war pushed to its utmost limits. I will not ponder over this aspect of the Terror here, as it has been studied at length.[46] The Law of Foreigners of 26 Germinal Year II completed the movement of inclusion/exclusion of this period. On the one hand, in the name of universal hospitality, foreigners could stay on French soil as guests. On the other, they had to wear an armband with the words "HOSPITALITY" signaling their difference as foreigners.

This type of movement belongs to what I call the "national universalist logic": the imposition of universal rules that tends to restrain the boundaries of the national body in order to make it coincide with the state. The situation after 1792 can be explained in great part by the war, which put a tremendous pressure on the republican government. There were, however, earlier signs of the same national universalist logic in 1789. The discussion of the summer of 1789 over freedom of religion exposed the same tension between universalism and nationalism: should those who had been historically excluded from the nation – the Protestants – benefit from the universal protection of religious freedom? Rabaut Saint-Etienne, a representative to the Constituent Assembly and a Protestant leader, successfully argued that it would be too much of a contradiction if they did not.

The discussion on religious minorities resumed on December 23, 1789 over the rights of Jews to apply to municipal and provincial functions as well as civil and military jobs just like the other citizens. The response of

45 Robespierre, "On the Principles of Political Morality," Discours du 17 Pluviôse An II [February 5, 1794], in Robespierre, *Œuvres complètes* t. X, 353.

46 Wahnich, *L'impossible citoyen. L'étranger dans le discours de la révolution française.*

Clermont-Tonnerre remains famous as a landmark in the history of Jews in France. His argument is also symptomatic of the national universalist logic. Clermont-Tonnerre argued that the current segregated situation of Jews in France was due to the laws that excluded them and forced them into some professions by barring them from exercising many other professions. Clermont-Tonnerre was not a republican; coming from old aristocracy, he was a monarchist, though a freemason with liberal leanings. His argument was the same as Robespierre's, as I argued in Chapter 3: one should not blame a minority for a behavior that was caused by its persecution. Clermont-Tonnerre concluded: "We must deny the Jews everything as a nation and grant them everything as individuals (...). They must not constitute a political body or order within the state."[47]

Clermont-Tonnerre's affirmation of the integration of Jews within the common law articulates a form of national universalism. It is only if Jews do not form a separate *nation* that they can be regular citizens to whom laws apply universally. They must be individually integrated within the body of the nation so that their religious particularity not threaten the homogeneity of the nation. Universalism can work only within the contours of national homogeneity.

In the minds of revolutionary representatives, foreigners recalled the possibility of intermediary bodies, factions, and societies within society that would prevent the general will to be expressed. What also appears in these examples was that the "particular" was perceived as particular only when characterizing a minority. The protestant and the Jew were potentially foreigners from within because they belonged to minority religious communities; but Catholics could not plausibly be considered foreigners because their community was the same as the majority.

An unpleasant conclusion can be drawn from observing the discussions of the nascent republic: the general argument (particularities destroy the republic) applies only to minorities, or those perceived as minorities – such as Protestants and Jews – because, in the perception of the majority, minorities threaten national unity. Particularities of the majority – for example, being Catholic – are not deemed particular: they define the "national," that is, the universal. The circle of national universalism is thus perfected and the paradox of national universalism emerges: Only those who are part of the historical nation can follow universal principles.

[47] *AP* X 756.

From Exemplarity to Conquest

Many republican revolutionaries thought that the idea of a universal republic in the style of Anarchasis Cloots was complete nonsense – impractical and undesirable. For many republicans, universalism should simply not take the form of cosmopolitanism. Rather they thought that France's republicanism was universal because it was *exemplary*: it gave the other people of the earth a model that they could emulate and achieve by themselves on their own terms within the confines of their history and territory. This form of republican universalism was probably the most widespread in the revolutionary period. I already invoked Robespierre and Saint-Just who often mentioned the glory of France as a model for oppressed people. See also the discourse of François Robert, which immediately preceded Cloots' presentation on the Conventional session of April 26, 1793.[48] Robert started by rejecting the mandate of a universal republic:

> We are not the representatives of the human race, we are not the representatives of savages [*sauvages*], we are not even the representatives of other policed nations [*nations policées*]. Let us not lose sight of our mission which is to represent the French people, and this is far enough for our glory! I want the lawgiver [*législateur*] of France to forget the universe for one moment and to be concerned only with their country (...). I want this type of national selfishness without which we would betray our duties (...). I love all men; I particularly love all free men; but I prefer the freemen of France over all the other men in the universe.[49]

While Robert rejected Cloots' cosmopolitan universalism, he argued that setting an example for the universe was the path to glory, this old republican ideal I presented in Chapter 1. Glory could be attained if the French focused on themselves and consolidated a "free and republican constitution based on the immutable principles of reason and eternal justice." By doing this, Robert argued, the French provided the "first stone of a durable monument for future generations and distant posterity."[50] This guidance, Robert insisted, was not quite the same as in previous republican traditions: the Romans and the Spartans had slaves whereas "now everything is different, and the great book of equality is open."[51] French republicanism offered a new type of political possibility – an expansive

[48] *AP* LXIII 385–90, April 26, 1793. In Chapter 3, I presented Robert as a committed republican very early in the revolutionary process.

[49] *AP* LXIII 385.

[50] Ibid.

[51] *AP* LXIII 386.

and egalitarian type of republicanism: sharing freedom with all fellow citizens.

The idea that the French Republic was guiding the world was shared by most, if not all, revolutionaries. However, just like in the previous type of universalism, the logic of inclusion reversed into exclusion under pressure of circumstances. From the goal of exemplarity came the related project of helping other countries liberate themselves and create their own free republics. From there, it was but a small step to expand military forces beyond the national boundaries.

On November 19, 1792 "the Convention declared in the name of the French nation that it will grant fraternity and aid to all peoples who wish to recover their liberty."[52] This declaration was fundamentally ambiguous. On that day, representatives wondered if France should "protect" these people, "reunite them" to the French Republic, and how this fraternal aid would be compatible with the respect of "the sovereignty of these peoples."[53] Others suggested that the aid to neighboring peoples was a way to constitute "a belt of free peoples around France" to protect its political position.[54] Representatives – all republicans at that time – sensed the deep ambiguity of a military invasion of a foreign country to help emancipate its inhabitants. How could "the sovereignty of the people" be ensured? What about the role, duty, and interests of the liberating nation? How would France be compensated for the expenses that inevitably would come with that military help?

The decree of December 15, 1792 suppressed this ambiguity and provided some answers to these questions. From a vague principle of fraternity, the Convention moved to the declaration that the revolutionary army should impose its principles on its conquered territories in the very name of their liberation. "The peoples to which the armies of the [French] Republic brought freedom do not have the necessary experience to set their rights. We need to declare revolutionary government and destroy the old regime that kept them subjugated."[55] What matters here is that instead of waiting for the local inhabitants to act as liberated people, the French army should impose its order and principles: "If we are a revolutionary power, everything that is contrary to the rights of people has to be destroyed as soon as we enter in the country [Clapping]; therefore we

[52] *AP* LIII 474, November 19, 1792.

[53] *AP* LIII 472–73.

[54] *AP* LIII 475.

[55] *AP* LV 71, December 15, 1792. Cambon speaking.

have to proclaim our principles, destroy all tyrannies and nothing that existed before will survive the power that we exercise."[56] In the word of the historian Lynn Hunt, "the French started the war in a spirit of self-defense that rapidly morphed into a war of liberation and then a war of conquest and occupation."[57]

By 1792, France started revolutionary wars, which had a long life as the republic gave way to Napoleon's power and his urge for conquest. The revolutionary wars to "help" the bordering nations to access to republicanism effectively led to the creation of protectorates, or client states. What started as a project to help liberate other peoples from oppression turned into a campaign for the benefit of France. From 1792 till the Napoleonic Empire, the exemplarity of republican France and its desire to grant fraternity to neighboring people seeking emancipation turned into a quest for glory, power, and conquest. While it is possible here to see only a mere expression of national self-interest, this period can, and in my view should also, be interpreted as an ambivalence of the French Republic towards the martial spirit that existed in the republican tradition, for instance in Machiavelli's work, as I argued in Chapter 1.

From Generalization to Homogenization

Thus far, I have discussed two types of universalism: cosmopolitanism and exemplarity. Yet the process of universalizing did not necessarily entail international politics. It also meant spreading, generalizing, and equalizing principles within the French territory. It was an eminently domestic process through which the diversity of the *Ancien Régime* was eradicated in order to give place to common and equal law.

By the same token, generalization implied homogenization, as it meant reducing the particularities that prevented the application of the same laws and principles to all. This process arguably spanned the whole revolutionary period over all policies and administration. Let me give one example of universalization as homogenization that proved an enduring concern for republicans: language.

In the summer of 1790, Abbé Grégoire started a survey of language use in the different regions of France.[58] While his survey does not meet today's

[56] *AP* LV 71.

[57] Hunt, "The French Revolutionary Wars."

[58] De Certeau, Julia, and Revel, *Une politique de la langue. La révolution française et les patois: l'enquête de Grégoire.*

methodological standards, he still received forty-nine answers coming from a range of different places throughout France. The survey tried to determine how different the "patois" (regional languages) were from French, how many variations were used, whether standard French was spoken in the provinces, what was the level of literacy of locals, and so on. The analysis of these data led him to publish a report whose goal was clearly set in the title: *Report on the necessity and the means to eliminate all local languages [patois] and universalize the use of the French language.*[59] Universalism required the eradication of all different local and regional languages.

Grégoire was concerned that only a small minority of French (3 million over 25 million) exclusively spoke the national language whereas over 6 million French people had no knowledge of it. His survey made clear what was already well known. One main obstacle to the consolidation of the French nation was the lack of a common language. Most of them, in fact, spoke another language in their daily life, and used French only occasionally for administrative purposes. Many of them did not understand or speak French at all. The creation of the nation therefore required the destruction of regional allegiances and the restriction of minority languages. Having French as a universal language, Grégoire thought, would strengthen the nation and make it into a nation-state for good.

The process of universalization of French was also necessitated for Grégoire for republican reasons, and not simply for national(ist) ones: if citizens did not know how to speak, read, and write French, they would be incapable of understanding the laws of the Republic and participating in the law-making process. In his *Rapport du Comité de salut public sur les idiomes,* presented a few months before Grégoire's *Report*, Barère had followed a similar reasoning. He accused all local languages, from *basque* to *bas -breton*, of fostering ignorance and anti-republicanism:

> A monarchy has to look like a Tower of Babel. There is only one language for the tyrant: the language of force to gain obedience and the language of taxation to gain money. In a democracy, by contrast, each citizen is in charge of keeping the government in check. In order to be able to do this, they have to know this government, and, above all, know the language it uses.[60]

As Barère summarized his point, the republic needed linguistic homogeneity: "Citizens! The language of a free people has to be one and the same for all."

[59] 16 Prairial An II, June 4, 1794, *AP* XCI 318–26.

[60] Barère, "Rapport du Comité de Salut Public sur les Idiomes," January 27, 1794 [8 pluviôse Year II], *AP* LXXXIII, 715–16. Barère here uses democracy and republic interchangeably.

It should be noted that on the language issue, revolutionaries oscillated between two opposed policies: on the hand, translations that would make it immediately possible for all non-French speaking citizens to know the law, and on the other, the enforcement of French as a universal language. The first path was pursued during the first years of the Revolution. On December 12, 1792, the Convention passed a decree mandating the translation of laws into "German, Italian, Castillan, Basque and Bas-Breton."[61] Yet the theoretical and practical arguments against the politics of translation abounded. Ultimately, the republican consensus became that the imposition of French as a universal language was necessary to shape a homogenous nation. In a circular of the Committee of Public Safety, published on June 16, 1794, we read that: "In the one and indivisible Republic, there ought to be but one language. The variety of dialects is federalism: it is the spring of tyranny; we must break it entirely or malevolent use would be made of it."[62]

To make sure that there would be only one language in the Republic, the circular proclaimed the necessity to appoint an elementary school teacher speaking French in each village where the locals spoke *patois*. Here again we can note how a paradox is generated: only those who belong to the nation (by speaking French, the common language of the nation) can be considered republican. That is to say: to access the universal (of the Republic), one must behave according to the imposed particular (of the nation).

The National Universalist Logic

Let me now develop the most striking example of the national universalist logic at play in this period: the Declaration of the Rights of Man and the Citizen (August 4, 1789). Before drafting the new Constitution, representatives in the Constituent Assembly wondered whether they should draft a declaration of rights as a preliminary to the Constitution. The Americans had given a great model, but the French wanted to move from a regional to a universal model. In the words of the representative Mathieu de Montmorency: "Let us follow the example of the United States: they have set a great example in the new hemisphere; let us give one to the universe, let us offer a model worthy of admiration."[63] The

[61] *AP* LV 17.
[62] June 16, 1794 (28 Prairial Year II).
[63] *AP* VIII 320, August 1, 1789.

French should do better than the regional example given by the American Revolution and Constitution.

The Declaration of Rights is often taken to embody the universal ambition of the French Revolution. The Declaration also shows how universalism is entangled with the construction of a nation. In 1789, the function of the Declaration of Rights was not primarily to offer a standard to assess the constitution of all nations, as it came to be understood in the twentieth century, but as a principle of legitimacy for the creation of the French State. The ambivalence between universalism and nationalism can be seen in the very title of the Declaration of the Rights of *Man and the Citizen,* which leaves open to interpretation which rights belong to man and which to the citizen, or to what extent these two categories overlap.

The rights of man and the citizen thus play a primary role in the foundation of the French nation. Rather than giving principles to other nations, the Declaration was "about a whole people incorporating itself in a state."[64] As many scholars have noted, the Declaration of Rights used universality for the national purpose of constituting a nation-state.[65] Article 2 unambiguously stated that "the aim of every political association is the preservation of the natural and imprescriptible rights of *man,*" and Article 3 proclaimed that "the principle of any Sovereignty lies primarily in the *Nation.*"

The discussion about drafting a preamble to the Constitution started on August 1, 1789. The representative inaugurating the debate, a delegate from Vendômes called Crénière, expressed the idea that the "constitution of the people" came from "the natural and imprescriptible rights that are anterior to positive laws."[66] For this reason, there was no meaningful difference between legitimate constitutions and the rights of man: "We can see, thanks to this simple and true definition, that what the French ask is not new. All the people have the same constitution, whether implicit or explicit, because they all have the same rights. These rights come from nature and no power, no will can take them away from them."[67] In this reasoning, the enterprises of constitutional state-building and universalism are not distinct. Importantly, nature is what gives the

[64] Moyn, *The Last Utopia: Human Rights in History*, 26.

[65] Baker, *Inventing the French Revolution*, 127; Edelstein, *On the Spirit of Rights*, 179; Moyn, *The Last Utopia: Human Rights in History*, 26.

[66] *AP* VIII 318.

[67] Ibid.

foundational basis to affirm this universality of rights and political principles.[68] Crénière continued: "The act of the constitution of the French people, expressing these incontestable principles, will necessarily be the natural code of all the societies of the universe."[69]

The confusion implicit in national universalism was perhaps best perceived by royalist representatives at the Constituent Assembly on the opening day of discussion on the preamble on August 1, 1789.[70] The "Monarchien" Malouet described a declaration of rights as an abstraction denying the distance between a real existing people – the French – and an ideal nonexistent people.[71] Imitating the Americans was a terrible mistake, he claimed. They were not proposing an adequate model for the constitution of an old nation like France. They did not have a diverse society but one that could easily be shaped by a new and abstract constitution:

> I know that the Americans have not taken similar precautions; they took man from the bosom of nature and presented him to the universe in all his primitive sovereignty. But American society, newly formed, is entirely composed of landowners already accustomed to equality, strangers to luxury as well as to poverty, barely acquainted with the yoke of taxes or the prejudices that dominate us, having found on the land that they cultivate no trace of feudalism. Such men were without doubt prepared to receive liberty in all its vigor: for their tastes, their customs, their position called them to democracy.[72]

For Malouet, a declaration of rights, by negating the existence of a people full of dependents, was criminal in neglecting to take into consideration the reality of dependence: "But we, Sirs, we have for fellow citizens an immense multitude of men without property who expect above all their subsistence from guaranteed labor, a just system of rules and continual protection."[73] For Malouet, the greatest objection to an abstract declaration was the material reality of a vast people of dependents, who would not be better off when declared all political equal.

[68] For reasons of space and focus, I have not analyzed the relation of French republicanism to the notion of "nature" and "natural rights." For an in-depth analysis, see Edelstein, *The Terror of Natural Right. Republicanism, The Cult of Nature and the French Revolution.*

[69] *AP* VIII 318.

[70] See also the reaction of the conservative representative Lally-Tolendal, in *AP* VIII 222.

[71] For a further analysis of Malouet's thought (from a perspective quite different from mine) and a presentation of Monarchiens' views, see Craiutu, *A Virtue for Courageous Minds*, 69–108.

[72] *AP* VIII 322.

[73] Ibid.

If the first level of national universalism was the use of universalism for nation-building readily expressed by the Declaration of Rights, the second level was the confusion between the national subject and the citizen, that is, the confusion between the national community of dependent people and the political community of abstract citizens.

The national universalism of the Republic took form around a basic and inescapable problem, the dual existence of the people in a republic: as a people and as a nation; as members of the universal and members of a historical community. The preliminary discussions on the Declaration of Rights abounded in references to Rousseau's *Social Contract* and in particular to the question of the institution of the people. For the representatives of the Constituent Assembly, Rousseau's discussion of the paradox of founding (*SC* I.5.2) was not philosophical speculation but an analysis of the very problem they were facing: whether a particular people that already exists can be instituted anew on a universal basis. And if it could be instituted anew, how?

EDUCATION

The national universalist logic at play in revolutionary discourses found an institutionalization in two public policies that durably defined French republicanism: public education and civil religion. How to institute a republican people? How to shape a nation? Revolutionaries across the political spectrum agreed on at least a central part of the answer: the necessity of mass public education. As the historian David Bell has argued, this was a completely new project revealing the birth of nationalism in France.[74] Indeed, even Louis XIV, who had great ambitions for France, would not have dreamt of shaping his subjects and was content with them simply obeying and paying taxes. Nationalism and republicanism converged into the realization of a massive public policy project that monarchy could not have achieved.

First, on the republican side, revolutionaries perceived education as the most straightforward solution to the paradox of emancipation, as I presented it in Chapter 4: how could the mass of the people be emancipated when they were ignorant, dependent, and lacking virtuous devotion to the republic? In the republican tradition, education had always been seen as necessary to shape the republican elite. The exemplary citizen of the Roman Republic needed be educated in the art of rhetoric to acquire

[74] Bell, 8.

virtue and knowledge.[75] In the modern democratic republic, education was tasked to answer the three challenges articulated by Montesquieu – unity, motivation, knowledge. Education could *unite* citizens through shared habits and a shared culture; it could instruct them to become *virtuous* and *epistemically competent* citizens. Education appeared as the solution to the problem of the large republic: it could create the missing citizen elite in France and provide a broad basis of devoted patriots.

On the nationalist side, education was the perfect place to strengthen the construction and self-awareness of a national identity in a people with so many languages and customs. Schools would be the place where peasants could be turned into Frenchmen, where an army of devoted soldiers could be created, and where the union of the citizen and the French national could be realized. Public education, therefore, was from the start a very complex matter, where all the republican ambivalence towards nationalism was expressed.

Revolutionary events created an immediate crisis of education. Until then, the basic schooling needs of the poor had been provided by village priests, who were the *de facto* teachers in rural areas. With the "civil constitution of the clergy" in 1790, that is the subordination of the Church to the State which provoked the defection of many priests, schools became deprived of their most fundamental teaching staff. Whatever public education would look like, an "army" of new teachers would need to be recruited. The very goals of education became a topic of debate. On the one hand, revolutionaries needed to negotiate the transition from elite private education to mass public education. The increase of scale was not simply quantitative – it required a transformation of the nature of education. On the other hand, republicans had to determine which goals education was to achieve and in what order of priority. Education was, from the start, the place where the republic was to define itself – it was therefore, essentially, a battle ground between conflicting interpretations of the republic.

In any case, the republicans needed a plan. On this topic as on so many others, revolutionaries tried to find guidance in the writings of the illustrious Jean-Jacques. In his treatise on education, *Émile,* Rousseau had noted the fundamental problem that would preoccupy the French revolutionaries. On the one hand, if education's goal was to help the individual become autonomous, it should foster independence and teach self-reliance and critical thinking. In Rousseau's words, education should

[75] Kapust, "Cicero on Decorum and the Morality of Rhetoric"; Rousselière, "*Audi Alteram Partem*: Rhetoric and Republican Political Thought."

raise a man. On the other hand, if education's goal was to form a citizen, it should emphasize obedience to the political tenets of one's community and the development of political virtue. If "natural man is entirely for himself," "civil man is only a fractional unity dependent on the denominator; his value is determined by his relation to the whole, which is the social body" (*E* 39–40). Trying to do both at once, Rousseau warned, would be a catastrophe. What would happen "when, instead of raising a man for himself, one wants to raise him for others? Then their harmony is impossible. Forced to combat nature or the social institutions, one must choose between making a man or a citizen, for one cannot make both at the same time" (*E* 39).[76]

The duality of the goal – becoming a man or becoming a citizen – was doubled by the duality of citizenship itself for Rousseau. Becoming a citizen means two different things at once: a citizen is one who follows the general will, but, as I have argued in Chapter 2, the general will is always the expression of a particular community for Rousseau, which means that the citizen is he who follows the will of his particular political community. The citizen is therefore subject to the rule of the social contract and his particular nation. The citizen, for Rousseau, is never a citizen in the abstract: he is the citizen of a particular society. In words that the Jacobins would not repudiate, Rousseau noted: "Every particular society, when it is narrow and unified, is estranged from the all-encompassing society. Every patriot is harsh to foreigners. They are only men. They are nothing in his eyes. This is a drawback, inevitable but not compelling. The essential thing is to be good to the people with whom one lives" (*E* 39).

The idea of particular national belonging may be compatible with republican citizenship (as it was in Rome or Sparta for Rousseau), but in most cases, and certainly in modern cities, there is no compatibility. Meet the bourgeois: "Always in contradiction with himself, always floating between his inclinations and his duties, he will never be either man or citizen. He will be good neither for himself, not for others. He will be one of these men of our days: a Frenchman, and Englishman, a bourgeois. He will be nothing" (*E* 40). Rousseau describes civil

76 Classical formulations of this thesis can be found in Shklar, *Men and Citizens* and Melzer, *The Natural Goodness of Man*. For the argument that Rousseau aims to provide an education to both autonomy and citizenship in *Émile*, see Oprea, "Rousseau's *Émile:* Education for Citizenship by Consent" in *Children or Citizens: Children, Education, and Politics in Modern Political Thought.*

man – the man in society who does not have the citizen's ethos – as a bourgeois, that is, a man in contradiction with himself. If civil man could somehow be at the same time a citizen, the conflict would be alleviated. Yet it remains unclear how the citizen and the man can be aligned. To know what the goal of education should be requires that three terms be considered: natural man, civil man (the bourgeois), and the citizen.

To make things even more complicated, Rousseau does not propose any blueprint for a republican public education in *Émile*: "Public instruction no longer exists and can no longer exist, because where there is no longer a fatherland, there can no longer be citizens. These two words, *fatherland* and *citizen,* should be effaced from modern languages" (*E* 40). For revolutionaries interested in instituting public education from scratch, Rousseau's guidance in the enigmatic *Émile* was simply unhelpful.[77]

The revolutionaries nonetheless tried to imagine plans for public education. Amid military wars with the whole of Europe, complete administrative overhaul, internal dissent and even civil war, they never ceased to develop educational projects in surprisingly high numbers.[78] Among those, the most notable ones were written by Mirabeau (1791), Talleyrand (1791), Condorcet (1792), Romme (1792), Rabaut Saint-Étienne (1792), Daunou (1793), Lepeletier (1793), and Lakanal (1795). All these plans varied along lines of obligation (should schools be mandatory? Until what age?), cost (should education be free?), gender accessibility (should girls have the same education as boys?), and the relative importance of religion and moral education. Most importantly they disagreed on the goals of education: whether it should prioritize the autonomy of the person, the political shaping of the citizen, or the modelling of the ideal French national.

The two most important plans, Condorcert's and Le Peletier's, showed the republican oscillation between the goals of individual emancipation and nation-building in the revolutionary period. I suggest here that the national universalist logic trapped both of them albeit for opposite reasons – Condorcet's plan got rejected for being insufficiently sensitive to

77 I argue elsewhere that *Émile* proposes an education to private independence in order to cope with living in modern societies. This education, however, is only accessible to the few. See Rousselière, "Rousseau on Freedom in Commercial Society."

78 Baczko, *Une éducation pour la démocratie. Textes et projets de l'époque révolutionnaire*, 10.

the demands of nation-building, whereas Le Peletier's almost entirely lost track of individual emancipation.

After rejecting Talleyrand's plan for its excessive emphasis on religion, the Legislative Assembly commissioned the Committee on Public Instruction, comprising Condorcet, Lacépède, Arbogast, Pastoret and Romme, to elaborate a new plan for education. Condorcet, the best qualified for that assignment, had already published his *Mémoires sur l'Instruction Publique* in 1790, and had the most important role in the redaction of the draft. The "Condorcet Plan" had the bad fortune of being reported to the Legislative Assembly in April 1792 at the outbreak of the war with Austria. The urgent military situation completely eclipsed the discussions on education for a few months.

Condorcet proposed an ambitious emancipatory goal for his education plan: "provide all humans with the means of satisfying their needs, ensuring their well-being, knowing and exercising their rights (...) and duties, as well as give to each the capacity to perfect their skills, become capable of exercising social functions (...), and develop their talents (...)." Such a program of education would "make the political equality proclaimed by the law real."[79] Contrary to Talleyrand, Condorcet did not believe religious education should take place in schools, and insisted on the importance of grounding all education on scientific truth.[80]

Two distinct motivations framed the Condorcet Plan. First, it aimed at alleviating domination by providing everyone with the basic knowledge necessary to exercise their rights. Second, it aimed at improving knowledge in all sciences for the common benefit of mankind. These two goals were not opposed to one another, yet they were also importantly distinct: the former concerned primary school, the mass, and individual emancipation; the latter concerned institutions of higher education, a refined elite, and the collective improvement of mankind. The tension between these two goals created intense hostility toward Condorcet's proposal.[81]

A key feature of the Condorcet Plan was the elaboration of different levels of instruction from elementary schools (the universal level) up to a learned society of Arts and Sciences (a rarefied level).[82] In his

79 Condorcet, "Rapport et projet de décret sur l'organisation générale de l'instruction publique," 181.

80 Palmer, *The Improvement of Humanity: Education and the French Revolution*, 125.

81 See the discussion of the Condorcet Plan at the Convention on December 12, 1792 (*AP* LV 25–33).

82 Condorcet, "Rapport et projet de décret sur l'organisation générale de l'instruction publique," 204.

Mémoires, this gradation of levels is subsumed under a structuring distinction between instruction and education. The purpose of instruction, for Condorcet, was first and foremost to protect the many against domination by increasing their capacity for autonomy and their judgment. Instruction was therefore aimed at freedom. "The obligation [of society to provide public instruction to all] consists in leaving no inequality that leads to dependence."[83] In the *Sketch,* Condorcet later reiterated that "the degree of equality in education that we can reasonably hope to attain, but that should be adequate, is that which excludes all dependence, either forced or voluntary."[84]

Strongly opposed to the kind of communal education endorsed by the ancients, he thought instruction should aim to provide the basic skills necessary for living in a society of equals. For Condorcet, a good curriculum should provide the basic knowledge that makes individuals capable of living a decent life, ensures that they were protected from material dependence, and could "employ their labor and their faculties in freedom."[85] Instruction consisted primarily in literacy, basic arithmetic, and basic scientific knowledge with daily applications. While "inequality of instruction is one of the principal sources of tyranny,"[86] Condorcet was under no illusion that his plan would bring perfect equality. Yet it would surely reduce the great gap between the illiterate and the elite. Most importantly, it would eliminate dependence, an immensely valuable goal in itself.[87] Condorcet was faithful here to the core republican idea of expanding freedom as non-domination.

Yet Condorcet's goal was not to eradicate all inequalities, which would be neither possible nor desirable. The main reason was that individuals naturally have unequal talents. "It is impossible that even an equal instruction will not increase the superiority of those whom nature has endowed with a better disposition."[88] The talented would get more knowledge and skills than the less talented, thereby increasing rather than decreasing their difference. This type of inequality, however, was not a matter of concern for Condorcet as long as dependence would decrease overall.

For Condorcet, the attempt to achieve equality ought not to extend beyond insuring the protection against domination. The quest for

[83] *Premier Mémoire,* in Condorcet, *Cinq Mémoires sur l'instruction publique,* 61.
[84] *Condorcet: Political Writings,* 132.
[85] Ibid.
[86] *Premier Mémoire,* 62.
[87] Ibid.
[88] Ibid., 61.

absolute equality would run against the interest of all and would create a form of levelling down.[89] For Condorcet, inequality based on the development of higher intellectual faculties provided more to the common lot of mankind than the absolute equality of all. The natural superiority of some contributes to the common good as part of "the common endowment of society."

In the second part of this plan, focused on higher education, Condorcet imagined institutions that would help expand already well-known fields of knowledge and discover new areas for research. Condorcet's project of education was an enlightenment project, of indefinite progress toward perfection. For him, the universalization of education would be a way of emancipating mankind, of sharing the means for expanding individual freedom.[90] The project of universal enlightenment was best pursued by a combination of elementary instruction and an elite program for higher education fostering exceptional talents.

The core idea here is that freedom stems from truth, whether basic knowledge or advanced science. As long as part of the population is ignorant and follows prejudices, "the human race will remain separated in two classes: the reasoning men on the one hand, and the believing men on the other; that is to say masters and slaves."[91] Because of Condorcet's rejection of prejudice, his Plan took a certain distance from the goal of shaping national subjects. However, this was a desired outcome of any education plan for most republicans. In the words of the Convention representative Durand-Maillane, the goal of elementary schools should be less "filling minds with knowledge than directing hearts toward social and patriotic feelings."[92] Condorcet was offering to create a society of learned men, of philosophers, whereas, according to Durand-Maillane, what schools should produce is a society of "good and virtuous citizens."[93] For many representatives, preoccupied as they were with the war of the Republic with the whole of Europe, Condorcet's lack of concern for shaping individuals into virtuous and patriotic citizens was a grave shortcoming: France needed republican citizens and national subjects, ready to become soldiers in the war.

89 "Rapport et projet de décret sur l'organisation générale de l'instruction publique, de décret sur l'organisation générale de l'instruction publique," 208.

90 *Premier Mémoire*, 70.

91 "Rapport et projet de décret sur l'organisation générale de l'instruction publique, de décret sur l'organisation générale de l'instruction publique," 185.

92 *AP* LV 28.

93 Ibid.

In response to Condorcet's unsatisfactory plan, a Jacobin representative, Michel Le Peletier, proposed an alternative with a strong Spartan flavor. Le Peletier never got to present his plan to the Convention. Assassinated by a royalist named Pâris in January 1793 for having voted the death of the King, Le Peletier became a martyr of the Republic. His murder became a symbol of the devotion of the Convention representatives to the republican cause. Beyond his spectacular funeral, Le Peletier was also honored with a painting by Jacques-Louis David portraying him on his deathbed. In these circumstances, his educational plan needed to be resurrected in a posthumous homage.

Contrary to the Condorcet Plan, the Jacobin proposal emphasized the moral and political shaping of the nation over the epistemic formation of free-thinking individuals. Robespierre took up the task and presented the Le Peletier Plan on behalf of the Jacobins.[94] The plan announced the national universalist project of creating citizens who were also national subjects. The point of a system of education was explicitly "to create a new people" by promoting its regeneration.[95]

Just like Condorcet, Le Peletier distinguished instruction and education. Instruction had been well taken care of by the Condorcet plan, Le Peletier conceded. The latter plan, however, was completely lacking with regard to education. In response, Le Peletier called for "a universally national education" (*une éducation universellement nationale*), which he saw as a debt owed by the Republic to its citizens.

The first striking feature of Le Peletier's Plan was that shaping citizens meant eliminating familial, religious, and regional particularities. Universalism, as homogenization, required eliminating all signs of particular belonging. To be free, Le Peletier, claimed, children needed to be taken away from their family and raised in boarding schools from the age of five to twelve. At home, children only learnt "prejudices" and "old errors." They escaped "the vigilance of the legislator."[96] This is why: "All children without distinction and exception will be raised in common by the Republic. All, under the sacred law of equality, will

[94] *Plan d'éducation nationale de Michel Lepelletier [sic] présenté à la Convention Nationale par Maximilien Robespierre au nom de la Commission d'Instruction Publique.* Note that the name of Lepeletier is spelled in different ways in this period (notably Le Peletier, Le peletier, Lepeletier, and Lepelletier).

[95] Ibid., 3.

[96] Ibid., 4.

receive the same clothes, the same food, the same instruction, the same care."[97]

The first five years would be left to the care of the mother, described as "the care of nature." Despite their supposedly natural understanding of their task, mothers would receive instructions and advice from the (entirely male) Committee. "At five years old, the fatherland will receive the child from the hands of nature; at twelve years old it will give the child back to society."[98] After this education to citizenship, children at twelve years old (eleven for girls) would start learning professional skills.

The other characteristic dimension of the Jacobin plan was its paradoxical insistence on discipline for the formation of free citizens. Le Peletier imagined an entirely regimented system:

> Continually under the eye and hand of an active surveillance, every hour will be marked for sleep, food, work, rest; all the regimen of life will be invariably fixed; gradual and successive tasks will be determined; gymnastics hours will be indicated; a salutary and uniform rule will prescribe all details and a constant and easy execution will guarantee its results.[99]

The political goal of forming productive citizens was explicitly expressed in the plan.[100] Le Peletier could not help but imagine that the disciplined habit of labor would "make almost all crimes disappear."[101]

Le Peletier's plan had a collectivist and authoritarian dimension that certainly goes against liberal ideas. There is also an anti-Rousseauian flavor in the insistence that everything would be imposed on children, who would learn nothing by themselves. Nothing in this education plan aims towards the development of autonomy. We should note however that one aspect of it can be described as republican in character, at least in the Rousseauian sense. Just like the young boy in *Émile,* Le Peletier considered that children who learned how to work would be capable of being "independent" in a social setting.[102] They would not have to rely on others for their subsistence as they would be capable of generating it themselves. For Le Peletier, just as for Rousseau in *Émile*, manual labor was crucial in this process of self-reliance.[103]

97 Ibid., 7.
98 Ibid., 9.
99 Ibid., 15.
100 Ibid.
101 Ibid., 16.
102 Ibid.
103 Rousselière, "Rousseau on Freedom in Commercial Society", 356.

Yet, contrary to Rousseau, who thought of education as based on learning freely how to think by oneself, Le Peletier imagined schools as places of discipline where absolutely nothing would be left to autonomous choices. The "independence" that the plan wanted to foster was a strictly economic concept, not a moral and political one. When education becomes a "public institution," rather than the stuff of a few hours per day, Le Peletier wrote, "the totality of the child's existence belongs to us; the raw material, if I can say so, will not spill out of the mold; no outside object will inform the modification that you give to it."[104] Individuality needed to be eradicated for the citizen to be entirely adapted to the Jacobin understanding of republicanism. Education moved away from the idea of a universal teaching of autonomy to a tool of nation-building.

Finally, the experience of equality in schools would be decisive in shaping their republican spirit and being "thrown into the republican mold": "There, all equally treated, equally fed, equally clothed, equally taught, equality will be for these young students not a specious theory but a continually effective practice." This is how, Le Peletier concluded, "a renewed, strong, hard-working, ruled, disciplined race" will be formed.[105] Viewed from the twenty-first century, the formation of a "new disciplined race" is, of course, a frightful prospect. For the Jacobins, it was a matter of giving to the Republic the kind of citizens that would make its existence sustainable.

Needless to say, the Jacobin Plan of education shows a very worrying tendency toward republican nationalism, embracing a rhetoric that later centuries would attach to forms of totalitarian nationalism. Without projecting later political theories onto it, we can still see that it strongly emphasized the formation of the disciplined national subject at the detriment of the formation of the free-thinking individual, which was a priority in the Condorcet Plan. It left no space for individuality and was unabashedly certain that the state knew better than individuals what was good for them. This sort of republicanism expressed the kind of excesses that postrevolutionary liberals would have an easy time targeting as deeply offensive to individual freedom. What matters to my argument here is how the logic of national universalism got deployed in the realm of education: under the guise of shaping citizens of the Republic, children were first and foremost shaped into homogenous national subjects.

104 *Plan d'éducation nationale de Michel Lepelletier*, 22.
105 Ibid., 35.

CIVIL RELIGION AND *LAÏCITÉ*

After education, the most powerful tool to both build the nation and consolidate the universalism of the Republic was the creation of a form of civil religion replacing, or at least displacing, traditional religions, and in particular Christianity. I turn now to civil religion, another major area of revolutionary policy making, with the goal of connecting civil religion and *laïcité,* a pillar of contemporary French republicanism.

Laïcité is today one of the few principles durably attached to French republicanism. See for instance the law of August 24, 2021 aiming to "secure the respect of the principles of the Republic."[106] Its central disposition is a reaffirmation of the principle of *laïcité*. Yet the so-called *laïcité laws* were enacted long after the revolutionary period that is covered in this book. The law of December 9, 1905 established that "the Republic guarantees freedom of conscience. It secures the free exercise of religion within the restrictions dictated by the interest of public order listed below" (Article 1). Article 2 of the same law stated the separation of state and church, which meant that the state did not recognize or subsidize any religious sect.

The concept of *laïcité* presents the same conflicting marks of national universalism as public education. At face value, the 1905 law describes a principle of secular neutrality toward all religions, affirms freedom of religious conscience and exercise, and separates the State and the Church. It could be construed as a rather standard liberal law. Yet the interpretation of *laïcité* became the object of virulent battles. The *Comité Laïcité République* was created in 1991 by a masonic lodge, the *Grand Orient de France* for the very purpose of ensuring its proper interpretation.[107] The first president of the *Comité* was no less than Claude Nicolet, the historian who wrote the history of republicanism, *L'idée républicaine en France*. The law of March 15, 2004, explicitly framed as part of the *laïcité* laws, stated that "in public elementary, middle and high schools, students do not have the right to wear signs or clothes that ostensibly manifest their belonging to a religion."[108] Instead of a standard right guaranteeing

[106] Loi numéro 2021–1109 du 24 août 2021 confortant le respect des principes de la République.

[107] On the role of freemasonry in the history of French republicanism, see Nord, *The Republican Moment. Struggles for Democracy in Nineteenth-Century France*, 15–30.

[108] Loi numéro 2004–228 du 15 mars 2004 encadrant, en application du principe de laïcité, le port de signes ou de tenues manifestant une appartenance religieuse dans les écoles, collèges et lycées publics.

freedom of religion, *laïcité* was interpreted as a law rejecting religious clothing at school in the name of enforcing a space *free from* religion.

To many, the 2004 law expressed a form of militant *laïcité* constituting an assault on the free expression of religions, especially those which were not historically majoritarian in France. The very principle supposed to secure the cohabitation of different religions was reinterpreted to legitimize the repression of minority religious expressions. For others, contesting the militant interpretation of *laïcité* amounted to contesting the republic *tout court*. Two hostile camps were thus created in the argument over the meaning of the concept.[109] In *Les 7 laïcités françaises*, a leading scholar of *laïcité*, Jean Baubérot, analyzed the idea and denied the existence of one model of French *laïcité*.[110] If anything, he argued, seven distinct models can be drawn out of the positions taken on the public stage since the 1905 law which officially created *laïcité* as a French law. *Laïcité* is the name of an interpretive conflict over the idea of republic itself.

In this section, I aim to show that the deep ambivalence of the concept of *laïcité* can be found in the idea of civil religion in Rousseau and then during the French Revolution with Robespierre's promotion of the Cult of the Supreme Being. It shows an intrinsic tension between the openness of universal republicanism (which requires only a right to religious freedom) and the homogeneity needed for its national realization in France (which requires the creation of a quasi-religious common bond). I aim here neither to discredit nor praise the idea of *laïcité* but rather to demonstrate how we can trace a political problem to its origins: that *laïcité* is not simply a way of solving religious conflicts by formulating a right protecting religious freedom. From the start it has also been a policy of creation of a political social bond using the sentimental dimension of religion as a catalyst. This is why *laïcité* is always militant: at stake is the survival of the political community, forever on the verge of being dismembered, or so its defenders believe.

Tracing *laïcité* back to Rousseau may be surprising. Not only does Rousseau's work antedate the *laïcité* laws by over a century, but his conception of civil religion is an extremely contested idea that has puzzled generations of scholars.[111] In any case it does not seem any clearer than

[109] For an analysis of the contemporary debate, see Laborde, *Critical Republicanism: The Hijab Controversy and Political Philosophy*.

[110] Baubérot, *Les 7 laïcités françaises. Le modèle français n'existe pas.*

[111] Beiner, *Civil Religion: A Dialogue in the History of Political Philosophy*; Griswold, "Liberty and Compulsory Civil Religion in Rousseau's *Social Contract*"; Bachofen,

laïcité itself. First, Rousseau's civil religion can be interpreted as a protection against overbearing religions such as Christianity that rulers use to impose laws, as happened in Geneva.[112] It is a protection from the religious power that can encroach politics. It is also, very clearly, a principle of religious toleration to end religious wars. But it is also, I argue, a supplemental instrument to create a social bond.

One problem of the *Social Contract* is whether the social body will be stable and have the capacity to be self-sustaining. "The initial act by which the body assumes form and unity still leaves undetermined what it must do to preserve itself" (*SC* II.6.1), Rousseau worries. In the penultimate chapter of the book, Rousseau presents civil religion as an essential part of the solution to this problem. Analyzing different types of existing religions, he first vehemently rejects any that is not supportive of the social bond between citizens. "Everything which destroys social unity is worthless: All institutions that put man in contradiction with himself are worthless" (*SC* IV.8.17).

For Rousseau, religion ought to serve the state and consolidate the strength of the civil association. Rousseau clearly holds an instrumental view of religion, which needs to be useful to the state.[113] This is why he praises religions that are "inscribed in a particular country" and "give [them] [their] gods" (*SC* IV.8.15). Such a religion "regards everything outside the single Nation which adheres to it as infidel, alien, barbarous" (*SC* II.8.15). This kind of religion is praiseworthy for Rousseau because

> It combines divine worship and love of the laws, and in making the fatherland the object of the citizens' worship it teaches them that to serve the State is to serve its tutelary God. It is a kind of Theocracy, in which there ought to be no other pontiff than the Prince, nor other priests than the magistrates. Then to die for one's country is to be a martyr, to break the laws is to be impious, and to subject the guilty to public execration is to deliver him to the wrath of the Gods; *sacer estod.* (*SC* IV.8.18)

Rousseau describes in these terms a national religion similar to the Romans'. Such a religion seals the relation between nationalism and

"La religion civile selon Rousseau: une théologie politique negative"; Scott, *Rousseau's God. Theology, Religion, and the Natural Goodness of Man*, 201–28.

[112] I agree with Rosenblatt when she argues that "Rousseau's argument in his chapter on civil religion was thus much more about *laïcizing* the state than it was about coercing belief." See Rosenblatt, "On the Intellectual Source of Laïcité. Rousseau, Constant, and the Debates about a National Religion," 8.

[113] For the view that the two standards to assess religion are utility and truth, see Scott, *Rousseau's God. Theology, Religion, and the Natural Goodness of Man*, Ch.1.

patriotism, the nation and the people – a goal which, as we have seen, is central to French revolutionaries.

Rousseau, however, rejects the solution of a "national religion." First, such a national religion would be highly exclusionary by necessity as the reference to the Roman religious term for outlawing "sacer esto!" reminds us. Rousseau points out an important problem in this kind of religion: it makes a people "bloodthirsty and intolerant," as well as "exclusive and tyrannical" (*SC* IV.8.19). Being exclusionary is to be avoided at all costs. The exclusionary tendency of such a religion pushes against the necessary principle of toleration toward other religions.

The second problem of such a national religion is that it is false. Here we reach the second standard – truth. "Being founded on error and lies it deceives men, makes them credulous, superstitious, and drowns the true cult of the divinity in a vain ceremonial" (*SC* IV.8.19). While Rousseau does not shy away from using deception (beneficial manipulation)[114] as a tool for education in *Émile,* he refuses the idea that a false religion may actually be an adequate foundation for a social community.

"Religion," Rousseau writes, "is one of the great bonds of particular societies" (*SC* II.8.21). If it can be used to strengthen the rational political community, it would be of great help. This is why a purely spiritual form of religion, like the religion of the Gospel, is not to be recommended: "this Religion, since it has no particular relation to the body politic, leaves the laws with only the force they derive from themselves without adding any other force to them" (*SC* II.8.21).

This necessity to align religion with the duties of citizenship, all the while preserving truth, leads Rousseau to propose what he calls a "civil profession of faith": "There is therefore a purely civil profession of faith the articles of which it is up to the Sovereign to fix, not precisely as dogmas of Religion but as sentiments of sociability without which it is impossible to be either a good Citizen or a loyal subject" (*SC* II.8.32). A civil religion allows the regulation of the body politic by permitting the sovereign to exclude those who do not respect these dogmas and are thus unsociable. The justification for this exclusion is not nationalist but based on the universal principle according to which the sentiments of sociability have to be fostered in any state. Yet the interpretation of this exclusionary principle would be made by the people themselves,

[114] See Grant, *Hypocrisy and Integrity*, 125–39.

that is to say the already existing nation. The circle of national universalism is thus perfected.

Rousseau's concept of civil religion may appear to create more problems than it solves. For once, the imposition of religious principles runs against the idea of freedom underlying the social contract.[115] Furthermore Rousseau's civil religion seems an odd mixture of a principle of religious tolerance and the imposition of dogmatic tenets compensating for citizens' motivational lack in a society based on a rational social contract.[116] In any case, Rousseau can be credited for inaugurating an important idea in French republicanism. A properly republican civil religion has a political role to play in bridging a wide protection of religious freedom with a positive cult that bonds individuals across the republic.

If connecting Rousseau's civil profession of faith to *laïcité* might seem strange, it may be shocking to include Robespierre's cult of the Supreme Being in its genealogy. Yet Robespierre's proposal, like Rousseau's, associates the protection of a right (religious freedom) with the construction of a sentimental bond in a republic. I therefore would like to argue that there is a theoretical line connecting these three points: Rousseau's civil religion, Robespierre's Cult of Supreme Being (Cult of Reason) and *laïcité* as it is understood today. All three are variations of the same awkwardly composite idea – a principle allowing the toleration of a range of religions, the separation of the Church and State as well as the imposition of a civic communal bond of all citizens. All three posit that in a pluralist republic, citizens need to have a spiritual bond distinct from existing religions. While the 1905 *laïcité* law does not argue for this bond (it is purely a protection of religious freedom and a principle of separation of state and church), the subsequent interpretations of *laïcité* support my claim: if religious freedom matters in a republic with religious diversity, citizens must be connected through another spiritual sentimental bond, the bond of the republic to replace the former bond of the monarchy of divine right.[117]

If not their allegiance to the King, perhaps the strongest bond between the inhabitants of the French kingdom before the Revolution was their majoritarian religion: Catholicism. The revolutionary period marked a moment of religious transition. In the first months of the revolution, the clergy lost its main sources of revenue, its privileges and

[115] Griswold, "Liberty and Compulsory Civil religion in Rousseau's *Social Contract*," 295.

[116] On this, see Scott, *Rousseau's God* as well as Bachofen, "La religion civile selon Rousseau: une théologie négative."

[117] For an analysis of the complex relations of religion and nationalism during the Revolution, see Bell, *The Cult of the Nation in France*.

soon after its land, which was seized and sold by the state. While the common people showed strong allegiance to the Catholic Church, as the civil war in Vendée demonstrated, the successive assemblies tried to republicanize the clergy. All they achieved was a deep schism between the constitutional clergy, who accepted to take the republican oath, and the "refractory" clergy. In 1793–1794, the republic moved toward an explicit and violent campaign of de-Christianization. Catholicism was no more a bond and was rather a principle of division and discord.

The relations between republicans and Christianity were complex during the Revolution and remain so till this day. I do not intend to analyze them here. What matters is that in this period, republicans started thinking that they should develop a republican (quasi)religion that would bond people together and overcome dissensions over Catholicism. This attempt to create a civil religion was not the endeavor of one isolated group. I will present Robespierre's Cult of the Supreme Being, but it is far from being the only one in the period. There were hundreds of such cults throughout France.[118] After Robespierre's death, the Thermidorian Convention, which went again many Jacobin decisions, still upheld the project of a republican religion based on the revolutionary calendar with periodical republican festivals.[119]

The main elements of Robespierre's proposal for a cult of the Supreme Being can be found in his Discourse of 18 Floréal Year II (May 7, 1794).[120] This lengthy and convoluted speech is at face value quite problematic.[121] As historians have debated at length, the spring of 1794 is a moment of intense struggle for power at the Convention. Robespierre tried to maintain the political power that was slowly escaping him even as he systematically eradicated his rivals. The 18 Floréal Discourse is indeed full of references to traitors and insists on Robespierre's winning position vis-à-vis the treasons of his opponents.[122] Even if we should take this context into consideration, Robespierre's view on the Supreme Being cannot be discounted as purely *ad hoc*. The idea of a cult of Reason had long been established among revolutionaries.[123]

[118] Tackett, "The French Revolution and Religion to 1794," 554.
[119] Desan, "The French Revolution and Religion, 1795–1815."
[120] "Rapport présenté par Robespierre au nom du Comité de Salut Public, concernant le culte à l'Être Suprême," *AP* XC 132–40, May 7, 1794.
[121] See Mathiez, "Robespierre et le culte de l'Être Suprême."
[122] See for instance Robespierre's accusatory remarks on Danton, 134, on Guadet, Hébert, Vergniaud and Gensonné, 137.
[123] Mathiez, "Robespierre et le culte de l'Être Suprême"; Vovelle, *La Révolution contre l'Eglise. De la Raison à l'Être suprême.*

Robespierre started his discourse by stating his goal: "strengthening the principles on which the stability and happiness of the Republic rely."[124] The presentation of the Cult of the Supreme Being was instrumental to the goal of securing the Republic's principles. Robespierre may initially seem to argue that all religions should disappear, stating that "all sects ought to dissolve within the universal religion of reason."[125] Here is another occurrence of the logic we already encountered: particularities must be eradicated for universality to prevail. Yet he then proposed an idea close to the *laïcité* principle: "May the freedom of religions be respected for reason to be triumphant! But this freedom ought not to trouble public order."[126] Despite affirming freedom of religion, Robespierre then proceeded to ridicule sects which, in his view, had "disfigured the Supreme Being."

For Robespierre, man needed "to hold a religious respect for man, a deep sentiment of his duties, which is the sole guarantor of social happiness."[127] What Robespierre had in mind was a purely republican cult which would shape citizens' character and behavior. Following Rousseau's proposal in the *Considerations on the Government of Poland,* revolutionaries organized countless celebrations in Paris and everywhere in French cities and villages.[128] The most important one, and in a sense a model for all revolutionary *fêtes,* remained the *Fête de la Fédération* (July 14, 1790), when thousands of *fédérés* came from provinces to attend and celebrate French national unity before returning to their provinces and spreading the spirit of the Revolution.[129] Robespierre deemed public gatherings for national celebration central to the creation of a republican spirit. The Cult of the Supreme Being should be their continuity. "A system of national celebrations well-understood should be the softest bond of fraternity and the most powerful means of regeneration."[130] Creating fraternity and instituting a new people thus needed a material way of citizens to bond together: these were precisely the goals of national celebrations and the civil religion of the Supreme Being.

124 *AP* XC 132, May 7, 1794.
125 Ibid., 138.
126 Ibid.
127 Ibid.
128 Ozouf, *La fête révolutionnaire, 1789–1799.*
129 The cover of this book shows a famous illustration of the *Fête de la Fédération.* This illustration became popular during the Revolution itself.
130 *AP* XC 128, May 7, 1794.

Laïcité finds its roots deep in the French republican tradition as an uncomfortable composite apparatus that combines a right to religious freedom with a policy creating social bonds. Its intrinsic tension, which is still at play today in endless public debates, bears the mark of the national universalism unleashed during the Revolution.

CONCLUSION

I have illustrated the tensions between two political goals: instituting a republican people and shaping a nation. These two goals characterize French revolutionary republicanism and create what I called a national universalist logic. I would like to suggest that this logic leads to exclusion as it traps individuals within a paradox that can be formulated as follows:

Paradox of national universalism: all individuals belong to the republic on the basis of their allegiance to universal principles, yet only those who already belong to the historical nation can belong to the republic.

I contend that this paradox comes from a fusion, and in fact a confusion, between republican citizenship and national belonging in this period. See how these two premises lead to the paradox:

(1) Republican citizenship is universalist. It is an inclusive status that demands allegiance to republican political principles and not to a particular culture.
(2) Republican citizenship is based on belonging to the nation. National belonging is an exclusive status that requires sharing a common culture.[131] What counts as the shared culture is defined by the majority of those who already belong to the nation.

This paradox explains many of the conundrums of republicans about the integration of minorities in the republic during and after the Revolution. The unresolved tension between the openness of universal principles and the closeness of nation-building can be seen in many domains. Should the laws of the republic be translated into the many languages spoken in the

[131] By "national belonging" I do not refer to nationality law but to the social perception of what it meant to be French. In the *Ancien Régime*, nationality law was mostly based on *jus soli* (being born in the French kingdom, meaning being *sujet naturel*) as well as on residence (being *régnicole*), but also incorporated *jus sanguinis* in some cases and processes of naturalization granted by the King. Being French meant being a subject of the French King. The collapse of the monarchy triggered a transformation of the notion of nationality toward both a legal fusion between nationality and citizenship on the one hand and a diffuse social notion of national belonging on the other.

French territory to foster citizenship? Or should these many languages be eradicated and French imposed over all? Should religious minorities be actively supported to compensate for the historical persecution they suffered under monarchy? Or should they be made to integrate into the majority by embracing a civil religion uniting all the French? Should individual emancipation be encouraged to compensate for the widespread ignorance of the people under the domination of the monarchy? Or should a new nation of obedient citizens be created? The paradox of national universalism took shape in France in the tension that shot through so many key questions.

The republican citizen is thus caught in a double injunction that will not appear contradictory to some (those for whom particular belonging aligns with both the nation and universal principles) but will prove difficult, if not impossible, for others – those who are minorities of various sorts. For them, abiding by the rules of the republic means that they have to let go of their particularity, thereby admitting that their particularities cannot give them access to republican citizenship in contradistinction with those of the majority. Peasants speaking regional languages can be recognized as republican citizens only in so far as they forego their inherited languages and speak French. Jews and Protestants can be recognized as part of the republic only insofar as they do not exhibit their religious faith through visible practices. The paradox here is not in the exclusion itself – after all, exclusion is the hallmark of any nationalism. The paradox lies in the conjunction of nationalism and universalism, which means that some citizens are faced with the fact that they can gain access to universal principles of republicanism only by embracing the particular practices of the national community and renouncing their own. Unless they want to bear the cost of exclusion, they can access freedom only by accepting national coercion.

Conclusion

On French Republicanism

REPUBLICANISM TODAY

In the 1990s, as the exaltation of the bicentenary celebrations wore off, republican universalism and citizenship met with increasing skepticism in the public sphere in France. Gay marriage, women's equal access to political power, migrants' rights, religious signs at schools: from all sides of society, accusations of exclusion were raised, and emphatic new demands for inclusion were made. The republican interpretation of citizenship needed to change.

The *fin-de-siècle* conceptual innovation, which was supposed to solve these different debates and make republicanism more inclusive, was yet a new one: integration (*intégration*). The imperative of integration became part of the official tenets of the Republic during these years. As an institutional response to the first "*affaire du foulard*" (the exclusion of three hijab-wearing Muslim girls from a middle school in Creil), the *Haut Conseil à l'Intégration* (High Council for Integration) was created on December 19, 1989. The *Conseil*'s mission was to "define and coordinate governmental policies on issues related to the integration of foreign residents or those of foreign origin."

As part of their state mission, the *Conseil* reinterpreted *laïcité* as "the fundamental principle of republican organization" (1998 report). Recall that, as I have shown in this book, *laïcité* was *not* a central principle of republicanism at the initial moment of its formation in France – neither before nor during the Revolution. *Laïcité* was ostensibly a product of the early twentieth century. In 2003, the political philosopher Blandine Kriegel, the author of several books on French republicanism, was nominated president of *The Haut Conseil à l'Intégration.*[1] Under her leadership, the *Conseil* wrote a report to the Prime Minister, entitled "Contract and Integration."[2] It proposed to understand integration as a republican obligation coming out of the social contract.

The report pedagogically defined the concept of "contract" and asked how contracts were related to republican integration. Founders of social contract theory, the report noted, include Duplessis-Mornay,[3] Grotius, Hobbes, Spinoza, Jurieu, and the "apex" *(le firmament)* of political thought, "Jean-Jacques Rousseau's *Social Contract.*"[4] The report then proceeded to present the political issue at stake following Jean-Jacques's guidance: asking how a people is a people.

The report was particularly interested in the conceptual difference that Rousseau draws between a multitude and a people. A multitude is a group of individuals without a common will, interacting with one another on the basis of "sedition, conspiracy, faction, force." By contrast, "proposing a social contract is proposing to move from an undifferentiated and particularized multitude to the unity of a people in a collectivity gathered together."[5] If this is how a people becomes a people, the report continued, it is also how a people "makes itself France" (*faire France*). The report placed the social contract as the act through which a people leaves particularities (*particularités*) behind in order to become a people united by law, and in this act of becoming a people, it also becomes one *particular* people: France. It should be noted that the report shows no anxiety concerning what I called the paradox of national universalism. The *Haut Conseil d'Intégration* had no doubt: the Republic and the nation, universal republican principles and France, were seamlessly reconciled within the Rousseauan social contract duly interpreted as a contract of integration.

One important consequence of this republican contract for the *Conseil* was that "not integrating," that is, failing to follow the behaviors expected from a citizen and a French national, meant threatening the dissolution of the whole nation: "The disintegration (*délitement*) of the

[1] Kriegel, *Philosophie de la république* and *The State and the Rule of Law.*

[2] Rapport à Monsieur le Premier Ministre, *Le contrat et l'intégration,* Haut Conseil d'Intégration, 2003 (henceforth HCI 2003).

[3] The French Monarchomach Duplessis-Mornay is sometimes considered a founder of social contract theory. The report refers to 1579, the date of the publication of *Vindiciae contra tyrannos,* the pamphlet written under the pseudonym of Stephanus Junius Brutus.

[4] HCI 2003, 107. Note the conspicuous absence of Locke from this list.

[5] HCI 2003, 107.

republican social bond leads to the disintegration through which a people reverts to a multitude and in which everyone goes back to their first identities (*chacun se replie sur ses identités premières*)."[6] Importantly, the Report noted, integration and assimilation are distinct concepts. While invoking Renan positively as a reference against the ethnic conception of the nation, the Report stated that "cultures evolve and there is no culture that is fixed forever." It would therefore be up to newer generations to "build the national community." In a word, "the contract is always to be remade."[7]

With the injunction of integration, the French Republic found yet another answer, however problematic, to respond to – or maybe evade – what I have called the paradoxes of republican emancipation and national universalism. While I cannot analyze here the results of republican policies of integration from the 1990s onward, we should note that they have been significantly criticized, indicating that once again the republican desire to emancipate found obstacles in its way. Most of the actions of the *Haut Conseil d'Intégration,* for instance, were interpreted as proposing measures that made immigration more difficult, increased controls of foreigners on French soil, and restricted their rights.[8] For many scholars studying race, gender, and poverty, integration has proven to be a highly deficient tool to alleviate exclusion.[9] The problem of republican exclusion persists in France today.

In the course of this book, I have described the mechanisms through which republicanism as a theory of emancipation unwittingly creating forms of exclusion. The chronological limits of this book have constrained the scope of my analysis. One important question only mentioned in this manuscript is colonization, whose legacy underlines major forms of exclusion in France today. As the end of the twentieth century was a moment of reckoning for French republicans, they had to face the ugly and overwhelming reality that their republican predecessors had not only engaged in but also justified colonization. In the nineteenth century, France accelerated its colonial expansion in a scramble to become a world power. After World War II, decolonization forced the French to reflect on the reasons they had invoked

6 Ibid., 109.

7 Ibid., 112.

8 See for instance the critical diagnostic of Lochak, "Le Haut Conseil à la (dés)intégration."

9 Mazouz, *La république et ses autres. Politiques de l'altérité dans la France des années 2000*; Brenner, *Les territoires perdus de la république*.

to legitimate their policies of conquest and exploitation. Given the chronological limits of this book, I have only briefly touched on the connection between the republican idea of glory and the republican temptation to colonize. One important reason is that it is only with the Third Republic that the justification of colonization took full force in republican discourse.[10] Some elements analyzed in these chapters indicate how the *mission civilisatrice* (civilizing mission) could become a core tenet of the Third Republic and motivate its colonizing enterprise.[11] Tracing the missing connections would be, however, a subject for another book focusing on a different period.

What then should we make of French republicanism as I have described and analyzed it in its historical complexity in this book? I have focused on understanding how republicanism, a dominant political theory today, particularly in France, conceptualized freedom and how it generated exclusion while aiming at inclusive and equal freedom. Returning to the revolutionary period, I have argued that French republicanism was plagued with internal paradoxes from the start as it aimed to achieve a formidable revolutionary enterprise by universalizing freedom on the basis of a tradition that had not been meant for this purpose. I explored the structure of exclusion, in particular the embedded elitism that generated a series of obstacles in the emancipatory process, as well as the difficulty of dealing with the multifaceted realities of dependence in different subordinated groups.

While I asked the French to take a long, hard look at the history of their republicanism, I hope to have shown Anglophone readers that French republicanism was in fact, despite or maybe because of its struggles, an original form of revolutionary republicanism worth exploring for its emancipatory impulse and for the theoretical innovations it offered as a conjunction between republicanism and democracy. French republicanism, I argued, should not be excluded from the international history of republicanism as it so often is in the neo-republican scholarship. Its example and ambition are unparalleled in the republican tradition: it aimed at no less than making the republican idea of freedom available to all, including all those who had never been deemed worthy of freedom, those Burke had called "low-born servile wretches."

[10] Vergès, "Colonizing, Educating, Guiding: A Republican Duty," 251. See also Blanchard and Bancel, "La fondation du républicanisme colonial. Retour sur une généalogie politique."

[11] Conklin, *A Mission to Civilize: The Republican Idea of Empire in France and West Africa, 1895–1930*.

SHARING FREEDOM

As much as I have tried to lay out the shortcomings of French republicanism, my goal in this book has also been to show what this political theory can contribute to strengthen republicanism today. What can we take from this journey into the origins of French republicanism? The historical period I have investigated is rather narrow. However, a few traits have emerged as particularly robust during the formative periods of French Republicanism, that is in the phase I called "revolutionary republicanism."

Let us first note how revolutionary republicanism in France remains faithful to well-established aspects of the republican tradition. Recall that for Pettit, republicanism as a political theory is characterized by three core ideas: freedom as non-domination, the mixed constitution, and the contestatory (vigilant) citizenry.[12] For Lovett, republicanism is marked by a commitment to three claims: the non-domination principle, the empire of law principle, and the popular control principle.[13] From what I have presented in this book, we can see that an important continuity exists between French republicanism and what neo-republicans have identified as the core elements of the tradition.

First, the struggle against domination was central to all the different moments of the revolutionary project and motivated many republican arguments in this period, from the parliamentary discussion to get rid of the king's veto to the treatises advocating for minorities' rights. Even if republicans concurrently used other definitions of freedom (as I have extensively argued), the trope of domination remained an extremely strong one, and I would argue one that took priority in that period as an emancipatory motivation.

Second, while the revolutionary republicans certainly did not advocate for a mixed constitution (and therefore did not follow Pettit's second principle), they did endorse the importance of "the empire of laws." I have shown in Chapter 3 the immense constitutional work that revolutionary republicans undertook. From the start, French republicanism appeared as a theory in which constitutionalism and the rule of law were the pillars of a just, free and stable society. Indeed, even during the period of "revolutionary government" (fall 1793-July 1794) when the Constitution was suspended, revolutionaries claimed

[12] Pettit, *On the People's Terms*, 5–8.

[13] Lovett, *The Well-Ordered Republic*, 3–9.

that their ultimate goal was to overcome the state of exception and provide legal foundations for the republic.

Third, revolutionary republicans strongly believed in the importance of popular control. I have shown in this book that this was a deeply entrenched belief in all French republicans from Rousseau on. However one conceptualizes the acceptable republican forms of representation and control, they all believed that popular control should be established. As for the principle of the "vigilant citizenry," it may be more complicated to recognize whether there is a continuity. On the one hand, it is undeniable that there is a strong element of popular insurgency in this form of republicanism – it is, after all, the historical reality of the French Revolution. The Declaration of the Rights of Man and the Citizen formulates a right of defense against oppression, which puts the people in a position of vigilance. But on the other hand, as Pettit notes, it is unclear whether, outside revolutionary moments, the people is given a normalized and ordinary role of checking the government. I agree that the institutions elaborated in this period do not provide us with a strong sense of the type of accountability that elected officials would have to the public. This is something that remains still vague in this period.

These are the main lines of continuity that can be traced. But what is the originality of French republicanism in this revolutionary moment? How did it transform the tradition? What is its normative attraction? I have suggested that its main appeal is in its understanding of politics as sharing freedom. French republicans have insisted that freedom carries its own injunction to be shared, that is, freedom has to be universalized. Revolutionary republicans also held that in the process of sharing freedom, citizens create a bond with one another. Its originality thus lays in three characteristics: that it is a theory of emancipation, a theory of republican democracy, and a theory of solidarity.

First, it is a *theory of emancipation* and not just a theory of freedom. The emancipation of the dependent and the vulnerable was a very difficult and fragile process, in great part because the theory underlying their emancipation had been originally conceived by powerful and secure individuals who thought of freedom from their own privileged perspective. Thinking from the point of view of the vulnerable and the dependent required that revolutionaries stop reasoning primarily from the point of view of independent individuals, that is, wealthy individuals secure in their social and economic power. It required understanding what actual dependence implies materially, relationally, and psychologically. The radical form of the Revolution, which scandalized Burke, cannot simply be attributed to an irrational overflow of violence from the mob. It is also, so to speak, an epistemic overflow, the emergence of the point of view of the dominated and the dependent. The different forms of classical republicanism could not simply be applied *tel quel,* as if a theory of freedom just needed to expand to be a theory of emancipation. In order for the vulnerable and the dependent to become free, a conceptual bridge needed to be created to democratize republicanism.

Second, French republicanism in its revolutionary form is a democratic theory of republicanism, or, to say the same thing, it is a theory of *republican democracy.* I showed that the idea of "democracy" was very much in flux during the Revolution and did not have a stable meaning. What I mean here is simply that for the French republicans, the republic ought to rely on the power of the people, that is to say, *popular sovereignty.* This was very much an innovation from the earlier tradition that was reluctant to attribute any form of absolute power to any group. For the French republicans, any admission of mixed sovereignty would be an admission to being dominated by a group other than the people. In order to avoid the problems associated with absolute sovereignty, the French republicans therefore had to look for solutions other than the traditional mixed constitution.

The second sense in which French republicanism is a form of republican democracy is that it is based not only on freedom as non-domination, but also on freedom as self-government. I have shown in this book that the two kinds of freedom were often inextricably intertwined in the republican arguments of the period. Contrary to neo-republicans, they did not conceptualize self-government as instrumental to freedom as non-domination. The political involvement of citizens could not be separated from their freedom. Any attempt to separate them was interpreted as a slide towards elitism and a loss of control from the people. It is not that they thought of popular power romantically, as something always inherently good. In fact, as I have argued, many revolutionaries were wary of the power of the *sans-culottes*, always unpredictable and often violent, as well as the voice of the rural masses – in their view, ignorant peasants, often inclined to follow tradition and religion. But they thought that being deprived of a political voice meant being subjected, and therefore becoming dependent. Self-government implied that republicanism was by necessity inclusive and participatory. For French republicans, freedom implied the act of *sharing* it, that is, having a part in it and participating in its distribution to everyone.

Finally, French republicanism emerges from this period as a form of *social theory* emphasizing the importance of socio-economic conditions and the constitution of solidarity for freedom. French republicans were extensively concerned with the question of social and economic dependence, which a large part of the population was subjected to. Their work bears witness to the necessity for any political theory to consider the social and economic situations of citizens as conditioning the type of political government that can be possible. If agency requires competence and assets, both need to be distributed not on the atomistic model of already existing individuals, but on the solidaristic model where citizens rely on each other for their own freedom. This makes French republicanism a type of political thought that is intrinsically committed to social justice, forms of egalitarianism, and social solidarity. In the revolutionary period, there were intense disagreements on how these ideas (justice, equality, solidarity) should be interpreted. Yet revolutionary republicans agreed that there was no free republic without the constitution of a social bond between citizens: they therefore considered the constitution of solidarity an integral part of the republican project. A republic, they thought, should be based on the mutually beneficial interdependence of all under the rule of law. It was only through this social bond that citizens could secure for themselves the freedom that they were sharing with others.

Bibliography

Abizadeh, Arash. "On the Demos and Its Kin: Nationalism, Democracy, and the Boundary Problem." *American Political Science Review* 106, no. 4 (2012): 867–82.

Adams, John. *The Adams Papers*. Vol. 16. Cambridge: The Belknap Press of Harvard University Press, 2012.

Addante, Luca. "Machiavel et les jacobins." *La Pensée* 2, no. 406 (2021): 109–19.

Agulhon, Maurice. *La république au village*. Paris: Plon, 1970.

Agulhon, Maurice. *Marianne au combat: l'imagerie et la symbolique républicaine de 1789 à 1880*. Paris: Flammarion, 1979.

Agulhon, Maurice. "Aspects du nationalisme francais." *Raison présente* 103, no. 3 (1992): 59–69.

Anonymous [Robespierre]. *A la nation artésienne. Sur la nécessité de réformer les états d'Artois*, 1789.

Appleby, Joyce. "America as a Model for the Radical French Reformers of 1789." *The William and Mary Quarterly* 28, no. 2 (1971): 267–86.

Arena, Valentina. "The Roman Republic of Jean-Jacques Rousseau." *History of Political Thought* 37 (2016): 8–31.

Arendt, Hannah. *On Revolution*. New York: Viking Press, 1963.

Atkins, Jed W. *Cicero on Politics and the Limits of Reason: The Republic and Laws*. Cambridge: Cambridge University Press, 2013.

Audier, Serge. *Les théories de la république*. Paris: La Découverte, 2004.

Audier, Serge. *Léon Bourgeois: Fonder la solidarité*. Paris: Édition Michalon, 2007.

Audier, Serge. *La pensée solidariste. Aux sources du modèle social républicain*. Paris: Presses Universitaires de France, 2010.

Aulard, Alphonse. *Histoire politique de la révolution française. Origines et développement de la démocratie et de la république (1789–1804)*. Paris: Colin, 1901.

Bachofen, Blaise. "La religion civile selon Rousseau: une théologie politique négative." In *La théologie politique de Rousseau*, edited by Ghislain Waterlot, 37–62. Rennes: Presses universitaires de Rennes, 2010.

Baczko, Bronisław. *Une éducation pour la démocratie. Textes et projets de l'époque révolutionnaire*. Paris: Droz, 2000.

Badinter, Elisabeth, and Robert Badinter. *Condorcet: un intellectuel en politique*. Paris: Fayard, 1988.

Bailyn, Bernard. *The Ideological Origins of the American Revolution*. Cambridge: Belknap Press of Harvard University Press, 1967.

Baker, Keith. *Condorcet: Selected Writings*. Indianapolis: The Bobbs-Merrill Company, 1976.

Baker, Keith. *Inventing the French Revolution*. Cambridge: Cambridge University Press, 1990.

Baker, Keith. "Transformations of Classical Republicanism in Eighteenth-Century France." *Journal of Modern History* 73, no. 1 (2001): 32–53.

Balibar, Etienne. "Ce qui fait qu'un peuple est un peuple. Rousseau et Kant." *Revue de Synthèse* 3–4 (1989): 391–417.

Bandoch, Joshua. *The Politics of Place: Montesquieu, Particularism, and the Pursuit of Liberty*. Rochester: University of Rochester Press, 2017.

Barny, Roger. *Rousseau dans la révolution. Le personnage de Jean-Jacques et les débuts du culte révolutionnaire (1778–1791)*. Oxford: Voltaire Foundation-Oxford University Press, 1986.

Baron, Hans. *The Crisis of the Early Italian Renaissance: Civic Humanism and Republican Liberty in an Age of Classicism and Tyranny*. Princeton: Princeton University Press, 1955.

Baubérot, Jean. *Histoire de la laïcité en France*. Paris: Presses Universitaires de France, 2000.

Baubérot, Jean. *Les 7 laïcités françaises. Le modèle français n'existe pas*. Paris: Editions de la Maison des sciences de l'homme, 2015.

Baumier, M. *De la monarchie françoise*. Paris, 1791.

Bayle, Pierre. *Dictionnaire historique et critique*. Genève: Slatkine, 1995.

Beiner, Ronald. *Civil Religion: A Dialogue in the History of Political Philosophy*. Cambridge: Cambridge University Press, 2011.

Bell, David A. *The Cult of the Nation in France: Inventing Nationalism, 1680–1900*. Cambridge: Harvard University Press, 2001.

Bell, David A. "Questioning the Global Turn: The Case of the French Revolution." *French Historical Studies* 37, no. 1 (February 2014): 1–24.

Bellamy, Richard. *Political Constitutionalism: A Republican Defence of the Constitutionality of Democracy*. Cambridge: Cambridge University Press, 2007.

Bergès, Sandrine. "Is Motherhood Compatible with Political Participation? Sophie de Grouchy's Care-Based Republicanism." *Ethical Theory and Moral Practice* 18, no. 1 (2015): 47–60.

Bergès, Sandrine. "Sophie de Grouchy and the Cost of Domination in 'The Letters on Sympathy' and Two Anonymous Articles in 'Le Républicain'." *The Monist* 98, no. 1 (2015): 102–12.

Berlin, Isaiah. "Two Concepts of Liberty." In *Four Essays on Liberty*, 118–72. Oxford: Oxford University Press, 1969.

Bertram, Christopher. "Rousseau's Legacy in Two Conceptions of the General Will: Democratic and Transcendent." *Review of Politics* 74, no.3 (2012): 403–19.

Billaud-Varenne, Jacques-Nicolas. *L'acéphocratie ou le gouvernement fédératif démontré le meilleur de tous pour un grand empire, par les principes de la politique et les faits de l'histoire.* Paris, 1791.

Blackburn, Robin. *The American Crucible: Slavery, Emancipation and Human Rights.* London: Verso, 2011.

Blais, Marie-Claude. *La solidarité: histoire d'une idée.* Paris: Gallimard, 2007.

Blanchard, Pascal, and Nicolas Bancel. "La fondation du républicanisme colonial. Retour sur une généalogie politique." *Mouvements* 2, no. 38 (2005): 26–33.

Blum, Carol. *Rousseau and the Republic of Virtue: The Language of Politics in the French Revolution.* Ithaca: Cornell University Press, 1986.

Bodin, Jean. *On Sovereignty. Four Chapters from The Six Books of the Commonwealth.* Edited by Julian H. Franklin. Cambridge: Cambridge University Press, 1992.

Bosc, Yannick. "Robespierre libéral." *Annales historiques de la Révolution française*, March 2013.

Bouniol, Béatrice. "Les gilets jaunes représentent la part de rêve de la révolution française." *La Croix*, February 18, 2019.

Bourke, Richard, and Quentin Skinner, eds. *Popular Sovereignty in Historical Perspective.* Cambridge: Cambridge University Press, 2016.

Bouteldja, Houria. *Les Blancs, les Juifs et nous.* Paris: La fabrique, 2016.

Boyd, Richard. "Rousseau and the Vanishing Concept of the Political?" *European Journal of Political Theory* 12, no. 1 (2013): 74–83.

Brenner, Emmanuel, ed. *Les territoires perdus de la république.* Paris: Mille et Une Nuits, 2002.

Brenner, Michael. "Je ne suis pas Charlie Hebdo." *Huffington Post*, February 16, 2015.

Brette, Armand. *Les limites et les divisions territoriales de la France.* Paris: E. Cornély, 1907.

Brissot, Jacques-Pierre, and Etienne Clavière. *De la France et des Etats-unis ou de l'importance de la révolution d'Amérique pour le bonheur de la France*, 1787.

Buck-Morss, Susan. *Hegel, Haiti, and Universal History.* Pittsburgh: University of Pittsburgh Press, 2009.

Burke, Edmund. *Reflections on the Revolution in France.* Edited by J. G. A. Pocock. London: Hackett Publishing Company, 1987.

Burke, Edmund. "Letters on a Regicide Peace." In *Selected Works. Volume 3.* Indianapolis: Liberty Fund, 1999.

Cassirer, Ernst. *The Question of Jean-Jacques Rousseau.* New Haven: Yale University Press, 1989.

Césaire, Aimé. *Toussaint-Louverture: La révolution française et le problème colonial.* Paris: Présence Africaine, 1962.

Chabal, Emile. *A Divided Republic. Nation, State and Citizenship in Contemporary France.* Cambridge: Cambridge University Press, 2016.

Charvet, John. "Rousseau, the Problem of Sovereignty, and the Limits of Political Obligation." In *Rousseau and Liberty*, edited by Robert Wolker, 139–151. Manchester and New York: Manchester University Press, 1995.

Cheney, Paul. *Revolutionary Commerce. Globalization and the French Monarchy.* Cambridge: Harvard University Press, 2010.

Chérel, Albert. *Fénelon au XVIIIe siècle en France (1715–1820)*. Paris: Hachette, 1917.

Clarkson, Thomas. *Essay on the Slavery and Commerce of the Human Species, Particularly the African*. London: T. Cadell and J.Phillips, 1786.

Cobban, Alfred. *The Social Interpretation of the French Revolution*. Cambridge: Cambridge University Press, 1999.

Coffee, Alan. "Mary Wollstonecraft, Freedom and the Enduring Power of Social Domination." *European Journal of Political Theory* 12, no. 2 (2013): 116–35.

Cohen, Joshua. *Rousseau: A Free Community of Equals*. Oxford: Oxford University Press, 2010.

Cohler, Anne M. *Montesquieu's Comparative Politics and the Spirit of American Constitutionalism*. Lawrence: University Press of Kansas, 1988.

Compagnon, Antoine. "Le dieu de la IIIe République." In *Ernest Renan*, 311–28. Paris: Travaux du Collège de France. Odile Jacob, 2013.

Condorcet, Jean-Antoine-Nicolas de Caritat (marquis de). *Réflexions sur l'esclavage des nègres*. Neufchâtel, 1781.

Condorcet, Jean-Antoine-Nicolas de Caritat (marquis de). *Essai sur la Constitution et les fonctions des Assemblées provinciales, Tome Premier*. Paris, 1788.

Condorcet, Jean-Antoine-Nicolas de Caritat (marquis de). *Examen sur cette question: est-il utile de diviser une assemblée nationale en plusieurs chambres*. Paris, 1789.

Condorcet, Jean-Antoine-Nicolas de Caritat (marquis de). "De la république ou un roi est-il nécessaire à la conservation de la liberté?" *Archives Parlementaires de 1787 à 1860* 28 (July 15, 1791): 336–38.

Condorcet, Jean-Antoine-Nicolas de Caritat (marquis de). *Réflexions sur la révolution de 1688 et sur celle du 10 août 1792*. Paris, 1792.

Condorcet, Jean-Antoine-Nicolas de Caritat (marquis de). "Ce que les citoyens ont le droit d'attendre de leurs représentants." In *Œuvres Complètes, Vol. XVIII*. Paris, 1804.

Condorcet, Jean-Antoine-Nicolas de Caritat (marquis de). "Influence de la révolution de l'Amérique sur les opinions et la législation de l'Europe [1786]." In *Œuvres*, 8: 1–68. Paris, 1847.

Condorcet, Jean-Antoine-Nicolas de Caritat (marquis de). "On the Principle of the Constitutional Plan Presented to the National Convention (1793)." In *Selected Writings*, edited by Keith Michael Baker. Indianapolis: The Bobbs-Merrill Company, 1976.

Condorcet, Jean-Antoine-Nicolas de Caritat (marquis de). *Cinq mémoires sur l'instruction publique*. Edited by Catherine Kintzler and Charles Coutel. Paris, 1994.

Condorcet, Jean-Antoine-Nicolas de Caritat (marquis de). "Rapport et projet de décret sur l'organisation générale de l'instruction publique" (avril 1792-décembre 1792). In *Une éducation pour la démocratie. Textes et projets de l'époque révolutionnaire*, edited by Bronislaw Baczko, 181–262. Genève: Droz, 2000.

Condorcet, Jean-Antoine-Nicolas de Caritat (marquis de). *Condorcet: Political Writings*. Edited by Steven Lukes and Nadia Urbinati. Cambridge: Cambridge University Press, 2012.

Conklin, Alice. *A Mission to Civilize: The Republican Idea of Empire in France and West Africa, 1895–1930*. Stanford: Stanford University Press, 1997.

Constant, Benjamin. *Political Writings*. Cambridge: Cambridge University Press, 1988.

Cooper, Anna Julia. *Slavery and the French and Haitian Revolutionists*. Translated by Frances Richardson Keller. Lanham: Rowman & Littlefield, 2006.

Courtney, Cecil Patrick. "*L'Esprit des Lois* dans la perspective de l'histoire du livre (1748–1800)." In *Le temps de Montesquieu*, edited by Michel Porret and Catherine Volpihac-Auger. Genève: Droz, 2002.

Cousin, Jean. "JJ Rousseau, interprète des institutions romaines dans le *Contrat Social*." In *Etudes sur le Contrat Social*, 13–34. Paris, 1964.

Craiutu, Aurelian. *A Virtue for Courageous Minds: Moderation in French Political Thought, 1748–1830*. Princeton: Princeton University Press, 2012.

Crook, Malcolm. *Elections in the French Revolution. An Apprenticeship in Democracy, 1789–1799*. Cambridge: Cambridge University Press, 2009.

Dagger, Richard. *Civic Virtues: Rights, Citizenship, and Republican Liberalism*. Oxford: Oxford University Press, 1997.

D'Argenson, Marquis. *D'Argenson, Considérations sur le gouvernement. A Critical Edition, with Other Political Texts*. Edited by Andrew Jainchill. Oxford: Oxford University Press, 2019.

De Certeau, Michel, Dominique Julia, and Jacques Revel. *Une politique de la langue. La révolution française et les patois: l'enquête de Grégoire*. Paris: Gallimard, 2002.

De Lolme, Jean-Louis. *Constitution de l'Angleterre ou état du gouvernement anglais, comparé avec la forme républicaine & avec les autres monarchies de l'Europe*. Amsterdam, 1771.

De Staël, Germaine. *Des circonstances actuelles qui peuvent terminer la révolution*. Paris: Droz, 1979.

Dent, N. J. H. *Rousseau. An Introduction to His Psychological, Social and Political Theory*. Oxford: Basil Blackwell, 1988.

Desan, Suzanne. "The French Revolution and Religion, 1795–1815." In *The Cambridge History of Christianity. Enlightenment, Reawakening and Revolution 1660–1815*, edited by Stewart J. Brown and Timothy Tackett, 556–574. Cambridge: Cambridge University Press, 2006.

Di Lorenzo, Anthony, and Mathieu Ferradou. "The Early Republic of France as a Cosmopolitan Moment." *La Révolution française* [online] 22 (2022).

Dijn, Annelien de. *French Political Thought from Montesquieu to Tocqueville: Liberty in a Levelled Society*. Cambridge: Cambridge University Press, 2008.

Dijn, Annelien de. "Was Montesquieu a Liberal Republican?" *The Review of Politics* 76 (2014): 21–41.

Dijn, Annelien de. "Rousseau and Republicanism." *Political Theory* 46, no. 1 (2015): 59–80.

Dijn, Annelien de. *Freedom. An Unruly History*. Cambridge: Harvard University Press, 2020.

Douglass, Robin. "Montesquieu and Modern Republicanism." *Political Studies* 60 (2012): 703–19.

Douglass, Robin. *Rousseau and Hobbes: Nature, Free Will, and the Passions*. Oxford: Oxford University Press, 2015.

Douglass, Robin. "Egalitarian Sympathies? Adam Smith and Sophie de Grouchy on Inequality and Social Order." *European Journal of Philosophy*, Online First (2023): 1–15.

Dubois, Laurent. *Avengers of the New World: The Story of the Haitian Revolution*. Cambridge: Harvard University Press, 2004.

Dubois, Laurent. *A Colony of Citizens. Revolution and Slave Emancipation in the French Caribbean, 1787–1804*. Chapel Hill: University of North Carolina Press, 2004.

Dubois, Laurent, and John D. Garrigus. *Slave Revolution in the Caribbean, 1789–1804*. Boston-NY: Palgrave Macmillan, 2006.

Dunn, John. "The Identity of the Bourgeois Liberal Republic." In *The Invention of the Modern Republic*, edited by Biancamaria Fontana, 206–25. Cambridge: Cambridge University Press, 1994.

Duong, Kevin. "The People as a Natural Disaster: Redemptive Violence in Jacobin Political Thought." *American Political Science Review* 111, no. 4 (November 2017): 786–800.

Edelstein, Dan. *The Terror of Natural Right. Republicanism, the Cult of Nature and the French Revolution*. Chicago: The University of Chicago Press, 2009.

Edelstein, Dan. *On the Spirit of Rights*. Chicago: University of Chicago Press, 2018.

Edelstein, Melvin. *The French Revolution and the Birth of Electoral Democracy*. New York: Routledge, 2014.

Elazar, Yiftah. "The Downfall of All Slavish Hierarchies: Richard Price on Emancipation, Improvement, and Republican Utopia." *Modern Intellectual History* 19 no. 1 (2022): 81–104.

Elazar, Yiftah, and Geneviève Rousselière, eds. *Republicanism and the Future of Democracy*. Cambridge: Cambridge University Press, 2019.

Farr, James, and David Lay Williams, eds. *The General Will: The Evolution of a Concept*. Cambridge: Cambridge University Press, 2015.

Fénelon, François. *Télémaque*. Paris: Hachette, 1927.

Fénelon, François. *Moral and Political Writings*. Edited by Ryan Patrick Hanley. Oxford: Oxford University Press, 2020.

Fink, Zera S. *The Classical Republicans: An Essay in the Recovery of a Pattern of Thought in Seventeenth Century England*. Evanston: Northwestern University, 1945.

Fontana, Biancamaria. *Benjamin Constant and the Post-Revolutionary Mind*. New Haven: Yale University Press, 1991.

Fontana, Biancamaria, ed. *The Invention of the Modern Republic*. Cambridge: Cambridge University Press, 1994.

Forsyth, Murray. *Reason and Revolution: The Political Thought of the Abbé Sieyès*. New York: Holmes and Meier Publishers, 1987.

Foucault, Michel. *Discipline and Punish*. New York: Vintage Books, 1995.

Fourest, Caroline. *La tentation obscurantiste*. Paris: Le Livre de poche, 2005.

Fraisse, Geneviève. *Muse de la raison. Démocratie et exclusion des femmes en France*. Paris: Gallimard, 1995.

Frank, Jason. "Populism and Praxis." In *Oxford Handbook of Populism*, edited by Cristóbal Rovira Kaltwasser, Paul Taggart, Paulina Ochoa Espejo, and Pierre Ostiguy, 629–43. Oxford: Oxford University Press, 2017.

Furet, Francois. *Penser la Révolution française*. Paris: Gallimard, 1978.

Furet, François. "The Ancien Régime and the Revolution." In *Realms of Memory*, edited by Pierre Nora, 79–108. New York: Columbia University Press, 1996.

Furet, Francois. *La Révolution en débat*. Paris: Gallimard, 1999.
Furet, François, and Mona Ozouf, eds. *A Critical Dictionary of the French Revolution*. Translated by Arthur Goldhammer. Cambridge: Belknap Press of Harvard University Press, 1989.
Furet, Francois, and Mona Ozouf, eds. *Dictionnaire critique de la révolution francaise*. Paris: Flammarion, 1989.
Gainot, Bernard. "Pierre Guyomar et la revendication démocratique dans les débats autour de la constitution de l'an III," in *1795, pour une République sans Révolution*, edited by Roger Dupuy. Rennes: Presses universitaires de Rennes, 1996.
Garsten, Bryan. "From Popular Sovereignty to Civil Society in Post-Revolutionary France." In *Popular Sovereignty in Historical Perspective*, edited by Richard Bourke and Quentin Skinner, 236–69. Cambridge: Cambridge University Press, 2016.
Gauchet, Marcel. *Robespierre: l'homme qui nous divise le plus*. Paris: Gallimard, 2018.
Gellner, Ernest. *Nations and Nationalism*. Oxford: Blackwell, 1983.
Getachew, Adom. "Universalism After the Post-Colonial Turn: Interpreting the Haitian Revolution." *Political Theory* 44, no. 6 (2016): 821–45.
Ghins, Arthur. "Representative Democracy versus Government by Opinion." *The Journal of Politics* 84, no. 3 (July 2022).
Gisler, Antoine. *L'esclavage aux Antilles françaises (XVII-XIXe siècles)*. Paris: Karthala, 1981.
Global Terrorism Database, 2023. www.start.umd.edu/gtd/about.
Godechot, Jacques. *France and the Atlantic Revolution of the Eighteenth Century, 1770–1799*. New York: Free Press, 1965.
Godechot, Jacques. *La Grande Nation. L'expansion révolutionnaire de la France dans le monde de 1789 à 1799*. Paris: Aubier, 1983.
Godechot, Jacques. *Les institutions de la France sous la Révolution et l'Empire*. Paris: Presses Universitaires de France, 1985.
Godineau, Dominique. *Citoyennes tricoteuses*. Paris: Perrin, 1988.
Gourevitch, Alex. "Labor Republicanism and the Transformation of Work." *Political Theory* 41, no. 4 (2013): 591–617.
Gourevitch, Alex. *From Slavery to the Cooperative Commonwealth: Labor and Republican Liberty in the Nineteenth Century*. Cambridge: Cambridge University Press, 2014.
Grant, Ruth W. *Hypocrisy and Integrity: Machiavelli, Rousseau, and the Ethics of Politics*. Chicago: University of Chicago Press, 1997.
Griswold, Charles. "Liberty and Compulsory Civil religion in Rousseau's *Social Contract*." *Journal of the History of Philosophy* 53 (2015): 271–300.
Grotius, Hugo. *The Rights of War and Peace*. Indianapolis: Liberty Fund, 2005.
Grouchy, Sophie de. *Letters on Sympathy*. Edited by Sandrine Bergès and Eric Schliesser. Oxford: Oxford University Press, 2019.
Grubb, James S. "Elite Citizens." In *Venice Reconsidered: The History and Civilization of an Italian City-State, 1297–1797*, edited by John Jeffries Martin and Dennis Romano, 339–64. Baltimore: Johns Hopkins University Press, 2000.
Gueniffey, Patrice. *Le nombre et la raison: la Révolution francaise et les élections*. Paris: Editions de l'EHESS, 1993.

Gueniffey, Patrice. "Girondins and Cordeliers: A Prehistory of the Republic?" In *The Invention of the Modern Republic*, edited by Biancamaria Fontana, 86–106. Cambridge: Cambridge University Press, 1997.

Guillon, Claude. "Pauline Léon, une républicaine révolutionnaire." *Annales historiques de la Révolution française* 344 [Online] (2006).

Guiraudet, Charles Philippe-Toussaint. *Qu'est-ce que la nation et qu'est-ce que la France?* Paris, 1789.

Hajjat, Abdellali. *Les frontières de l'"identité nationale". L'injonction à l'assimilation en France métropolitaine et coloniale.* Paris: La Découverte, 2012.

Hamel, Christopher. "L'esprit républicain anglais adapté à la France du XVIIIe siècle: un républicanisme classique?" *La Révolution française* 5 [Online] (2013).

Hamilton, Alexander, James Madison, and John Jay. *The Federalist: With Letters of Brutus.* Edited by Terence Ball. Cambridge: Cambridge University Press, 2003.

Hammersley, Rachel. "English Republicanism in Revolutionary France: The Case of the Cordelier Club." *Journal of British Studies* 43, no. 4 (2004): 464–81.

Hammersley, Rachel. *French Revolutionaries and English Republicans: The Cordeliers Club, 1790–1794.* Rochester: Rochester University Press, 2005.

Hammersley, Rachel. *The English Republican Tradition and Eighteenth-Century France: Between the Ancients and the Moderns.* Manchester: Manchester University Press, 2010.

Hammersley, Rachel. *Republicanism. An Introduction.* Cambridge: Polity, 2020.

Hampson, Norman. *The Life and Opinions of Maximilien Robespierre.* London: Duckworth, 1974.

Hankins, James. "Exclusivist Republicanism and the Non-Monarchical Republic." *Political Theory* 38, no. 4 (2010): 452–82.

Hanley, Ryan Patrick. "Commerce and Corruption: Rousseau's Diagnosis and Adam Smith's Cure." *European Journal of Political Theory* 7, no. 2 (2008): 137–58.

Hanley, Ryan Patrick. "The 'Science of the Legislator' in Adam Smith and Rousseau." *American Journal of Political Science* 52, no. 2, (2008): 219–34.

Hanley, Ryan Patrick. "Rousseau and Fénelon." In *The Rousseauian Mind*, edited by Eve Grace and Christopher Kelly, 87–97. New York: Routledge, 2019.

Hanley, Ryan Patrick. *The Political Philosophy of Fénelon*, Oxford: Oxford University Press, 2020.

Harrington, James. *The Commonwealth of Oceana and a System of Politics.* Edited by J. G. A. Pocock. Cambridge: Cambridge University Press, 1992.

Hasan, Rafeeq. "Rousseau on the Ground of Obligation: Reconsidering the Social Autonomy Interpretation." *European Journal of Political Theory* 17, no. 2 (2018): 233–43.

Hazareesingh, Sudhir. *Political Traditions in Modern France.* Oxford: Oxford University Press, 1994.

Hazareesingh, Sudhir. *Intellectual Founders of the Republic. Five Studies in Nineteenth-Century French Political Thought.* Oxford: Oxford University Press, 2001.

Higonnet, Patrice. *Sister Republics. The Origin of French and American Republicanism.* Cambridge: Harvard University Press, 1988.

Hobbes, Thomas. *The Leviathan*. Edited by Richard Tuck. Cambridge: Cambridge University Press, 1996.
Hobsbawm, E. J. *Nations and Nationalism since 1780*. Cambridge: Cambridge University Press, 1992.
Honig, Bonnie. "Between Decision and Deliberation: Political Paradox in Democratic Theory." *American Political Science Review* 101, no. 1 (2007): 1–17.
Honohan, Iseult. *Civic Republicanism*. London: Routledge, 2002.
Hont, Istvan. "The Permanent Crisis of a Divided Mankind: 'Contemporary Crisis of the Nation State' in Historical Perspective." *Political Studies* 42, no. 1 suppl (August 1994): 166–231.
Hont, Istvan. *Jealousy of Trade*. Cambridge: Harvard University Press, 2005.
Hont, Istvan. "The Early Enlightenment Debate on Commerce and Luxury." In *The Cambridge History of Eighteenth-Century Political Thought*, edited by Mark Goldie and Robert Wokler, 377–418. Cambridge: Cambridge University Press, 2008.
Hont, Istvan, and Michael Ignatieff, eds. *Wealth and Virtue: The Shaping of Political Economy in the Scottish Enlightenment*. Cambridge: Cambridge University Press, 1983.
Hörnqvist, Mikael. *Machiavelli and Empire*. Cambridge: Cambridge University Press, 2004.
Hörnqvist, Mikael. "Machiavelli's Three Desires. Florentine Republicans on Liberty, Empire, and Justice." In *Empire and Modern Political Thought*, edited by Sankar Muthu, 7–29. Cambridge: Cambridge University Press, 2017.
Hulliung, Mark L. *Citizen Machiavelli*. Princeton: Princeton University Press, 1983.
Hume, David. *Political Essays*. Cambridge: Cambridge University Press, 1994.
Hunt, Lynn. *The Family Romance of the French Revolution*. Berkeley and Los Angeles: University of California Press, 1992.
Hunt, Lynn. "The French Revolutionary Wars." In *The Cambridge History of the Napoleonic Wars, Volume I*, edited by Michael Broers and Philip Dwyer, 127–46. Cambridge: Cambridge University Press, 2022.
Israel, Jonathan. *Democratic Enlightenment. Philosophy, Revolution and Human Rights. 1750–1790*. Oxford: Oxford University Press, 2013.
Jack, Malcolm. "One State of Nature: Mandeville and Rousseau." *Journal of the History of Ideas* 39, no. 1 (1978): 119–24.
Jainchill, Andrew. *Reimagining Politics after the Terror: The Republican Origins of French Liberalism*. Ithaca: Cornell University Press, 2008.
James, C. L. R. *The Black Jacobins: Toussaint L'Ouverture and the San Domingo Revolution*. New York: Vintage Books, 1963.
Jaume, Lucien. *Le discours jacobin et la démocratie*. Paris: Fayard, 1989.
Jaume, Lucien. "Robespierre chez Machiavel? Le culte de l'Etre Suprême et le 'retour aux principes'." *Droits* 1, no. 57 (2013): 177–88.
Jennings, Jeremy. "Citizenship, Republicanism and Multiculturalism in Contemporary France." *British Journal of Political Science* 30, no. 4 (2000): 575–97.
Jennings, Jeremy. *Revolution and the Republic. A History of Political Thought in France since the Eighteenth-Century*. Oxford: Oxford University Press, 2011.

Jurdjevic, Mark. "Virtue, Commerce, and the Enduring Florentine Moment: Reintegrating Italy into the Atlantic Republican Debate." *Journal of the History of Ideas* 62 (2001): 721–43.

Kalyvas, Andreas, and Ira Katznelson. *Liberal Beginnings: Making a Republic for the Moderns*. Cambridge: Cambridge University Press, 2008.

Kant, Immanuel. *Practical Philosophy*. Edited by Mary J. Gregor. Cambridge: Cambridge University Press, 1999.

Kant, Immanuel. *The Metaphysics of Morals*. Cambridge: Cambridge University Press, 2017.

Kapust, Daniel. "Skinner, Pettit and Livy: The Conflict of the Orders and the Ambiguity of Republican Liberty." *History of Political Thought* XXV, no. 3 Autumn (2004): 377–401.

Kapust, Daniel. "Cicero on Decorum and the Morality of Rhetoric." *European Journal of Political Theory* 10, no. 1 (2011): 92–112.

Kasimis, Demetra. *The Perpetual Immigrant and the Limits of Athenian Democracy*. Cambridge: Cambridge University Press, 2018.

Kates, Gary. *The Cercle Social, the Girondins, and the French Revolution*. Princeton: Princeton University Press, 2014.

Kelly, Duncan. "Popular Sovereignty as State Theory in the Nineteenth Century." In *Popular Sovereignty in Perspective*, edited by Richard Bourke and Quentin Skinner, 270–96. Cambridge: Cambridge University Press, 2016.

Kepel, Gilles. *Banlieue de la république: société, politique et religion à Clichy-sous-Bois et Montfermeil*. Paris: Gallimard, 2012.

Kepel, Gilles. *Quatre-vingt-treize*. Paris: Gallimard, 2012.

Kirk, Linda. "Genevan Republicanism." In *Republicanism, Liberty and Commercial Society, 1649–1776*, edited by David Wooton, 270–309. Stanford: Stanford University Press, 1994.

Kirshner, Alexander S. *Legitimate Opposition*. New Haven: Yale University Press. 2022.

Kloppenberg, James T. *Toward Democracy: The Struggle for Self-rule in European and American Thought*. Oxford: Oxford University Press, 2016.

Krause, Sharon. "The Spirit of Separate Powers in Montesquieu." *The Review of Politics* 62, no. 2 Spring (2000): 231–65.

Krause, Sharon. *Liberalism with Honor*. Cambridge: Cambridge University Press, 2002.

Kriegel, Blandine. *The State and the Rule of Law*. Translated by Jeffrey Cohen and Marc LePain. Princeton: Princeton University Press, 1995.

Kriegel, Blandine. *Philosophie de la république*. Paris: Plon, 1998.

La Rochefoucauld d'Enville, Louis-Alexandre, and Benjamin Franklin, eds. *Constitution des treize Etats-unis de l'Amérique*. Philadelphie & Paris: Pissot, Père et fils, libraires, 1783.

Laborde, Cécile. *Critical Republicanism: The Hijab Controversy and Political Philosophy*. Oxford: Oxford University Press, 2008.

Laborde, Cécile, and John Maynor, eds. *Republicanism and Political Theory*. Oxford: Blackwell, 2008.

Lakanal, Joseph. *Rapport sur J.J. Rousseau fait au nom du Comité d'Instruction Publique*. Paris, 1794.

Landes, Joan B. *Women and the Public Sphere in the Age of French Revolution*. Ithaca and London: Cornell University Press, 1988.

Larcher, Silyane. *L'autre citoyen: L'idéal républicain et les Antilles après l'esclavage*. Paris: Armand Colin, 2014.

Larrère, Catherine. "Montesquieu et l'idée de fédération." In *L'Europe de Montesquieu*, edited by Alberto Postigliola and Maria-Grazia Bottaro-Palumbo, *Cahiers Montesquieu* 2, 137–152. Naples: Liguori, 1995.

Laurentin, Emmanuel. "Pourquoi la république?" In *Histoire d'une république fragile, 1905–2015. Comment en sommes-nous arrivés là?* Paris: Fayard/France Culture, 2015.

Lavicomterie, Louis-Charles. *Du peuple et des rois*. Paris, 1790.

Le Cour Grandmaison, Olivier. *Les citoyennetés en révolution (1789–1794)*. Paris: Presses Universitaires de France, 1992.

Le Cour Grandmaison, Olivier. *De l'indigénat. Anatomie d'un monstre juridique: le droit colonial en Algérie et dans l'Empire français*. Paris: Zones, 2010.

Lee, Daniel. *Popular Sovereignty in Early Modern Constitutional Thought*. Oxford: Oxford University Press, 2016.

Lefebvre, Georges. *The Coming of the French Revolution*. Translated by R. R. Palmer. Princeton: Princeton University Press, 1975.

Levy, Jacob. "Beyond Publius: Montesquieu, Liberal Republicanism and the Small-Republic Thesis." *History of Political Thought* 27, no. 1 (2006): 50–90.

Levy, Jacob. *Rationalism, Pluralism, and Freedom*. Oxford: Oxford University Press, 2014.

Linton, Marisa. "Robespierre's Political Principles." In *Robespierre*, edited by Colin Haydon and William Doyle, 37–53. Cambridge: Cambridge University Press, 1999.

Linton, Marisa. *Choosing Terror: Virtue, Friendship, and Authenticity in the French Revolution*. Oxford: Oxford University Press, 2013.

Lintott, Andrew. *The Constitution of the Roman Republic*. Oxford: Oxford University Press, 1999.

List, Christian, and Robert E. Goodin. "Epistemic Democracy: Generalizing the Condorcet Jury Theorem." *Journal of Political Philosophy* 9, no. 3 (September 2001): 277–306.

Livy. *The History of Rome*. London: J. M. Dent & Sons, 1905.

Lochak, Danièle. "Le Haut Conseil à la (dés)intégration." *Plein Droit* 4, no. 91 (2011): 12–15.

Locke, John. *Two Treatises of Government*. Cambridge: Cambridge University Press, 1960.

Lovett, Frank. *A General Theory of Domination and Justice*. Oxford: Oxford University Press, 2010.

Lovett, Frank. "Harrington's Empire of Law." *Political Studies* 60, no. 1 (March 2012): 59–75.

Lovett, Frank. *The Well-Ordered Republic*. Oxford: Oxford University Press, 2022.

Lovett, Frank. "Republicanism," online *Stanford Encyclopedia of Philosophy*. 2022.

Lovett, Frank, and Philip Pettit. "Neo-Republicanism: A Normative and Institutional Research Program." *Annual Review of Political Science* 12 (2009): 11–29.

Lutz, Donald S. "The Relative Influence of European Writers on Late Eighteenth-Century American Political Thought." *American Political Science Review* 78 (1984): 189–97.

Mably, Gabriel Bonnot de. *Observations sur les Grecs*. Geneva, 1749.

Mably, Gabriel Bonnot de. *Observations sur le gouvernement et les loix des Etats-Unis d'Amérique*. Amsterdam & Paris, 1784.

Mably, Gabriel Bonnot de. *Collection complète des œuvres de l'Abbé de Mably*. 15 vols. Paris: Desbrières, 1795.

Mably, Gabriel Bonnot de. *Entretiens de Phocion sur le rapport de la morale avec la politique*. Paris, 1797.

Mably, Gabriel Bonnot de. *Des droits et des devoirs du citoyen*. Paris: Marcel Didier, 1972.

MacGilvray, Eric. *The Invention of Market Freedom*. Cambridge: Cambridge University Press, 2011.

Machiavelli, Niccolò. *Discourses on Livy*. Translated by Harvey C. Mansfield and Nathan Tarcov. Chicago: The University of Chicago Press, 1996.

Machiavelli, Niccolò. *The Prince*. Translated by Peter Bondanella and Mark Musa. Oxford: Oxford University Press, 1998.

Madec, Annick, Numa Murard, Smain Laacher, and François Gèze. "A propos des indigènes de la république." *Mouvements* 41 (2005): 112–26.

Manin, Bernard. "Rousseau." In *Dictionnaire critique de la Révolution française*, edited by François Furet and Mona Ozouf. Paris: Flammarion, 2007.

Mathiez, Albert. "Robespierre et le culte de l'Etre Suprême." *Annales révolutionnaires* 3, no. 2 (1910): 209–38.

Mazeau, Guillaume, and Clyde Plumauzille. "Penser avec le genre: trouble dans la citoyenneté révolutionnaire." *La Révolution française* 9 [online] (2015).

Mazouz, Sarah. *La république et ses autres. Politiques de l'altérité dans la France des années 2000*. Lyon: ENS-Lyon, 2017.

McCormick, John P. "Rousseau's Rome and the Repudiation of Populist Republicanism." *Critical Review of International Social and Political Philosophy* 10, no. 1 (March 2007): 3–27.

McCormick, John P. *Machiavellian Democracy*. Cambridge: Cambridge University Press, 2011.

McNeil, Gordon H. "The Cult of Rousseau and the French Revolution." *Journal of the History of Ideas* 6, no. 2 (April 1945): 197–212.

McPhee, Peter. *Robespierre. A Revolutionary Life*. New Haven: Yale University Press, 2012.

Melon, Jean-François. *Essai politique sur le commerce [1734]*. Edited by Francine Markovits. Caen: Presses Universitaires de Caen, 2014.

Melzer, Arthur M. *The Natural Goodness of Man: On the System of Rousseau's Thought*. Chicago: University of Chicago Press, 1990.

Mercier, Louis-Sébastien. *De Jean-Jacques Rousseau, considéré comme un des premiers auteurs de la révolution*. Paris, 1791.

Miqueu, Christophe. "Le républicanisme. Présentation d'un champ de recherches en philosophie politique." *Klesis* 2 (2006): 1–19.

Monnier, Raymonde. *Républicanisme, patriotisme et Révolution française*. Paris: L'Harmattan, 2005.

Montesquieu, Charles de. *The Spirit of the Laws*. Edited by Anne M. Cohler, Basia C. Miller and Harold S. Stone. Cambridge: Cambridge University Press, 1989.
Montesquieu, Charles de. *Considerations on the Causes of the Greatness of the Romans and Their Decline*. Edited and translated by David Lowenthal. Indianapolis: Hackett Publishing Company, 1999.
Morgan, Edmund S. *Inventing the People: The Rise of Popular Sovereignty in England and America*. New York: W. W. Norton, 1988.
Moyn, Samuel. *The Last Utopia: Human Rights in History*. Cambridge: The Belknap Press of Harvard University Press, 2010.
Muthu, Sankar. *Enlightenment against Empire*. Princeton: Princeton University Press. 2003.
Näsström, Sofia. "The Legitimacy of the People." *Political Theory* 35, no. 5 (2007): 624–58.
Necker, Jacques. *Réflexions philosophiques sur l'égalité*. Paris: Les Belles Lettres, 2005.
Necker, Jacques. *On Executive Power in Great States*. Edited by Aurelian Craiutu. Indianapolis: Liberty Fund, 2020.
Neidleman, Jason Andrew. *The General Will is Citizenship: Inquiries into French Political Thought*. New York: Rowman and Littlefield, 2000.
Nelson, Eric. *The Greek Tradition in Republican Thought*. Cambridge: Cambridge University Press, 2004.
Nesbitt, Nick. *Universal Emancipation: The Haitian Revolution and the Radical Enlightenment*. Charlottesville: University of Virginia, 2008.
Neuhouser, Frederik. *Rousseau's Theodicy of Self-love: Evil, Rationality, and the Drive for Recognition*. Oxford: Oxford University Press, 2008.
Nicolet, Claude. *L'idée républicaine en France: Essai d'histoire critique (1789–1924)*. Paris: Gallimard, 1982.
Noiriel, Gérard. *Les origines républicaines de Vichy*. Paris: Fayard, 2013.
Noiriel, Gérard. *Les gilets jaunes à la lumière de l'histoire*. Paris: Editions de l'Aube, 2019.
Nora, Pierre. *Les lieux de mémoire. Tome I: la république*. Paris: Gallimard, 1984.
Nord, Philip. *The Republican Moment. Struggles for Democracy in Nineteenth-Century France*. Cambridge: Harvard University Press, 1995.
Ober, Josiah. *The Athenian Revolution: Essays on Ancient Greek Democracy and Political Theory*. Princeton: Princeton University Press, 1996.
Ochoa Espejo, Paulina. *The Time of Popular Sovereignty. Process and the Democratic State*. University Park: Penn State University Press, 2011.
Oprea, Alexandra. "Pluralism and the General Will: The Roman and Spartan Models in Rousseau's Social Contract." *Review of Politics* 81, no. 4 (September 2019): 573–96.
Oprea, Alexandra. *Children or Citizens: Children, Education, and Politics in Modern Political Thought*. [unpublished manuscript], 2023.
Outram, Dorinda. *The Body and the French Revolution: Sex, Class and Political Culture*. New Haven: Yale University Press, 1989.
Ozouf, Mona. *La fête révolutionnaire, 1789–1799*. Paris: Gallimard, 1976.
Ozouf, Mona. "Varennes." In *Dictionnaire critique de la révolution française. Evénements*, edited by François Furet and Mona Ozouf, 325–40. Paris: Flammarion, 2007.

Paine, Thomas. *Lettre de Thomas Paine au peuple français sur la journée du 18 Fructidor*. Paris: Imprimerie du Cercle Social, 1797.

Palmer, Robert Roswel. *The Age of the Democratic Revolution: A Political History of Europe and America. 1760–1800*. Princeton: Princeton University Press, 1970.

Palmer, Robert Roswell. *The Improvement of Humanity: Education and the French Revolution*. Princeton: Princeton University Press, 1985.

Pangle, Thomas. *Montesquieu's Philosophy of Liberalism: A Commentary on the Spirits of the Laws*. Chicago: The University of Chicago Press, 1973.

Pasquino, Pasquale. *Sieyes et l'invention de la constitution en France*. Paris: Editions Odile Jacob, 1998.

Pateman, Carole. *Participation and Democratic Theory*. Cambridge: Cambridge University Press, 1970.

Peabody, Sue. *"There Are No Slaves in France": The Political Culture of Race and Slavery in the Ancien Régime*. Oxford: Oxford University Press, 1996.

Peillon, Vincent. *Liberté, égalité, fraternité. Sur le républicanisme français*. Paris: Le Seuil, 2018.

Pettit, Philip. *Republicanism: A Theory of Freedom and Government*. Oxford: Oxford University Press, 1997.

Pettit, Philip. *On the People's Terms: A Republican Theory and Model of Democracy*. Cambridge: Cambridge University Press, 2012.

Pettit, Philip. "Two Republican Traditions." In *Republican Democracy: Liberty, Law and Politics*, edited by Andreas Niederberger and Philipp Schink, 169–204. Edinburgh: Edinburgh University Press, 2013.

Pictet, Charles. *Tableau de la situation actuelle des Etats-Unis d'Amérique*. Paris: Du Pont, 1795.

Piquet, Jean-Daniel. "Le discours abolitionniste de Danton (16 pluviôse an II)." *Revue d'histoire et de philosophie religieuses* 90, no. 3 (2010): 353–77.

Pitkin, Hanna Fenichel. *Fortune is a Woman. Gender and Politics in the Thought of Niccolò Machiavelli*. Chicago: the University of Chicago Press, 1984.

Pitts, Jennifer. *A Turn to Empire. The Rise of Imperial Liberalism in Britain and France*. Princeton: Princeton University Press, 2006.

Pocock, J. G. A. *The Machiavellian Moment: Florentine Political Thought and the Atlantic Republican Tradition*. Princeton: Princeton University Press, 1975.

Pocock, J. G. A. *Virtue, Commerce, and History: Essays on Political Thought and History, Chiefly in the Eighteenth Century*. Cambridge: Cambridge University Press, 1985.

Pocock, J. G. A. "Virtues, Rights, and Manners: A Model for Historians of Political Thought." *Political Theory* 9, no. 3 (1981): 353–68.

Polybius. *The Histories*. Translated by William R. Paton. 6 vols. Loeb. Cambridge: Harvard University Press, 2011.

Prochasson, Christophe. "Introuvable modèle républicain." *Cahiers français: Les valeurs de la République* 336 (2007).

Putterman, Ethan. "Realism and Reform in Rousseau's Constitutional Projects for Poland and Corsica." *Political Studies*, vol. 49 no 3 (2001):481–494.

Raab, Felix. *The English Face of Machiavelli: A Changing Interpretation 1500–1700*. London: Routledge and Kegan Paul, 1964.

Rahe, Paul A. *Republics Ancient and Modern: Classical Republicanism and the American Revolution*. Chapel Hill: University of North Carolina Press, 1992.

Ramsey, James. *An Essay on the Treatment and Conversion of African Slaves in the British Sugar Colonies*. London: J. Phillips, 1784.

Rasmussen, Dennis C. *The Problems and Promise of Commercial Society: Adam Smith's Response to Rousseau*. University Park: Pennsylvania State University Press, 2008.

Rawls, John. *Lectures on the History of Political Philosophy*. Cambridge: Harvard University Press, 2007.

Raynal, Guillaume-Thomas. *Révolution de l'Amérique*. London, 1781.

Recueil des loix constitutives des colonies angloises, confédérées sous la dénomination d'Etats-Unis de l'Amérique-Septentrionale, 1778.

Reinert, Sophus A. *Translating Empire. Emulation and the Origins of Political Economy*. Cambridge: Harvard University Press, 2011.

Reisert, Joseph R. *Jean-Jacques Rousseau. A Friend of Virtue*. Ithaca, NY: Cornell University Press, 2003.

Renan, Ernest. *What Is a Nation? And Other Political Writings*. Edited by Matteo F. N. Giglioli. New York: Columbia University Press, 2018.

Riley, Patrick. "Rousseau, Fénelon, and the Quarrel between the Ancients and the Moderns." In *The Cambridge Companion to Rousseau*, edited by Patrick Riley, 78–93. Cambridge: Cambridge University Press, 2001.

Riot-Sarcey, Michèle. *Histoire du féminisme*. Paris: La Découverte, 2002.

Robbins, Caroline. *The Eighteenth-Century Commonwealthman*. Cambridge: Harvard University Press, 1959.

Robert, François. *Le républicanisme adapté à la France*. Paris, 1790.

Robespierre, Maximilien. *Œuvres complètes de Maximilien de Robespierre*. Paris: Presses Universitaires de France, 1967.

Robespierre, Maximilien. *Robespierre. Virtue and Terror*. New York: Verso, 2007.

Robine, Jérémy. "Les 'indigènes de la république': nation et question postcoloniale." *Hérodote* 1, no. 120 (2006): 118–48.

Rosanvallon, Pierre. *Le sacre du citoyen: histoire du suffrage universel en France*. Paris: Gallimard, 1992.

Rosanvallon, Pierre. *La démocratie inachevée: histoire de la souveraineté du peuple en France*. Paris: Gallimard, 2000.

Rosanvallon, Pierre. *Le modèle politique français. La société civile contre le jacobinisme de 1789 à nos jours*. Paris: Seuil, 2004.

Rosenblatt, Helena. *Rousseau and Geneva. From the First Discourse to the Social Contract, 1749–1762*. Cambridge: Cambridge University Press, 1997.

Rosenblatt, Helena. "On the Intellectual Source of Laïcité. Rousseau, Constant, and the Debates about a National Religion." *French Politics, Culture & Society* 25, no. 3 (Winter 2007): 1–18.

Rosenblatt, Helena. *The Cambridge Companion to Constant*. Cambridge: Cambridge University Press, 2009.

Rousseau, Jean-Jacques. *Œuvres complètes. Tome III*. Paris: NRF Gallimard (Pléiade), 1964.

Rousseau, Jean-Jacques. *Émile or On Education*. Edited by Allan Bloom. New York: Basic Books, 1979.

Rousseau, Jean-Jacques. *The Discourses and Other Early Political Writings*. Cambridge: Cambridge University Press, 2010.

Rousseau, Jean-Jacques. *The Social Contract and Other Later Political Writings*. Cambridge: Cambridge University Press, 2010.

Rousseau, Jean-Jacques. *Affaires de Corse*. Edited by Christophe Litwin and James Swenson, Paris: Vrin, 2018.

Rousselière, Geneviève. "Rousseau on Freedom in Commercial Society." *American Journal of Political Science* 60, no. 2 (April 2016): 352–63.

Rousselière, Geneviève. "On Political Responsibility in Post-Revolutionary Times: Kant and Constant's Debate on Lying." *European Journal of Political Theory* 17 no.2 (2018): 214–32.

Rousselière, Geneviève. "Can Popular Sovereignty Be Represented? Jacobinism from Radical Democracy to Populism." *American Journal of Political Science* 65, no. 3 (July 2021): 670–82.

Rousselière, Geneviève. "Rousseau's Theory of Value and the Case of Women." *European Journal of Philosophy* 29, no. 2. (2021): 285–98.

Rousselière, Geneviève. "Audi Alteram Partem: Rhetoric and Republican Political Thought." In *The Oxford Handbook of Rhetoric and Political Theory*, edited by Keith Topper and Dilip Gaonkar. Oxford: Oxford University Press, 2022.

Rousselière, Geneviève. "Rousseau and the Puzzle of the Roman Republic." In *The Cambridge Companion to Rousseau's Social Contract*, edited by David Lay Williams and Matthew Maguire, 223–51. Cambridge: Cambridge University Press, 2023.

Roussin, Juliette. "La démocratie épistémique: une perspective condorcétienne." *Cahiers philosophiques* 160 (2020): 55–74.

Rubinelli, Lucia. "How to Think beyond Sovereignty: On Sieyes and Constituent Power." *European Journal of Political Theory* 18, no. 1 (2019): 47–67.

Rubinelli, Lucia. "Sieyès versus Bicameralism." *The Review of Politics* 81 (2019): 255–79.

Rudé, George. *Robespierre: Portrait of a Revolutionary Democrat*. New York: Viking Press, 1975.

Saada, Emmanuelle. "The Republic and the Indigenes." In *The French Republic. History, Values, Debates*, edited by Edward Berenson, Vincent Duclert, and Christophe Prochasson, 223–31. Ithaca: Cornell University Press, 2011.

Saada, Emmanuelle. *Empire's Children: Race, Filiation, and Citizenship in the French Colonies*. Chicago: University of Chicago Press, 2012.

Saint-Victor, Jacques de, and Thomas Branthôme. *Histoire de la République en France*. Paris: Economica, 2018.

Sala-Molins, Louis. *Le Code Noir ou le calvaire de Canaan*. Paris: Presses Universitaires de France, 2018.

Schaeffer, Denise. "Realism, Rhetoric and the Possibility of Reform in Rousseau's *Considerations*." *Polity* 42, no. 3 (July 2010): 377–97.

Schliesser, Eric. "Sophie de Grouchy: The Tradition(s) of Two Liberties, and the Missing Mother(s) of Liberalism." In *Women and Liberty: 1600–1800*, edited by Jacqueline Broad and Karen Detlefsen, 109–22. Oxford: Oxford University Press, 2018.

Schnapper, Dominique. "L'universel républicain revisité." *Ville-Ecole-Intégration Enjeux*, no. 121 (June 2000): 10–22.

Schwartzberg, Melissa. "Political Equality among Unequals." In *The Cambridge Companion to Rousseau's "Social Contract,"* edited by David Lay Williams and Matthew W. Maguire, 223–51. Cambridge: Cambridge University Press, 2023.

Scott, Joan Wallach. *Only Paradoxes to Offer: French Feminists and the Rights of Man*. Cambridge: Harvard University Press, 1996.

Scott, John T. *Rousseau's God. Theology, Religion, and the Natural Goodness of Man*. Chicago: The University of Chicago Press, 2023.

Scurr, Ruth. *Fatal Purity. Robespierre and the French Revolution*. New York: Metropolitan Books, 2006.

Selinger, William. *Parliamentarism. From Burke to Weber*. Cambridge: Cambridge University Press, 2019.

Sellers, Mortimer N. S. *American Republicanism: Roman Ideology in the United States Constitution*. New York: New York University Press, 1994.

Shalhope, Robert E. "Republicanism and Early American Historiography." *William and Mary Quarterly* 3, no. 39 (1982): 335–56.

Shepard, Todd. *The Invention of Decolonization*. Ithaca: Cornell University Press, 2006.

Shklar, Judith. *Men and Citizens: A Study of Rousseau's Social Theory*. Cambridge: Cambridge University Press, 1969.

Shklar, Judith. "Montesquieu and the New Republicanism." In *Machiavelli and Republicanism*, edited by Gisela Bock, Quentin Skinner, and Maurizio Viroli, 266–78. Cambridge: Cambridge University Press, 1990.

Sidney, Algernon. *Discourses Concerning Government*. Edited by Thomas G. West. Indianapolis: Liberty Fund, 1996.

Sieyès, Emmanuel Joseph. *Observations sur le rapport du comité de constitution concernant la nouvelle organisation de la France*. Versailles: Chez Baudouin, 1789.

Sieyès, Emmanuel Joseph. *Ecrits politiques*. Edited by Roberto Zapperi. Paris: Editions des archives contemporaines, 1985.

Sieyès, Emmanuel Joseph. *Des Manuscrits de Sieyès. 1773–1799*. Edited by Christine Fauré. Paris: Honoré Champion, 1999.

Sieyès, Emmanuel Joseph. *Political Writings. Including the Debate between Sieyès and Paine*. Indianapolis/Cambridge: Hackett Publishing Company, 2003.

Simpson, Matthew. *Rousseau's Theory of Freedom*. London: Continuum, 2006.

Skinner, Quentin. *The Foundations of Modern Political Thought*. 2 vols. Cambridge: Cambridge University Press, 1978.

Skinner, Quentin. "The Paradoxes of Political Liberty." In *The Tanner Lectures on Human Values*, Volume VII, edited by Sterling McMurrin, 225–50. Cambridge; Cambridge University Press, 1986.

Skinner, Quentin. *Liberty before Liberalism*. Cambridge: Cambridge University Press, 1998.

Skinner, Quentin, "John Milton and the Politics of Slavery." In *Visions of Politics: Volume 2: Renaissance Virtues*, edited by Quentin Skinner, 2: 286–307. Cambridge: Cambridge University Press, 2002.

Soboul, Albert. "Anarchasis Cloots, l'orateur du genre humain." *Annales historiques de la Révolution française* 239 (1980): 29–58.

Sonenscher, Michael. *Before the Deluge: Public Debt, Inequality and the Intellectual Origins of the French Revolution.* Princeton: Princeton University Press, 2007.

Sonenscher, Michael. *Sans-Culottes. An Eighteenth-Century Emblem in the French Revolution.* Princeton: Princeton University Press, 2008.

Spector, Céline. "Montesquieu: Critique of Republicanism?" *Critical Review of International Social and Political Philosophy* 6, no. 1 Spring (2003): 38–53.

Spector, Céline. *Montesquieu: Pouvoirs, Richesses et Sociétés.* Paris: Presses Universitaires de France, 2004.

Spector, Céline. "'Pour vous, peuples modernes, vous n'avez point d'esclaves.' Le silence sur la traite dans le *Second Discours*, *Émile* et le *Contrat social.*" In *Silence, Implicite et Non-dit chez Rousseau*, edited by Brigitte Weltmann-Aron, Ourida Mostefai, and Peter Westmoreland, 189–201. Paris: Brill Rodopi, 2020.

Spitz, Jean-Fabien. *La liberté politique. Essai de généalogie conceptuelle.* Paris: Presses Universitaires de France, 1995.

Spitz, Jean-Fabien. "La culture républicaine en question. Pierre Rosanvallon et la critique du 'jacobinisme' français." *Raisons Politiques* 3, no. 15 (2004): 111–24.

Spitz, Jean-Fabien. *Le moment républicain.* Paris: Gallimard, 2005.

Spitz, Jean-Fabien. *La république? Quelles valeurs? Essai sur un nouvel intégrisme.* Paris: Gallimard, 2022.

Sreenivasan, Gopal. "What Is the General Will?" *The Philosophical Review* 109, no. 4 (2000): 545–81.

Stilz, Anna. *Liberal Loyalty: Freedom, Obligation, and the State.* Princeton: Princeton University Press, 2009.

Sullivan, Vickie. *Machiavelli, Hobbes, and the Formation of a Liberal Republicanism in England.* Cambridge: Cambridge University Press, 2004.

Sullivan, Vickie. *Montesquieu and the Despotic Ideas of Europe: An Interpretation of the "Spirit of the Laws."* Chicago: University of Chicago Press, 2017.

Swenson, James. *On Jean-Jacques Rousseau, Considered as One of the First Authors of the Revolution.* Stanford: Stanford University Press, 2000.

Tackett, Timothy. "The French Revolution and Religion to 1794." In *The Cambridge History of Christianity. Vol.7. Enlightenment, Reawakening and Revolution 1660–1815*, edited by Stewart J. Brown and Timothy Tackett, 536–55. Cambridge: Cambridge University Press, 2006.

Taylor, Robert. *Exit Left. Markets and Mobility in Republican Thought.* Oxford: Oxford University Press, 2017.

Todd, Emmanuel. *Qui est Charlie? Controverse d'une crise religieuse.* Paris: Le Seuil, 2016.

Tuck, Richard. *The Sleeping Sovereign: The Invention of Modern Democracy.* Cambridge: Cambridge University Press, 2016.

Turgot, Anne-Robert-Jacques. "Lettre du Docteur Price sur les constitutions américaines." In *Œuvres de Turgot et documents le concernant*, edited by Gustave Schelle, Vol. 5, 532–40. Paris, 1923.

Turgot, Anne-Robert-Jacques. *Œuvres de Turgot et documents le concernant.* Edited by Gustave Schelle. 5 vols. Paris, 1923.

Turner, Brandon P. "Mandeville against Luxury." *Political Theory* 44, no. 1 (February 2016): 26–52.
Urbinati, Nadia. "Condorcet's Democratic Theory of Representative Government." *European Journal of Political Theory* 3, no. 1 (January 2004): 53–75.
Urbinati, Nadia. *Representative Democracy: Principles and Genealogy*. Chicago: University of Chicago Press, 2006.
Urbinati, Nadia. "Competing for Liberty: The Republican Critique of Democracy." *The American Political Science Review* 106, no. 3 (2012): 607–21.
Van Gelderen, Martin, and Quentin Skinner, eds. *Republicanism: A Shared European Heritage*. 2 vols. Cambridge: Cambridge University Press, 2002.
Venturi, Franco. *Utopia and Reform in the Enlightenment*. Cambridge: Cambridge University Press, 1971.
Vergès, Françoise. "Colonizing, Educating, Guiding: A Republican Duty." In *Colonial Culture in France since the Revolution*, edited by Pascal Blanchard, Sandrine Lemaire, Nicolas Bancel, and Dominic Thomas, 250–56. Bloomington: Indiana University Press, 2014.
Vergès, Françoise. *Monsters and Revolutionaries. Colonial Family Romance and Métissage*. Durham: Duke University Press, 1999.
Verjus, Anne. *Le cens de la famille. Les femmes et le vote, 1789–1848*. Paris: Belin, 2002.
Viroli, Maurizio. *For Love of Country: An Essay on Patriotism and Nationality*. Oxford: Clarendon Press, 1997.
Viroli, Maurizio. *Machiavelli*. Oxford: Oxford University Press, 1998.
Vovelle, Michel. *La mentalité révolutionnaire: société et mentalités sous la révolution française*. Paris: Messidor, 1985.
Vovelle, Michel. *La Révolution contre l'Eglise. De la Raison à l'Etre suprême*. Bruxelles: Complexe, 1989.
Vovelle, Michel, ed. *Révolution et république. L'exception française*. Paris: Kimé, 1994.
Wahnich, Sophie. *L'impossible citoyen. L'étranger dans le discours de la révolution française*. Paris: Albin Michel, 1997.
Wahnich, Sophie. *La Révolution française*. Paris: Hachette, 2012.
Watkins, William J. *Reclaiming the American Revolution: The Kentucky and Virginia Resolutions and Their Legacy*. New York: Palgrave MacMillan, 2008.
Watson, Alan, ed. *The Digest of Justinian, Volume 1*. Philadelphia: University of Pennsylvania Press, 2009.
Weber, Eugen. *Peasants into Frenchmen. The Modernization of Rural France, 1870–1914*. Stanford: Stanford University Press, 1976.
Weil, Patrick, and Nicolas Truong. *Le sens de la république*. Paris: Grasset, 2015.
Williams, David Lay. "Ideas and Actuality in the Social Contract: Kant and Rousseau." *History of Political Thought* 28, no. 3 (2007): 469–95.
Williams, David Lay. *Rousseau's Platonic Enlightenment*. University Park: Pennsylvania State University Press, 2007.
Williams, David Lay. "Political Ontology and Institutional Design in Montesquieu and Rousseau." *American Journal of Political Science* 54, no. 2 April (2010): 525–42.

Williams, David Lay. *Rousseau's Social Contract: An Introduction*. Cambridge: Cambridge University Press, 2014.

Wollstonecraft, Mary. *A Vindication of the Rights of Woman. A Vindication of the Rights of Men*. Oxford: Oxford University Press, 1993.

Wood, Gordon. *The Creation of the American Republic, 1776–1787*. Chapel Hill: University of North Carolina Press, 1969.

Wood, Gordon. *Power and Liberty: Constitutionalism in the American Revolution*. Oxford: Oxford University Press, 2021.

Wood, Neal. *Cicero's Social and Political Thought*. Berkeley: University of California Press, 1991.

Worden, Blair. "English Republicanism." In *The Cambridge History of Political Thought 1450–1700*, edited by James Henderson Burns, 443–76. Cambridge: Cambridge University Press, 1991.

Wright, Johnson Kent. *A Classical Republican in Eighteenth-Century France. The Political Thought of Mably*. Stanford: Stanford University Press, 1997.

Wright, Johnson Kent. "Montesquieuan Moments: *The Spirit of the Laws* and Republicanism." *Proceedings of the Western Society for French History* 35 (2007): 149–69.

Zuckert, Catherine. "Machiavelli's Democratic Republic." *History of Political Thought* XXXV, no. 2 (Summer 2014): 262–94.

Index

www.ingramcontent.com/pod-product-compliance
Lightning Source LLC
Chambersburg PA
CBHW020002180125
20576CB00003B/74

9781009477277